PROTESTANT SPIRITUAL TRADITIONS

PROTESTANT SPIRITUAL TRADITIONS

EDITED BY
FRANK C. SENN

PAULIST PRESS
New York/Mahwah

Library of Congress Catalog Card Number: 85-62876

ISBN: 0-8091-2761-X

Published by Paulist Press
997 Macarthur Boulevard
Mahwah, N.J. 07430

Printed and bound in the United States of America

CONTENTS

ESSAYISTS

PETER C. ERB. Professor of English and Religion and Culture, Wilfrid Laurier University, Waterloo, Ontario; Associate Director, Schwenkfelder Library, Pennsburg, Pennsylvania

HOWARD G. HAGEMAN. Past President, New Brunswick Theological Seminary, New Brunswick, New Jersey

E. GLENN HINSON. David T. Porter Professor of Church History, The Southern Baptist Theological Seminary, Louisville, Kentucky

PAUL V. MARSHALL. Rector, Christ Church (Episcopal), Babylon, New York; Associate Professor of Liturgics and Homiletics, The George Mercer School of Theology, Garden City, New York

FRANK C. SENN. Pastor, Christ the Mediator Lutheran Church, Chicago, Illinois; Lecturer in Worship, the Divinity School of the University of Chicago

DAVID LOWES WATSON. Board of Discipleship of the United Methodist Church, Nashville, Tennessee

JOHN WEBORG. Associate Professor of Theology, North Park Theological Seminary, Chicago, Illinois

Frank C. Senn

INTRODUCTION

There has been a widespread interest in spirituality in recent years. The reasons for this may have to do with a reaction to the values which emerged in a mass, urban, technocratic society. There is a growing concern that life should be valued for its quality and authenticity rather than for its quantitative achievements. As Nathan Mitchell put it, "There seems to be a growing disinclination to identify either people or prayer in terms of function. Simultaneously there is a burgeoning impulse to identify them according to personal categories of wholeness, clarity, depth, and integrity."[1]

The "individualism, superficiality, and utilitarianism" of modern Western life which Abbot Gabriel Braso listed as obstacles to the cultivation of a deep spiritual life are precisely what many people in our society are eschewing.[2] It is not surprising, therefore, that the initial search for forms of self-knowledge and self-development, prayer and meditation, and traditions of spirituality should lead Westerners to the East and away from the spiritual traditions which are identified with the development of Western culture. In North America the Protestant spiritual traditions especially have been found wanting because of the dominant role they played in the formation of our way of life.

Catholic authors, such as the Trappist monk Thomas Merton, have popularized the term "spirituality" for Protestants who are searching for a deeper spiritual life. "Spirituality" is not a word that has been current in Protestant vocabulary, although it is familiar to Roman Catholics and the Eastern Orthodox. It is a standard idiom in the French language. On the other hand, Anglo-Saxon Protestantism is not lacking in other terms to express what is meant by "spirituality." But such terms as "god-

1

liness," "piety," "holiness of life," "the devout life," etc., have acquired unfortunate connotations. The word "spirituality" seems a clearer, more virile, less sentimental term by which to express the subject of communion with God and the way of life which emanates from that.

It is not easy to agree on what is meant by the subject of spirituality. Louis Bouyer distinguished between the "religious life," the "interior life," and the "spiritual life."[3] He pointed out examples of religious life which involve nothing more than carrying out certain rites, and which are therefore void of any interior life. He provided examples of great artists, like James Joyce and Marcel Proust, who cultivated a rich interior life but were indifferent or even hostile to religion or any sense of transcendent reality. A spiritual life is not attained until the interior life develops in awareness of a spiritual reality which may or may not be identified as "God." If the spiritual reality which is apprehended, however, is some One rather than some thing, it is likely to include the cultivation of a religious life. "From this point of view," wrote Bouyer, "Christianity is seen to be a form of 'spiritual life' in which our most personal, most interiorized relationship with God Himself in His transcendent reality is fully recognized and formally cultivated."[4]

Spirituality, therefore, has to do with one's relationship with God, with the way in which that relationship is conceived and expressed. The way in which one conceives *of God* is theology. There is an obvious relationship between theology and spirituality. If one conceives of God as being "just" or "sovereign," then the way in which one conceives of one's relationship with God might be defined in terms of "justification" (Luther) or "obedience" (Calvin). Thus it would seem that much Protestant theologizing has really been in the area of spirituality—articulating the divine-human relationship and working out the concrete ways in which it is expressed in prayer, liturgy, ethics, mission, etc.

It appears therefore that it is possible to delineate a Protestant spirituality. Franz Leenhardt has tried to do it by contrasting a Protestant spirituality with a Catholic one. In *Two Biblical Faiths: Protestant and Catholic,* he identified Protestant and Catholic spiritualities with two strands of biblical tradition which he labels "Abrahamic" and "Moseic."[5] The Abrahamic/Protestant strand of tradition is traced from Abraham through the prophets of Israel to Paul and the reformers. The Moseic/Catholic strand is traced from Moses through the priesthood of Israel to Peter and the papacy. For a symbol of Protestant spirituality Leenhardt takes "the word"; the "burning bush" represents Catholic spirituality (the original French title of Leenhardt's book was *La Parole et le Buisson de Feu*). In Christian terms, the Abrahamic spirituality is one in which persons hear the call of the word of God, break with their past through repentance, and move on in hope toward the eschatological kingdom. As Abraham was called "out of the blue," as it were, so the believer lives each day in utter dependence on the promise of God as his or her sole security. Any ritual forms which seem to get in the way of this absolute dependence on the word, or which might become a substitute security, will be distrusted and rejected. In Protestantism, concern for ritual purity is replaced by concern for ethical purity. By way of contrast, Moses' call is mediated through the burning bush. He also sets out on a journey of faith, but does so with and on behalf of a people who are already heirs of a tradition. In Christian terms, the Moseic spirituality is one in which the gospel is mediated through concrete, sacramental instruments, and is expressed in brotherly love in community. Ritual forms are not seen as getting in the way of one's relationship with God, but of actualizing it. The sacraments fulfill and apply what the word of the gospel proclaims. Ethical purity flows from the same source as ritual purity: the presence of God among his people.

Leenhardt's book bears careful reading. But undoubtedly many Protestants will see something of their own spirituality expressed in the Moseic strand, while many Catholics will identify with Abraham, the prophets, and St. Paul. The book may be criticized not only for forcing certain historical personalities into preconceived molds, but also from the standpoint of biblical scholarship. For example, it is clear that the Abrahamic cultus utilized external signs (see Genesis 14–15). Whatever the deficiencies of his comparisons, however, Leenhardt has rooted both Catholic and Protestant spirituality in the biblical tradition. That in itself is a significant ecumenical contribution. But the problem is that by painting Protestantism and Catholicism with such broad strokes, significant nooks and crannies are missed or glossed over.

These are often the aspects which make the whole edifice distinctive.

In order to get at these nooks and crannies, this book brings together essays on spirituality written by persons within particular Protestant traditions. While there are a number of disparate spiritualities living together under the roof of Catholicism (often expressed in the different religious orders), spirituality was often a factor causing organizational disunity among Protestants. Indeed, each Protestant tradition may be viewed as a "school of spirituality." If there are differences between them, then how can it be determined that certain spiritual traditions belong together in this book?

We have endeavored to solve that problem by appealing to historical relationships. The original Protestant traditions are Lutheran, originating in Germany and spreading north to Scandinavia and the Baltic countries, and the Reformed, emerging in cantons of Switzerland, in trading centers along the Rhine River (e.g. Strasbourg), and spreading into France, The Netherlands, Scotland, and England. The English Church was significantly influenced by both the Lutheran and the Reformed reformations during the reigns of Edward VI and Elizabeth I. Some members of the English Church, the Puritans, desired the English Reformation to go farther in the Reformed direction than it did, and during the reign of Elizabeth some of their numbers moved into exile in The Netherlands where they were influenced also by the Anabaptists (i.e. Mennonites) who surfaced there. The Anabaptists come out of what has been called the Radical Reformation. They may be regarded as a sixteenth century resurgence of certain radical tendencies in Medieval Christianity expressed in such groups as the Cathari, Waldensians, Lollards, and Franciscan Spirituals, and therefore they might not be regarded as Protestant at all. Nevertheless, they were influential on the Free Church tradition which played so large a part in early American Christianity. "Free Church" really means free of the obligatory use of the *Book of Common Prayer.* Among the English and Scotch Calvinists (i.e. Presbyterians) there emerged a preference for a *Book of Common Order* or a Directory of Worship which provided an outline for worship rather than a set of liturgical texts and rubrics. The Puritan Separatists, influenced by the Anabaptists, did not even provide this, although descriptions of worship abound.[6] The Anabaptists also influenced the Puritans to move toward the ideal of a pure gathered church, separated from the world—a model which was difficult to apply in New England where the Separatists (i.e. Congregationalists) became the established church. On the other hand, as Peter Erb points out in his essay, the Anabaptists were later influenced by Pietism, a movement which originated in the German Lutheran and Reformed Churches in the seventeenth century, and which has contributed to the character of the present-day Anabaptist Churches, bringing them closer to conventional Protestantism. John Wesley was also influenced by such Pietists as Count Nicholas von Zinzendorf and the Moravian Brethren, and Methodism can be viewed as a Pietist movement within and then outside of the Anglican Church. Methodism was important in the spiritual awakenings, or revivals, which played such an important role in the history of American Protestantism.

Out of this welter of relationships it is possible to establish which traditions should be included in a book on Protestant spirituality. In the somewhat chronological order in which we shall deal with them they are: Lutheran, Reformed, Anabaptist, Anglican, Puritan, Pietist and Wesleyan. These traditions comprehend an even broader spectrum of denominations. This book must be more than a history of Protestant Christianity or a history of Christian thought, although that cannot be ignored by the nature of the subject and the approach taken in these presentations. But the essays seek to establish ways in which Christians have conceived and expressed their relationship with God within these major Protestant traditions. Thus they deal with prayer as well as faith, public worship as well as private devotion.

The essays are offered in the conviction that Protestants and non-Protestants alike will appreciate a survey of the spiritualities which have nurtured the faith and life of so many adherents who have contributed in a formative way to Western, and especially North American, culture. At the same time it may be that many Protestants who are searching for a deeper spiritual life will find what they are looking for at home as well as abroad. It may be that what passes for the copy in current circulation betrays the original. For this reason the essays emphasize the experiences and reflections of the "founders" of these spiritual traditions—e.g.

Martin Luther, John Calvin, Menno Simons, Thomas Cranmer and the Anglican divines and mystics, Richard Baxter, Philip Jacob Spener, John Wesley, and others. Communities in search of renewal need to begin by returning to their origins.

The "return to the sources" which characterizes these essays offers some remarkable discoveries. One is the esteem which certain reformers and pietist leaders had for certain Medieval mystics such as St. Bernard of Clairvaux, Meister Eckhart, Johann Tauler, and Thomas à Kempis. Mysticism has been defined as a "quest for immediacy" in the God-human relationship.[7] The mystical element in Protestantism would explain both the aversion to ritual ceremonies and also the reliance on the Word and the Sacraments as means of grace. Indeed, this is another discovery: the sacraments of Baptism and the Lord's Supper played a much more important role in the formative stages of Protestantism than much recent practice would suggest. The sacraments, including the sacramental act of preaching (both Luther and Calvin made much of the real presence of God in the oral proclamation of His Word), relate the individual to Christian community, which provides the support system for living the godly life. The role of the community of faith—whether an established and/or folk church (as in Lutheranism, the Reformed Churches, and Anglicanism), or the pure, gathered community (as in the Anabaptist Churches and in Puritanism), or small groups devoted to the mutual cultivation of godliness (as in the collegia pietatis and the Methodist class meetings)—is an important aspect of Protestant spirituality. Far from cultivating a rugged individualism, each of these Protestant traditions was concerned with the renewal and revitalization of Christian community. Protestantism cannot be solely blamed for the individualism of American life. Indeed, it would seem to be the other way around: American individualism, a product of both the Enlightenment and the pioneer conditions on the American frontier, has had a deleterious effect on Protestant spirituality.

These introductory remarks indicate some common threads in the various Protestant traditions. We would also note some significant divergences between the mainline Reformation spirituality and Puritanism, Pietism, and Revivalism. The latter place a far greater emphasis on the immanence of God, rather than the transcendence of God. There is also an increasing emphasis on personal religious experiences, rather than trust in the promises of God, as constituting the central validation of one's faith. The discerning reader will discover areas where dialogue might fruitfully take place between the Protestant traditions as well as the ties that bind them together.

NOTES

1. Nathan Mitchell, "Useless Prayer," in John Gallen, ed., *Christians at Prayer* (Notre Dame: University of Notre Dame Press, 1977), p. 2.

2. Gabriel M. Braso, *Liturgy and Spirituality*, 2nd ed., trans. by Leonard J. Doyle (Collegeville: The Liturgical Press, 1971), p. xiv.

3. Louis Bouyer, *Introduction to Spirituality*, trans. by Mary Ryan Perkins (Collegeville: The Liturgical Press, 1961), pp. 1ff.

4. *Ibid.*, p. 5

5. Franz J. Leenhardt, *Two Biblical Faiths: Protestant and Catholic*, English trans. (London: Lutterworth Press, 1964).

6. See Doug Adams, *Meeting House to Camp Meeting. Toward a History of American Free Church Worship From 1620 to 1835* (Austin: The Sharing Company, 1981).

7. Margaret Lewis Furse, *Mysticism: Window on a World View* (Nashville: Abingdon, 1977).

Frank C. Senn

LUTHERAN SPIRITUALITY

In order to define "Lutheran spirituality" we must specify how Lutherans conceive of and express their relationship to God. This immediately presents problems. Those who have borne the name "Lutheran," or who are members of Churches which are Lutheran in doctrine and practice, span five centuries and six continents. Lutheranism has been a state church and a folk religion in much of Central and Northern Europe. It has become a major denomination in North America and a growing ecclesial community in South America, Africa, Asia, and Australia. What binds all these people together is a common commitment to some or all of the confessional writings included in *The Book of Concord*.[1] What separates them are cultural factors, such as language and custom, and historical influences, both ecclesiastical and secular.

The roots of Lutheran church life and spirituality are to be found in the Reformation which swept Europe in the sixteenth century. As a conservative Reformation, Martin Luther's movement retained a "critical reverence" for the dogmas, liturgical orders, and church polity received from the Western Catholic tradition.[2] At the same time subsequent Lutheran church bodies, groups, and persons have been shaped by the Age of Orthodoxy (late sixteenth–early seventeenth centuries) with its scholastic theology, Pietism (late seventeenth–early eighteenth centuries in Germany; nineteenth century in Scandinavia), the Enlightenment (eighteenth century rational theology and its continuation in nineteenth century liberal theology), Neo-Lutheranism (nineteenth century repristination theology and the Erlangen School), and the modern Ecumenical Movement. To this must be added the complication of modern American pluralism and mobility, which has encouraged a shopping around for a church which

9

suits one's personal needs and interests. Many people join a local congregation because of the personality of the pastor, the hospitality of the people, the vitality of the congregation's liturgical life, and/or the challenge and edification of the parish programs. Thus, many people who bear the religious identification "Lutheran" may not conceive and express their relationship to God along traditional Lutheran lines.This is most evident in the widespread preference for Anglo-American hymnody among American Lutherans instead of the sixteenth and seventeenth century German chorales and the Scandinavian folk hymns which have played such a formative role in Lutheran piety. Of course, people do not check their culture at the church door when they enter to worship. To the extent that Lutheranism makes claims to catholicity it must be open to all forms of cultural expression. Depending on where one is on the continuum of relationships between cult and culture one might view this as a watering down or an enriching of Lutheran piety.

In view of this problem of culture and history, how shall we articulate the characteristics of a "Lutheran spirituality"? It seems that the most productive approach is to look at the spirituality of Martin Luther himself (1483–1546). There is no doubt that it has been upheld as a model by Lutherans of all times and places. Two problems present themselves in this approach. The first is that Luther and Lutheranism are not the same. Very often they have served as correctives of each other. Secondly, it is difficult to get at Luther himself.Each age has tended to view Luther through its own eyes.[3] Furthermore, the mass of historical-critical studies of Luther and his thought in the last hundred years is intimidating to an amateur in Luther studies such as myself. But one thing has become increasingly clear from recent research: it is that Luther's spiritual experience cannot be separated from his exegetical discoveries and theological reflections. It is amazing how many older interpretations of Luther failed to recognize the significance of the fact that his basic convictions were not arrived at as a result of purely academic research but as a consequence of his struggles with God. It was his personal experience of a gracious God who forgives sinners for the sake of Jesus Christ which set his reform movement on its way. Because it was the Bible which brought him to this experience, he emphasized its authority. Because the Bible taught that man lives before God by faith, he de-emphasized the role of religious works. Because faith comes from what is heard, Luther emphasized the preaching of the gospel rather than the performance of ritual acts. Because the Church's testimony did not lead others to the same kind of experience, he emphasized the divinely-instituted means of grace (Word and Sacrament) over human institutions (e.g. the papacy, monasticism, etc.). A certain kind of spirituality is the consequence of these theological emphases with their implications for institutional reordering.

If modern Luther research has emphasized the experiential basis of Luther's theology and reform proposals, it has also wanted to understand Luther in the light of the beliefs and practices of the late Middle Ages. Catholic scholars especially have seen Luther in relationship to late Medieval Nominalism, mysticism, and renewal movements.[4] This has been a helpful correction of the interpretations of older Protestant scholars who tended to see Luther in radical discontinuity with the age which preceded him. The liability of stressing Luther's continuity with the late Middle Ages is that it blurs his own distinctive insights and the way in which he came to them. After all, there had been many attempts at church renewal in the fourteenth and fifteenth centuries, associated with William of Occam, Jean Gerson, and Cardinal Nicholas von Cusa, not to mention John Wycliffe, Jan Hus, and Savanarola. But it was Luther's idea of reform that picked up an age and carried it away in new directions. Nevertheless, it is instructive to see where Luther's ideas fit in with the age which preceded him, in spirituality as well as doctrine.

While there have been many forms or models of spirituality in Christian history, two dimensions have remained constant in all times and places: asceticism and mysticism. Asceticism represents an active or expressive kind of spirituality while mysticism represents a more passive or contemplative kind. They are not mutually exclusive. As Louis Bouyer suggests, "The necessary counterpart of Christian asceticism is found in Christian mysticism, just as the cross cannot be understood apart from the resurrection. Asceticism makes us take up and carry our cross. Mysticism inaugurates in this life the life that comes to us by the cross."[5] Thus, the great practitioners of the ascetic disciplines have also been the great mystics. This is already the case with St. Paul. He clearly emphasizes the dualistic combat of the Spirit against the "flesh" (Romans 8:5–9) and compares the Christian life to a rigorous athletic training (1 Corinthians 9:24–27). The "flesh," for St. Paul, is not matter, but the lifestyle of this world which militates against living the new life in Christ to which we are assimilated by Baptism. "Spirit" is the indwelling Spirit of the risen Christ who effects union with Christ (Romans 8:9–11).[6] The Christian martyrs are preeminent examples of both asceticism and mysticism. In their sufferings they participate in the Lord's passion and fulfill the Lord Jesus' invitation to take up their crosses and follow him to glory the way he went. But at the moment of death the martyrs have a radiant experience of the Savior's presence, as, for example, St. Stephen, the proto-martyr, "full of the Holy Spirit, gazed into heaven and saw the glory of God, and Jesus standing at the right hand of God" (Acts 7:56). The asceticism of the cross leads to the beatific vision. Likewise, the neo-platonic-inspired doctrine of the "three ways" propounded by Evagrius Ponticus and in the writings of Pseudo-Dionysius the Areopagite in the fifth century regarded the *via purgativa,* "the way of purification," which uses ascetic disciplines to achieve detachment from the cares of the world, as the first step toward the way of illumination and the way of union with God. This doctrine of spiritual progress found a natural home in monasticism generally, and in eastern monasticism especially. It was certainly the case that many of the great mystics of the Middle Ages were monks or religious who purposely lived the ascetic life as they undertook vows of poverty, chastity, and obedience. These examples are meant to suggest that elements of asceticism and mysticism will be found in all forms of spirituality. We should therefore look for them also in Luther's spirituality.

ASCETICISM AND MYSTICISM
IN LUTHER'S SPIRITUALITY

The story of Luther's terror-stricken vow to St. Anne, in the midst of a thunderstorm on a summer day in 1505, that he would straightway become a monk if she would save him, is legendary.

While there may have been signs of religious disquietude in the young Luther, his biographer Roland Bainton points out an important datum that "This man was no son of the Italian Renaissance, but a German born in remote Thuringia, where men of piety still reared churches with arches and spires straining after the illimitable. Luther was himself so much a gothic figure," wrote Bainton, "that his faith may be called the last great flower of the religion of the Middle Ages."[7] He also came from the most religiously conservative part of the population, the peasants (although his father, Hans, had moved from the farm to the mines). In 1496 Luther was sent to a school in Magdeburg which was run by the Brethren of the Common Life, who had spread a spiritual doctrine known as the *devotio moderna,* which advocated an eminently interior piety based on self-analysis achieved through meditation and the use of the confessional. In 1501 he matriculated at the University of Erfurt, where he earned his Master of Arts. This was not a university much influenced by the Renaissance. It was an old university which had become a stronghold of Nominalism and the *Via Moderna.* This does not mean that Luther was unacquainted with the work of the humanists, but it does mean that everything in Luther's background indicates that the decision to enter a monastery was not hastily made, even if the incident which forced a decision was impromptu.

Much against his father's will, Luther entered the monastery of the Hermits of St. Augustine, which was by far the strictest of the religious houses of the city. There is a solid core of evidence in his lectures, sermons, letters, and Table Talk that Luther took his vows seriously and even went beyond the ordinary requirements of the Rule. Both during his career as a monk and later in life he attacked those monks who sought "exemption" from the strict observance of the Rule. As he later commented on his own observance,

> It's true. I was a good monk, and kept my order so strictly that I could say that if ever a monk could get to heaven through monastic discipline, I should have entered in. All my companions in the monastery who knew me would bear me out in this. For if it had gone on much longer, I would have martyred myself to death, what with vigils, prayers, readings, and other works.[8]

Luther retained a lifelong appreciation for ascetic discipline. In his irenic treatise on *The Freedom of a Christian* (1520) Luther suggested that ascetic discipline does for the outward man what faith does for the inner man.

> Although, as I have said, a man is abundantly and sufficiently justified by faith inwardly, in his spirit, and so has all that he needs, except insofar as this faith and these riches must grow from day to day even to the future life; yet he remains in this mortal life on earth. In this life he must control his own body and have dealings with men. Here the works begin; here a man cannot enjoy leisure; here he must indeed take care to discipline his body by fastings, watchings, labors, and other reasonable discipline and to subject it to the Spirit so that it will obey and conform to the inner man and faith and not revolt against faith and hinder the inner man, as it is the nature of the body to do if it is not held in check.[9]

Luther, the Pauline theologian, had a great appreciation of the fact that the life of faith is a life of struggle. Asceticism is therefore to be taken seriously. As late as the 1532 Commentary on the Sermon of the Mount Luther castigated the frivolous attitude toward fasting he had experienced under the papacy.

> How can I call it a fast if someone prepares a lunch of expensive fish, with the choicest spices, more and better than for two or three other meals, and washes it down with the strongest drink, and spends a hour or three at filling his belly till it is stuffed? Yet that was the usual thing and a minor thing even among the very strictest monks.[10]

He recommended that the civil government impose a fast of one or two days a week to curb gluttony and that Christians observe a spiritual fast a few days before Easter, Pentecost, and Christmas as a way of marking off these festivals. But by this time he saw the role of fasting primarily as a spiritual discipline which helps one live the life of faith, and not as a good work by which one tries to please God.

> But above all, you must see to it that you are already pious and a true Christian and that you are not planning to render

God a service by this fasting. Your service to God must be only faith in Christ and love to your neighbor, simply doing what is required of you. If this is not your situation, then you would do better to leave fasting alone. The only purpose of fasting is to discipline the body by outwardly cutting off both lust and the opportunity for lust, the same thing that faith does inwardly in the heart.[11]

In reaction to the excessive legalism of the late Middle Ages, Luther and his followers preferred not to make rules and regulations that would bind the consciences of believers. But by not making a requirement of fasting, it eventually passed out of use as a common spiritual discipline among Lutherans. Very often evangelical freedom has been interpreted in terms of what one does not have to do instead of in terms of what one may do. In the twentieth century, Dietrich Bonhoeffer castigated this attitude as "cheap grace," in the area of fasting and other forms of spiritual discipline as well as in ethics.

We claim liberty from all legal compulsion, from self-martyrdom and mortification, and play this off against the proper evangelical use of discipline and asceticism; we thus excuse our self-indulgence and irregularity in prayer, in meditation and in our bodily life. But the contrast between our behavior and the word of Jesus is all too painfully evident. We forget that discipleship means estrangement from the world, and we forget the real joy and freedom which are the outcome of a devout rule of life. . . . Any objection that asceticism is wrong, and that all we need is faith, is quite beside the point. . . . When all is said and done, the life of faith is nothing if not an unending struggle of the spirit with every available weapon against the flesh.[12]

In the area of ascetic discipline Luther serves as a corrective of Lutheran laxity. This is the case in the use of private confession as well. When Luther returned to Wittenberg from his temporary hideout in the Wartburg in 1522, and found that Karlstadt and the radicals had carried out an iconoclastic campaign, he preached eight sermons in eight days to try to restore order and to teach a proper use of evangelical freedom. The Eighth Sermon dealt with the confessional. While Luther admitted that we must have many forms of absolution, and that those who are firm in their faith may confess to God alone, he asked: "How many have such a strong faith? Therefore, as I have said, I will not let this private confession be taken from me. But I will not have anybody forced to it, but left to each one's free will."[13]

These and many other passages indicate that long after Luther left the monastery, its ascetic discipline was still a part of his life. But he could not impose these disciplines on others because his own experience had been that " . . . the more I sweated it out like this, the less peace and tranquility I knew."[14] Luther's problem was not overscrupulosity. The use of private confession and the advice of spiritual directors provided remedies for those suffering from a bad case of scruples. Luther called his problem *Anfechtung*, which suggests spiritual combat rather than temptation (the word for "temptation" would be *Versuchung*). *Anfechtung* has to do with the experience of being in the presence of God *(coram Deo)* and experiencing God's wrath against the sinner.

> When one is tormented in "Anfechtung" it seems to him that he is alone: God is angry only with him, and irreconcilably angry against him: then he alone is a sinner and all the others are in the right, and they work against him at God's orders. There is nothing left for him but this unspeakable sighing through which, without knowing it, he is supported by the Spirit and cries, "Why does God pick on me!"[15]

Anfechtung was a condition Luther experienced all his life. It was only later when he understood it in the light of Scripture that he could deal with it effectively, as the marvelous exposition of Jonah (1526) and the sermons on the story of the Canaanite woman (Matthew 15:21–28) illustrate. "I find in the Scriptures that Christ, Abraham, Jacob, Moses, Job, David, Ezekiel and many more have experienced hell in this life." Luther identified with these biblical personalities who murmured against God, thus committing the sin of blasphemy as Luther had done.

In his own struggle, Luther's greatest help came from the kindly Vicar-General of the Augustinians, Johannes von Staupitz, who was alarmed by Luther's abnormal introspection but impressed by his gifts. Staupitz ordered Luther back to his studies to earn a doctorate in theology and to teach Scripture at the newly-founded University of Wittenberg. In his biblical studies Luther found a way of dealing with *Anfechtung* as he wrestled with the interpretation of *iustitia Dei* in Romans 1:17. This phrase, "the righteousness of God," troubled him as he worked through his lectures on the Psalms in 1513–14 because he was conceiving "righteousness" and other divine attributes in a passive way, as that which God is and possesses, rather than in an active way, as that which God does and gives. Luther described his own discovery of a different meaning of *iustitia Dei* in one of his most autobiographical writings, the Preface to the Complete Edition of his Latin Writings in 1545.

> At last, by the mercy of God, meditating day and night, I gave heed to the context of the words, namely, "In it the righteousness of God is revealed, as it is written, 'He who through faith is righteous shall live.'" There I began to understand that the righteousness of God is that by which the righteous lives by a gift of God, namely, by faith. And this is the meaning: the righteousness of God is revealed by the gospel, namely, the passive righteousness with which merciful God justifies us by faith, as it is written, "He who through faith is righteous shall live." Here I felt that I was altogether born again and had entered paradise itself through open gates. There a totally other face of the entire Scripture showed itself to me. Thereupon I ran through the Scriptures from memory. I also found in other terms an analogy, as, the work of God, that is, what God does in us, the power of God, with which he makes us strong, the wisdom of God, with which he makes us wise, the strength of God, the salvation of God, the glory of God.[16]

In the light of this experience Luther turned to the teachers of the church to see if his insight checked out with the tradition. He was pleased to discover a similar interpretation of *iustitia Dei*, as that righteousness with which God endues us when he justifies us, in St. Augustine's treatise *On the Spirit and the Letter*. In this same period he turned again to the Medieval mystics.

As Erich Vogelsang pointed out in his famous essay on "Luther and the Mystics,"[17] Luther rejected the mystical tradition stemming from Pseudo-Dionysius, rated highly the Romance mysticism of St. Bernard of Clairvaux, Hugh of St. Victor, and St.

Bonaventure, but had nothing but praise for the so-called German mysticism of Johann Tauler (ca. 1300–1361) and the anonymous writing known as the *Theologia deutsch*. We know that Luther bought an edition of Tauler's sermons which had been published in 1508 and annotated it carefully. In 1516 he published those parts of the *Theologia deutsch* which were available to him under the title *A Spiritually Noble Little Book*. Lest this be regarded as a momentary fascination, he published a complete edition of this work two years later.[18] In the preface of this edition he wrote: "To boast with my old fool (St. Paul), no book except the Bible and St. Augustine has come to my attention from which I have learned more about God, Christ, man, and all things."[19]

This German mysticism represents the line of St. Augustine that the goal of human life is union with God, the achievement of which is hindered by original sin, which is manifested in the fact that man seeks himself in all things and does not seek God, which situation God himself must overcome by his grace.[20] Man is essentially passive in the reception of grace. The Spirit prompts man to seek to be free from himself and turn to God. This involves a dying to oneself, a "resignation" rather than active deed. All self-will and humanly-generated activity must be extinguished in order for God to become the one who wills and works in man. Thus, everything that belongs to salvation is exclusively the work of God. "Justification" occurs when God comes to be present in man's inner being.[21]

As Bengt Hoffman points out, Luther was not interested in mysticism as a conceptual system; he was interested in "the inner side of the external creed, personally appropriated and felt."[22] He was interested in the knowledge of the God who is both hidden and revealed *(Deus absconditus et revelatus)* in the suffering and death of Christ. This mystical theology was expressed by Luther in his "Heidelberg Disputation" of 1518. In these theses he developed his theology of the cross for the first time. He rejected the Nominalist notion that man obtains grace by doing what is in him *(facere quod in se est)*. "While a person is doing what is in him," argued Luther, "he sins and seeks himself in everything."[23] This is not cause for despair because this knowledge of the way we really are arouses "the desire to humble oneself and seek the grace of Christ." This grace is revealed in the cross of Christ, so the knowledge of God we must seek is the knowledge of what Christ accomplished for us there. "Because men misused the knowledge of God through works, God wished again to be recognized in suffering . . . ."[24] "He who does not know Christ does not know God hidden in suffering. Therefore he prefers works to suffering, glory to the cross, strength to weakness, wisdom to folly, and, in general, good to evil."[25] Therefore, "He is not righteous who does much, but he who, without work, believes much in Christ." By "without work" Luther means "Not that the righteous person does nothing, but that his works do not make him righteous, rather that his righteousness creates works. For grace and faith are infused without our works."[26]

It is hard to exaggerate the radicality of what Luther was proposing. The true theology, he said, is one that discerns the omnipotent God not in manifestations of power and glory but in the midst of peril and suffering. The true God, he said, is not an omnipotent monarch whose glory should be reflected by his devotees but One who divests himself of power and is revealed as "the crucified God." The true Christian life, said Luther, is not a life of security lived out in a world where the triumph of the good is assured but where the only real security is the security of a beggar. Therefore the true faith is not one which relies on one's own works but one which trusts in the promises of God.

Luther is one with the mystics in emphasizing human passivity before the grace of God. We are beggars before the grace of God who rejoice that " . . . it is the sweetest righteousness of God the Father that he does not save imaginary, but rather, real sinners, sustaining us in spite of our sins and accepting our works and our lives which are all deserving of rejection, until he perfects and saves us."[27] This idea is expanded in the sermon on *Two Kinds of Righteousness*, preached early in 1519, in which Luther distinguished between the "alien righteousness . . . instilled from without" and "our proper righteousness, not because we alone work it, but because we work with that first and alien righteousness." "Through faith in Christ . . . Christ's righteousness becomes our righteousness and all that he has becomes ours; rather, he himself becomes ours."[28] This sense of mystical union with Christ is also developed in *The Freedom of a Christian*, a work of mystical serenity written in the turbulent year 1520, in which Luther says: "Just as the heated iron glows like fire because of the union of fire with it, so the Word imparts its qualities to the soul."[29] In this same treatise Luther speaks of the benefit of faith "that it unites the soul with Christ as a bride is united with her bridegroom."[30] This simile was used frequently by the Medieval mystics, and is especially associated with St. Bernard of Clairvaux in his Commentary on the Song of Songs.

The mystical characteristics in Luther's theology between 1516 and 1520 prepared the way for a resurgence of mystical piety among Lutherans in the Ages of Orthodoxy and Pietism. As we shall see, that piety flourished in the hymnody and devotional writings of the seventeenth century. But it was also a piety that was rooted in Luther's christology, doctrine of the Word, and doctrine of the sacraments in which there is a strong affirmation of a God who meets us in Christ "deep in the flesh."[31] The practical expression of Luther's incarnational-sacramental piety is found in the liturgical life that emerged in the Lutheran Churches during and after the period of the Reformation. Indeed, we may propose that in Lutheranism, at least in its classical period, there is the revitalization of a liturgical spirituality. This was because of the conviction that the gift of justifying faith comes primarily through the preaching of the Word and the administration of the Sacraments.

LUTHERAN LITURGICAL PIETY

The Reformation period may be viewed as one of the most creative periods in the history of Christian liturgy between the fourth and twentieth centuries. All of the great reformers involved themselves in the task of liturgical reform and revision.[32] Luther laid the theological groundwork for such reform in *The Babylonian Captivity of the Church* in 1520. He was slow to get involved in the practical work of liturgical revision, but once he did his efforts were prodigious. There was the revision of the Latin Mass in *An Order of Mass and Communion for the Church at Wittenberg* in 1523; the *German Mass and Order of Service* in 1526; the Order of Baptism in 1523 and its revision in 1526; an Order of Marriage in 1529; an Order for Ordination of Ministers in

1539; the German Litany and the Latin Litany corrected in 1529; translations and musical settings of other liturgical chants such as the Te Deum, Magnificat, Gloria in excelsis, and Agnus Dei; and some thirty-seven hymns which were either revisions of pre-Reformation Latin hymns or new creations.[33] Luther's liturgical works served as models for similar liturgical revisions in various territories which adopted Luther's Reformation. A remarkable unity in variety is evident in these various Church Orders. Some, like Brandenburg-Nuremberg 1533, Mark Brandenburg 1540, and Pfalz-Neuburg 1543, were very conservative; others, especially in Southern Germany, displayed more affinity with the Reformed tradition. Johannes Bugenhagen prepared a number of Church Orders for Northern Germany and the Kingdom of Denmark which followed the spirit of Luther's *German Mass*. The Swedish Mass of Olavus Petri in 1531 followed the spirit of Luther's *Formula Missae,* as mediated through Nuremberg.[34]

Our interest here is not an analysis of liturgical structure and content as much as how Lutheran liturgical reform affected piety. It is commonly thought that vernacularization and congregational hymn-singing are two of the major contributions of Luther's liturgical work. We would not want to minimize these directions in Lutheran Reformation liturgy, but we should note that Lutheran liturgical reform was not characterized by a rigid principle of vernacularization (indeed, parts of the Mass and Divine Office remained in Latin in some Lutheran territories for two centuries) and hymnody was not an invention of the Reformation (indeed, the more radical reformers eschewed non-biblical songs and criticized the Lutherans for singing them). On the contrary, we should have to say that the liturgical reforms which most directly affected piety were the emphases on preaching and frequent reception of communion. It became a principle of Lutheran liturgical life that there should be no worship without preaching and no Masses without communicants. It is in this connection that we should consider Luther's understanding of the Word and his own eucharistic piety.

Luther's understanding of the Word of God is surely one of the most creative and complex aspects of his theology.[35] It was occasioned by a hermeneutical shift in Luther's approach to biblical interpretation from allegory to event. From this it follows that the Word is essentially an act of proclamation which elicits a response from the hearer; it is not primarily written word but preached word. This does not imply any kind of dichotomy for Luther between Word of God and Scripture; rather it is the task of preaching "to make the Scriptures come alive," as we might say—to make them come alive for us. There are endless examples of Luther's own ability to do this in some 2,300 extant sermons of his which we have in print (he preached every day of the week and sometimes four times on Sundays—all on different texts of the Bible and sometimes on the Catechism). As Roland Bainton notes, Luther is at his best in his sermons on the Nativity, and he provides an utterly charming example, which ends as follows:

> Think, women, there was no one there to bathe the Baby. No warm water, nor even cold. No fire, no light. The mother was herself midwife and the maid. The cold manger was the bed and the bathtub. Who showed the poor girl what to do? She never had a baby before. I am amazed that the little one did not freeze. Do not make of Mary a stone. For the higher people are in the favor of God, the more tender are they.
>
> Let us, then, meditate upon the Nativity just as we see it happening in our own babies. Behold Christ lying in the lap of his young mother. What can be sweeter than the Babe, what more lovely than the mother! What fairer her youth! What more gracious than her virginity! Look at the Child, knowing nothing. Yet all that is belongs to him, that your conscience should not fear but take comfort in him. Doubt nothing. To me there is no greater consolation given to mankind than this, that Christ became man, a child, a babe, playing in the lap and at the breasts of his most gracious mother. Who is there whom this sight would not comfort? Now is overcome the power of sin, death, hell, conscience, and guilt, if you come to this gurgling Babe and believe that he is come, not to judge you, but to save.[36]

Such a preaching of the the Word creates faith in the hearer; it may even be described as bearing Christ's presence. As Luther wrote in the 1526 treatise on *The Sacrament of the Body and Blood of Christ—Against the Fanatics,*

> Again, I preach the gospel of Christ, and with my bodily voice I bring Christ into your heart, so that you may form him

within yourself. If now you truly believe, so that your heart lays hold of the word and holds fast within it that voice, tell me, what have you in your heart? You must answer that you have the true Christ, not that he sits in there, as one sits on a chair, but as he is at the right hand of the Father. How that comes about you cannot know, but your heart truly feels his presence, and through the experience of faith you know for a certainty that he is there.[37]

While this is a theory of the living word of God taking on flesh in the life of the believer through the act of preaching, it is also an argument developed by Luther in this treatise to defend the real presence of Christ's body and blood in the bread and wine of the Lord's Supper. Luther's view of Christ's real presence in the Word is the same as his view of Christ's real presence in the sacrament.

Luther's eucharistic piety is somewhat buried in the polemics resulting from the conflicts over the sacrament, but it is related to his primary insight into the nature of the sacrament that God meets us in Christ where we are. In one revealing exchange during the Marburg Colloquy the Swiss reformer Oecolampadius said to Luther, "You should not cling to the humanity and flesh of Christ, but rather lift up your mind to his divinity," to which Luther replied, "I do not know of any God except Him who was made flesh, nor do I want to have another."[38] In the classical Lutheran formulation that Christ is present "*under* the bread, *with* the bread, *in* the bread,"[39] there is an effort to avoid metaphysical speculation and to preserve the mystery of Christ's presence.[40] In making himself available *in* an earthly vessel, Christ's divinity does not dissolve his humanity. Christ is mysteriously joined *with* the bread and wine by his Word in order to feed us with his very body broken and blood spilled on the cross for our forgiveness and reconciliation with God. At the same time, this divine self-giving remains *veiled under* the earthly signs. In the sacrament as in the Word we are confronted by *Deus absconditus et revelatus* and the theology of the cross.

The church has not yet arrived triumphantly in heaven; it is still on the way. A pilgrim church is more interested in receiving nourishment from the sacrament than in stopping to adore the consecrated elements. Even so, Luther found it hard to give up the elevation, which had been such a conspicuous example of Medieval adoration piety. In his *Formula Missae* of 1523 he advised, "Let the bread and cup be elevated according to the customary rite for the benefit of the weak in faith who might be offended if such an obvious change in this rite of the mass were suddenly made."[41] Indeed, since Luther inserted the institution narrative *(Qui pridie)* into the eucharistic preface *(Vere dignum)*, the elevation after the consecration could occur in its usual place during the "Blessed is he who comes" of the *Sanctus*. In the *German Mass* of 1526 Luther said,

> We do not want to abolish the elevation, but retain it because it goes well with the German Sanctus and signifies that Christ has commanded us to remember him. For just as the sacrament is bodily elevated, and yet Christ's body and blood are not seen in it, so he is remembered and elevated by the word of the sermon and is confessed and adored in the reception of the sacrament.[42]

The elevation was eventually dropped in Wittenberg in 1542 in order to conform with the practice of other evangelical churches, but as late as 1544, in his *Brief Confession Concerning the Holy Sacrament*, Luther asserted that if the fanatics like Karlstadt insisted upon the abolition of the elevation "I would still today not only retain the elevation but, where one would not be enough, assist in introducing three, seven, or ten elevations."[43] Even the *Formula of Concord*, while resisting adoration piety, conceded parenthetically that "no one except an Arian heretic can or will deny that Christ himself, true God and man, who is truly and essentially present in the Supper when it is rightly used, should be adored in spirit and in truth in all places but especially where his community is assembled."[44]

Certainly the spirit of adoration, of mystical absorption in the presence of Christ, was not lacking in the evangelical eucharistic celebration. The moment of communion was a high moment in the mass, accompanied by the singing of such hymns of adoration as the *Agnus Dei* and Luther's "O Lord, we praise you, bless you and adore you,"[45] as communicants *knelt* to receive the host and chalice. Perhaps the Catholic liturgiologist, Louis Bouyer, was correct in his assessment that Lutheran worship was

more an extension of Medieval piety than a recovery of early
church practice (and there was no concern among Lutherans, as
there was among the Reformed, to try to repristinate the worship
of the New Testament church). As Bouyer wrote,

> . . . following a rather lengthy service of readings and chants
> in which nothing had been changed from the pre-Reforma-
> tion mass, the preface, the words of consecration uttered
> aloud, kneeling at the sound of the bell for the adoration of
> the holy presence, which was heralded by the *Sanctus* and
> *Benedictus*, not only retained but popularized whatever prop-
> erly eucharistic elements remained in the liturgy of the middle
> ages thanks to the vernacular and catechetical instruction.[46]

To this would have to be added, of course, the not insignificant
fact that Lutherans heard preaching at every mass and were
urged to receive communion frequently. Indeed, the sermon and
the reception of communion became what have been called the
"twin peaks" of the Lutheran liturgy, and both were surrounded
by the tender and virile piety of the chorales which simultaneously fostered a sense of the corporate nature of public worship and reinforced the understanding that the objective means
of grace must be personally appropriated.

Surely this kind of liturgical experience was a powerful factor in the formation of Lutheran spirituality. In addition to the
chief liturgy of Word and Sacrament, the church year with its
cycle of seasons and holy days provided the substance of the liturgical celebrations in terms of biblical readings and proper prayers. Along with this chief service the daily prayer offices of Matins
and Vespers were retained and even received a reinvigoration in
the Reformation period as suitable liturgies with which to replace
the daily masses when there were no communicants. Saturday
Vespers often became a service of preparation for Holy Communion which included corporate confession and individual
absolution with the laying on of hands.

The classical period of the Lutheran liturgy was the hundred
years following the implementation of the Reformation. The
deteriorization of these liturgical patterns occurred in the seventeenth and eighteenth centuries as a result of the total social
upheaval of the Thirty Years War (1618–48), the reaction of Pie-

tism to a dogmatic and lifeless orthodoxy, and the anti-ritualism of Rationalism.[47] The recovery of these liturgical orders and practices began in the confessional revival movement of Neo-Lutheranism in the nineteenth century, first in Europe, then in America. In America it resulted in the promulgation of the *Church Book* of the Ministerium of Pennsylvania (1868), continued with the Common Service (1888) and the *Common Service Book* (1917), and came to a culmination with the publication of the *Service Book and Hymnal* (1958). This whole period can be regarded as a time when Lutherans, settling down into life in the new world, were also recovering their heritage from the old world. The *Lutheran Book of Worship* [LBW] (1978) represents the influence of the modern liturgical movement on American Lutheranism and a growing ecumenical commitment. But it has not been a development antithetical to the classical Lutheran liturgical piety. The late Arthur Carl Piepkorn regarded the liturgical pattern of Holy Communion with sermon every Sunday and festival, the observance of the church year with its proper readings and customs, and the retention of the daily prayer offices as "the norm of Lutheran piety . . . honored among American Lutherans perhaps more in the breach than in the keeping."[48] American Lutherans may honor their liturgical heritage to a greater or lesser extent, but few would be comfortable without it. To the extent that it has been a way in which the relationship with God has been experienced and expressed, it is a liturgical spirituality. The chief Liturgy of Word and Sacrament especially has been a way in which Lutherans have appropriated God's grace by faith and responded with the sacrifice of praise and thanksgiving in prayer, liturgical chant, and hymnody. In their worship Lutherans have been nourished by the means of grace in order to put their faith to work in the everyday world. The liturgy has been formative of a genuine lay spirituality, which is also a major contribution of Luther to Protestant spirituality in general that we must take up here.

THE PRIESTHOOD OF ALL BELIEVERS

One of the reasons for desiring more active participation by the laity in worship through congregational singing and vernacular liturgies and better nurture of the laity through the preaching of the Word and the administration of the sacraments is to equip them to exercise the priesthood to which all Christians have been called in Baptism. Luther's doctrine of the priesthood of all believers emerged in his attack on the sacramental system of the Medieval Church with its clerical monopolization of the means of grace. As early as 1519, in his *Treatise on the Sacrament of Penance*, Luther attacked the teaching that the right of declaring forgiveness resides only in the ordained ministry by virtue of the power of the keys which had been transmitted to the ordained through Peter. Luther contended that the keys were indeed given to Peter (Matthew 16), but on behalf of the whole church (Matthew 18). The clergy, therefore, have no monopoly on absolution. Since God alone forgives sins, the important thing is to trust the Word of Christ. "It follows that in the forgiveness of penance, nothing more is done by a pope or a bishop than could be done by any ordinary priest, or, for that matter, by any Christian layman. Every Christian, even a woman, can declare in God's name that 'God forgives you of your sin,' and you may be faithfully certain that your sin has as surely been absolved as if God himself spoke to you."[49]

This thought is further developed in the 1520 *Treatise on the New Testament, that is the Holy Mass*, in which Luther denies that the priest may offer the sacrament to God for special intentions on behalf of the living and the dead. As Luther made clear in *The Babylonian Captivity* of the same year, we cannot offer the sacrament to God because that is the gift or testament which he offers to us. The *Treatise on the New Testament* does contain some of Luther's most positive comments on the mass as a sacrifice, but it is based on the idea that "we do not offer Christ as a sacrifice, but that Christ offers us. And in this way it is permissible, yes, profitable, to call the mass a sacrifice; not on its own account, but because we offer ourselves as a sacrifice along with Christ."[50] Luther has captured here the patristic idea that the Eucharist is the fulfillment of the pure offering of the Gentiles in the Messianic Age, the self-oblation of the church, which St. Augustine describes in *The City of God*, Book X. But the true priest of this sacrifice is Christ himself, who "takes up our cause, presents us and our prayer and praise, and offers himself for us in heaven."[51] The true Christian sacrifice, therefore, is the sacrifice of prayer,

praise, thanksgiving, and the offering of ourselves, in gratitude
for God's redeeming act in the death and resurrection of Jesus
Christ, and in the confidence that the righteousness of Christ covers our own shabby righteousness as we dare to present this offering to the Father. Such a sacrifice requires faith, and that is the
true priestly work. "For faith must do everything. Faith alone is
the true priestly office. It permits no one else to take its place.
Therefore all Christian men are priests, all women priestesses, be
they young or old, master or servant, mistress or maid, learned
or unlearned. Here there is no difference, unless faith be
unequal."[52]

The doctrine of the priesthood of all believers received deci-
sive expression in the three great reformatory treatises of 1520.
In his *Open Letter to the Christian Nobility of the German Nation*,
Luther asserts that the "first wall'" that must be torn down if the
church is ever to be reformed is the myth that "the spiritual is
above the temporal power." All Christians have responsibility for
the life of the church since "Through baptism all of us are consecrated to the priesthood . . . and there is no difference at all
[between clergy and laity] except that of office."[53] Since "the temporal authorities are baptized with the same baptism and have the
same faith and Gospel" as the spiritual authorities, they can take
responsibility for the reform of the church, just as the emperor
Constantine convened the Nicene Council. If the bishops would
not reform the Church, Luther saw no reason why the most emi-
nent lay persons, the princes, should not undertake this responsibility. The ordained priests are not a separate order of men
endowed with an "indelible character" whose service is "religious" while the service of princes and magistrates is only "temporal." All life belongs to God and therefore work which serves
neighbor and society is as pleasing to God as the work of preaching the gospel and administering the sacraments.

Luther developed these views more thoroughly in *The Babylonian Captivity of the Church*, which deals specifically with the
sacramental system. Luther extols the sacrament of Baptism
which God, in his mercy, "hath preserved . . . untouched and
untainted by the ordinances of men . . . " He develops the understanding of Baptism as conformation to the death and resurrection of Christ. This identification with Christ in Baptism raises

questions about religious vows which seem to compete with the baptismal vows and create the impression that there are two levels of Christians. Consequently,

> I advise no one to enter any religious order or the priest-hood—nay, I dissuade everyone—unless he be forearmed with this knowledge and understand that the works of monks and priests, be they never so holy and arduous, differ no whit in the sight of God from the works of the rustic toiling in the field or the woman going about her household tasks, but that all works are measured before Him by faith alone.[54]

The difference between clergy and laity is not one of greater or lesser standing in the sight of God but one of *office*. To make a spiritual distinction between clergy and laity redounds "to the incredible injury of the grace of baptism and the confusion of our fellowship in the Gospel."[55]

The view of the ordained ministry in *The Babylonian Captivity* seems to be that it is one vocation among many which the ordained exercise on behalf of the whole priestly community. ". . . we are all priests, as many of us as are Christians. But the priests, as we call them, are ministers chosen from among us, who do all that they do in our name." [56] This treatise is fiercely polem-ical and it was written before the schism with the papacy made it necessary to give greater thought to church structure. It was the layman, Philip Melanchthon, who provided Lutheranism with a "high" view of the ordained ministry in the Augsburg Confession and its Apology, articles V and XIV. In these Symbolical Books the ordained ministry of Word and Sacrament is regarded as a divine institution, essential to the church's existence, which no one should exercise without a proper call. As Arthur Carl Piep-korn notes, "The Symbolical Books nowhere attempt to derive the sacred ministry from the universal priesthood of the faithful. In fact, the doctrine of the universal priesthood of believers had receded into minor importance—also for Luther himself—by the time the Symbolical Books were being framed."[57]

The abiding importance of the doctrine of the universal priesthood lies not so much in its implication for church polity as in its implications for spirituality and social ethics. It asserts that all Christians have equal standing *coram Deo* by virtue of their Baptism. All priests offer to God the sacrifice of prayer and praise, and of their lives and work. The work of the ordained priest is to preach the gospel and administer the sacraments. But it is a calling no higher in God's sight than that of any other Christian vocation. Whether it is the pastor preaching the gospel, or the prince executing God's will for justice in the world, or the homemaker rearing children in the fear of the Lord, all Christians must live by grace alone through faith in the daily struggle between the "flesh" and the "Spirit," "between sinful self-centeredness and faithful God-centeredness."[58] Before God every person is either covered with the alien righteousness of Christ or stands naked in the guilt and shame of his own sin. But within such a stance Luther could tell the timid Melanchthon, "Be a sinner and sin bravely; but believe more bravely, and rejoice in Christ, who is the victor over sin, death, and the world."[59] We are all saints and sinners at the same time, but that is not cause for dispair for one who believes the gospel that we are justified by grace alone through faith. That gospel liberates us to live boldly, doing what God has called us to do.

It should also be evident that the doctrine of the universal priesthood has nothing in common with the "rugged individualism" espoused by some American Protestants, in which everyone is his own pastor because each person has his own personal "pipeline" to God. The pipelines to God are the means of grace which God has instituted, and which are celebrated in the Christian community. Furthermore, the ethical consequence of the doctrine of the universal priesthood aims at the building up of community. This view is developed in Luther's irenic treatise on *The Freedom of the Christian* with its paradoxical theses: "A Christian is a perfectly free lord of all, subject to none. A Christian is a dutiful servant of all, subject to all."[60] If no one can impose anything on the Christian other than faith in the God of grace, the grace of God also bespeaks his love which empowers the Christian to perform good works for the neighbor. This is the only way to serve a God who humbled himself, voluntarily assuming the form of a servant. Christ is not only the lord of faith, he is also the archetype of love. Saved by God's grace, for Christ's sake, through faith alone, the Christian is free to serve his neighbors with the good works that God's Spirit empowers. Lutheranism is not opposed to good works; it is only concerned that these be seen as a loving response to God's love for us. Such works are a sheer act of devotion; they are not a striving and devising to make oneself acceptable to God. Worksrighteousness is nothing else than the attempt to wring a blessing out of God without faith. Justified by faith, the Christian is liberated to perform all kinds of service to God and to his fellow human beings simply for the sake of doing it.

In Luther's eyes, one of the greatest acts of devotion and one of the most rewarding Christian vocations is to be a pastor and bishop to one's own family. He regarded marriage as a holy estate in which God desires the vast majority of his children to live in mutual love and faithfulness. Luther always allowed the possibility that God grants "supernatural gifts" to a minority to enable them to live a life of celibacy wholly committed to the work of the kingdom of God. Luther regarded his own situation, right up until the time of his marriage in 1525, as being one of celibacy. For some time, however, he had been encouraging monks and nuns to leave the cloister and enter into secular life. In April 1523, he was directly involved in a plot to help some nuns escape from the Cistercian convent in Nimschen, Saxony, one of whom, Katherine von Bora, eventually became Mrs. Martin Luther. The example of Luther's own married life and parental role has been regarded as one of the most profound influences on his followers, especially the picture of the parsonage family that emerges from portrayals of the Luther household. One can easily envision Luther gathering his family around him at the end of the day to tell stories, play his lute, and teach the faith to his children. It was for this kind of setting, with all its joys and pains, that Luther wrote his Small Catechism, and it was also in the household setting as well as in public worship that Lutheran hymnody developed. Catechism and hymnody, without doubt, constitute the most enduring forms of Lutheran faith and piety. No presentation of Lutheran spirituality could be complete without looking at these traditions.

CATECHISM AND HYMNODY

Many times during the 1520s Luther preached catechetical sermons on the Ten Commandments, The Apostles' Creed, the

Lord's Prayer, the Words of Institution, etc. The official visitation of parishes in electoral Saxony in 1528 disclosed the unhappy state of Christian education among both clergy and laity. Luther's *German Catechism* (later called the Large Catechism) appeared in April 1529. The material in the Large Catechism is drawn from the catechetical sermons Luther had preached in 1528 and 1529, and it was largely aimed at the clergy. Luther urged on them the spiritual discipline of reciting the catechism daily and chastised them for regarding the catechism as "a simple, silly teaching which they can absorb and master at one reading." "As for myself," he said, "let me say that I, too, am a doctor and a preacher—yes, and as learned and experienced as any of those who act so high and mighty. Yet I do as a child who is being taught the Catechism. Every morning, and whenever else I have time, I read and recite word for word the Lord's Prayer, the Ten Commandments, the Creed, the Psalms, etc. I must still read and study the Catechism daily, yet I cannot master it as I wish, but must remain a child and pupil of the Catechism, and I do it gladly."[61]

In December 1528, while still at work on the Large Catechism, Luther also began writing the Small Catechism, in the form of an Enchiridion or Handbook. It was published in pamphlet form in May 1529, and in that booklet Luther added the Preface and Table of Duties to the five main sections. The polemical tone which punctuates the Large Catechism is completely lacking in the Small Catechism, for it was written for use in the households of ordinary people. Thus, for example, the Ten Commandments with their "explanations" are presented "in the plain form in which the head of the family shall teach them to his household."[62] While the practice of parents teaching the catechism to their children has become an exception rather than the rule in modern Lutheranism, the Small Catechism has remained the basis of classes leading to confirmation in Lutheran parishes; and these classes are almost invariably taught by the pastor, who regards confirmation instruction as one of the principal responsibilities of his or her office. Lutheran young people, to this day, are expected to memorize the texts of the Ten Commandments, the Apostles' Creed, and the Lord's Prayer, along with the meanings of the commandments, the articles of the Creed, and the petitions of the Prayer, together with the explanations of Baptism and the Lord's Supper.

The Catechism nowhere takes up that chief article on justification by grace through faith, on which the Lutheran Confessions say everything else stands or falls. Yet the spiritual stance of man *coram Deo*, which the doctrine of justification articulates, pervades every section of the Catechism. Thus, in the explanations of the Ten Commandments, Luther has caught the biblical preamble, "I am the Lord your God, who brought you out of the land of Egypt, out of the house of bondage. [Therefore] You shall have no other gods before me" (Exodus 20:2–3). "What does this mean?" asks the Catechism. "We should fear, love, and trust God above all things." Each of the other commandments is interpreted in this light, each explanation beginning "We should fear and love God so that . . . " The basis for obeying the commandments is the divine election. Living life in conformity with the commandments is not a matter of legalistic compulsion but of loving response to the God who has saved us and made us his own. Thus, in each explanation there is not only a negative thrust—what we should *not* do—but also a positive thrust—what we *are* to do. For example, the explanation to the second commandment (Luther follows the traditional Catholic numeration) is: "We should fear and love God, and so we should not use his name to curse, swear, practice magic, lie, or deceive, but in every time of need call upon him, pray to him, praise him, and give him thanks."[63]

The loving response to the God who has created, redeemed, and sanctified me is emphasized in the explanations of the articles of the Creed. In article one, all that God the Father does to "preserve," "provide," and "protect" me is "out of his pure, fatherly, and divine goodness and mercy, without any merit or worthiness on my part. For all this I am bound to thank, praise, serve, and obey him."[64] In article two, it is clear that God the Son "has redeemed me, a lost and condemned creature, delivered me and freed me from all sins, from death, and from the power of the devil . . . in order that I might be his, live under him in his kingdom, and serve him in everlasting righteousness, innocence, and blessedness . . . ." In article three, God the Holy Spirit "has called me through the Gospel, enlightened me with his gifts, and sanctified and preserved me in true faith, just as he calls, gathers, enlightens, and sanctifies the whole Christian church on earth and preserves it in union with Jesus Christ in the one true faith."

This personal relationship with God receives even stronger emphasis in the explanations of the petitions of the Lord's Prayer. "Here God would encourage us to believe that he is truly our Father and we are truly his children in order that we may approach him boldly and confidently in prayer, even as beloved children approach their dear father."[65] A father knows his children so well that he is aware of their needs even before they ask. "To be sure, God's name is holy in itself. . . . To be sure, the kingdom of God comes of itself, without our prayer. . . . To be sure, the good and gracious will of God is done without our prayer. . . . To be sure, God provides daily bread, even to the wicked, without our prayer. . . ." If God does not need our prayer, why do we pray? "We pray in this petition that [God's name] may also be holy for us. . . . we pray in this petition that [God's kingdom] may also come to us. . . . we pray in this petition that [God's will] may also be done by us. . . . we pray in this petition that God may make us aware of his gifts and enable us to receive our daily bread with thanksgiving."

This personal relationship with God is established in holy Baptism, which "effects forgiveness of sins, delivers from death and the devil, and grants eternal salvation to all who believe, as the Word and promise of God declare."[66] The effects of Baptism are not accomplished by the water only, but by "the Word of God connected with the water." The Word of God is everything for Luther, because it is trustworthy. It is in the power of that Word that we live out our baptism in daily life, for baptism signifies a daily struggle: "that the old Adam in us, together with all sins and evil lusts, should be drowned by daily sorrow and be put to death, and that the new man should come forth daily and rise up, cleansed and righteous, to live forever in God's presence." Confession and absolution is a means of living out this daily putting to death of the old self which baptism signifies. But once again, it is the *word* of forgiveness to which one should cling. The confessor is directed by the Catechism to ask the penitent, "Do you believe that the forgiveness I declare is the forgiveness of God?" If the answer is "yes," the confessor declares: "Be it done for you as you have believed. According to the command of our Lord Jesus Christ, I forgive you your sins in the name of the Father and of the Son and of the Holy Spirit."[67] There is a profound psychological insight here; there is no point in forgiving someone who cannot believe that he is forgiven. But the theological emphasis is, in the words of the Large Catechism, God's work of absolution rather than the human work of confession, "when he absolves me of my sins through a word placed in the mouth of a man."[68] Likewise, in the sacrament of the altar the benefits of eating and drinking are given by virtue of the words "for you" and "for the forgiveness of sins." "These words, when accompanied by the bodily eating and drinking, are the chief thing in the sacrament, and he who believes these words has what they say and declare: forgiveness of sins."[69] Forgiveness of sins for Luther is a dynamic event which makes possible a new relationship with God, "for where there is forgiveness of sins, there are also life and salvation."

The Christian's new relationship with God finds concrete expression in prayer. The first appendix of the Small Catechism provides private prayer for rising in the morning and going to bed at night. Without saying so, the Catechism provides that the Christian's day is to begin and end in remembrance of one's Baptism. For "in the morning, when you rise," and again "in the evening, when you retire, make the sign of the cross and say, 'In the name of God, the Father, the Son, and the Holy Spirit. Then, kneeling or standing, say the Apostles' Creed and the Lord's Prayer." The sign of the cross, the trinitarian invocation, and the Apostles' Creed are all associated with Baptism; and in the Medieval rite of Baptism which Luther translated and revised in 1523, and revised further in 1526, the Lord's Prayer was also taught at the font. Luther's well-known (to Lutherans) morning and evening prayers are provided in the Catechism.[70]

MORNING PRAYER
I give Thee thanks, heavenly Father, through thy dear Son Jesus Christ, that Thou hast protected me through the night from all harm and dan-

EVENING PRAYER
I give Thee thanks, heavenly Father, through thy dear Son Jesus Christ, that Thou hast this day graciously protected me. I beseech Thee to forgive

ger. I beseech Thee to keep me this day, too, from all sin and evil, that in all my thoughts, words, and deeds I may please Thee. Into thy hands I commend my body and soul and all that is mine. Let thy holy angel have charge of me, that the wicked one may have no power over me. Amen.

all my sin and the wrong which I have done. Graciously protect me during the coming night. Into thy hands I commend my body and soul and all that is mine. Let thy holy angels have charge of me, that the wicked one may have no power over me. Amen.

There are very few prayers from Luther's pen. Like his postcommunion prayer in the *German Mass*, these prayers are based on traditional sources—in this case the Roman Breviary. And yet they display the essential characteristics of Luther's prayers and have been a model for praying Lutherans. They presuppose that God's grace has already been given to us, and therefore they begin on a note of thanksgiving. Following Paul's exhortation to the Philippians, "in everything by prayer and supplication with thanksgiving let your requests be made known to God," they include very specific petitions. It is one of the characteristics of Luther's prayers that they end in an expression of trust and surrender to God. Thus: "Into thy hands I commend my body and soul and all that is mine." The basis of this trust is the confidence that God is true to his promise. The morning and evening prayers conclude with a petition based on the promise in Psalm 91:11, "For he will give his angels charge of you to guard you in all your ways."

We should note that Luther's prayers, like the classical Latin collects and the Lord's Prayer, tend to be brief and to the point. It was Luther's rule on prayer that "one should pray briefly but often and fervently." He saw no contradiction between being spontaneous in prayer and using a devotional formula. In periods of spiritual dryness one may need classical models of prayer. Luther taught that "if one would pray by himself alone in church or at home and has no better words or form, let him recite the Lord's Prayer and rouse his own spirit of worship with these or similar words."[71]

The second appendix on prayer in the Catechism instructs the head of the family to offer blessing and thanksgiving at table. Luther took over the monastic meal graces with only minor changes.[72] The blessing before meals *(Benedicite)* is preceded with the verses of Psalms 145:15–16, "The eyes of all look to Thee, O Lord . . . " which teach us to be mindful of our utter dependence on our heavenly Father for all the gifts of life, including the nourishment we need for bodily existence. The thanksgiving after meals *(Gratias)* blends together Psalms 106:1, 136:26, and 147:9–11, which celebrate God's provision for his whole creation. His steadfast love is unvaryingly stable and dependable. The cattle in the field and the young ravens which scream overhead all receive God's care without merit or worthiness, and so do we. God takes no particular delight in the strength or fleetness of the horse, nor is he impressed by the strong thighs of the rider, but the Lord reserves his pleasure for those who revere him and wait patiently for his steadfast love to reveal itself.

Even this cursory survey of the Catechism reveals how its use over the years has nurtured a spirituality which centers on a personal response to the unfailing love of God in his works of creation, redemption, and sanctification. The believer hears the word of God and submits to it in expectation of the promise of a new and renewable relationship with God which it declares. For Lutherans, this word does not lead to a distrust of external means because the word is known only through the external means of Bible, preaching, and the sacraments. Nor is the emphasis on the personal relationship with God a form of individualism. The Christian's responsibility to others is more than adequately treated in the explanations of commandments four through ten. The Christian's relationship with the community of believers is memorably treated in the explanation of the third article of the Creed. The Christian's common dependence on God with all other creatures is amply discussed in the explanation of the meaning of "daily bread" in the fourth petition of the Lord's Prayer and in the gloss on Psalm 145:15–16 in the appendix on Grace at Table, which was intended to explain the meaning of "satisfy the desire of every living thing." The context of the administration of the sacraments, of course, is the *ecclesia*, the "assembly," although it must be admitted that the focus of the

Catechism's treatment of the sacraments is the personal appropriation of the benefits promised by the words of Christ. It is also
noteworthy that Lutheran sacramental practice remained as per-
sonally-oriented as Roman Catholic practice. Baptisms were privately arranged, private confession lingered on for some years
after the Reformation (and has always remained available in pastoral care), and Holy Communion "is offered to those who wish
for it after they have been examined and absolved" (*Apology*,
XXIV, 1).[73] In comparison, Reformed use of the sacraments
under Zwingli, Bucer, and Calvin was more corporate in practice.

The Catechism has been a mainstay of Lutheran spirituality
over the years, along with the hymnal. Luther had a better than
average musical ability, and he encouraged the writing of evangelical hymns both for liturgical purposes (to facilitate congregational participation in public worship) and for catechetical purposes (to inculcate true doctrine and piety). Among the early
Lutheran hymns which served liturgical purposes are those which
Luther wrote for his *German Mass*[74] and several of his versifica-
tions of sequences and canticles (e.g. "Christ Jesus lay in death's
strong bands" [*LBW* #134], based on *Victimae paschali laudes*,
and "Lord God, thy praise we sing" [*LW* 53:174], based on the
Te Deum). One of the most successful efforts along these lines is
Nikolaus Decius' versification of the *Gloria in excelsis*, "All glory
be to God on high" (*LBW* #166). Among the important catechetical hymns are two which appeared in the first Lutheran hymnal, the *Achtliederbuch* of 1524, Luther's "Good Christians, one
and all, rejoice" (*LBW* #299), which extols the saving merits of
Christ, and Paul Speratus' "Salvation unto us has come" (*LBW* #
297; see also *Lutheran Hymnal* #377), which has been called "a
poetic counterpart to Luther's preface to the Epistle to the
Romans."

As they had done in other spheres, Luther and his co-work-
ers made use of pre-Reformation musical traditions such as liturgical chants, German sacred *lieder*, and German folk and fraternal
songs.[75] Sometimes texts were simply translated or "improved in
a Christian manner," and the melody altered only slightly to fit
the revised text. Many of the Medieval office hymns and *Leisen*
(pre-Reformation folk hymns characterized by the words *Kyrie
eleison* at the end of each stanza) came into Lutheran use in this

way. Another group of hymns was procured through the *contra-factum* technique of providing a new text for a melody that was already popular. Such secular love songs as *O Welt, ich muss dich lassen* and *Mein G'müt ist mir verwirret* came into the church with such texts as Paul Gerhardt's "Now rest beneath night's shadows" (*LBW* #276, 282) and "O sacred Head, now wounded" (*LBW* #116, 117). Luther's own "From Heaven above to earth I come" (*LBW* #51) was based on the tune and text of the secular song, "Good news from far abroad I bring." Within such strictures, however, Luther achieved some of his tenderest lyrics as he expressed wonder at the divine condescension in the incarnation.

> O Lord, you have created all!
> How did you come to be so small,
> To sweetly sleep in manger-bed
> Where lowing cattle lately fed?
>
> Were earth a thousand times as fair
> And set with gold and jewels rare,
> Still such a cradle would not do
> To rock a prince so great as you.
>
> For velvets soft and silken stuff
> You have but hay and straw so rough
> On which as king so rich and great
> To be enthroned in humble state.
>
> O dearest Jesus, holy child,
> Prepare a bed, soft, undefiled,
> A holy shrine, within my heart,
> That you and I need never part.

The final source of hymns were new texts and tunes written and composed by the reformers. Certainly the most famous of these is Luther's "A mighty fortress is our God" (*LBW* #228, 229), based on Psalm 46 and set to a vigorous tune composed by Luther himself. The exact circumstances of the origin of the hymn are uncertain, although the days of uncertainty and persecution of Luther's followers in the years before the Diet of Augsburg (1530) undoubtedly provide a general background for this sturdy expression of reliance on God's Word to prevail over all spiritual enemies. It is for this reason that it has been called "the battle hymn of the Reformation," and a hundred years later the Swedish King Gustavus Adolphus caused it to be sung before the Battle of Leipzig in 1631. Hymns of a similar character by other reformers include Justus Jonas' "If God had not been on our side" and Paul Eber's "When in the hour of deepest need" (*LBW* #303).

Hymns expressing a childlike trust in a gracious God continued to be written in the generations after the Reformation. Such texts would include Nikolaus Selnecker's "Let me be yours forever" (*LBW* #490), Bartholomäus Ringwaldt's "The day is surely drawing near" (*LBW* #321), and Martin Schalling's masterful hymn of comfort, "Lord, Thee I love with all my heart" (*LBW* #325), with which Johann Sebastian Bach concluded his *St. John Passion*. It was in this period of Lutheran scholasticism, after the signing of the Formula of Concord in 1577, that Philipp Nicolai (1556–1608) wrote the two masterpieces which have been called respectively the king and queen of chorales, "Wake, awake, for night is flying" (*Wachet auf, LBW* #31) and "O Morning Star, how fair and bright" (*Wie schön Leuchtet, LBW* #76). Both hymns appear in Nicolai's devotional writing, *Mirror of Joy*. As a title to *Wachet Auf*, Nicolai wrote, "Of the voice at Midnight, and the Wise Virgins who meet their heavenly Bridegroom. Matthew 25." The title of *Wie schön Leuchtet* reads, "A spiritual bridal song of the believing soul concerning Jesus Christ, her Heavenly Bridegroom founded on the 45th Psalm of David." The theme of mystical union was prominent in the writings of Nicolai. He emphasized the dwelling of the baptized believer in Christ and the indwelling of the Triune God in the baptized believer.[76] In these hymns he used the image of marriage to describe this personal relationship between Christ and the believer, as many of the Medieval mystics had done. In both hymns the doxological conclusions reach incandescent proportions.

WACHET AUF	WIE SCHÖN LEUCHTET
Now let all the heav'ns adore you,	Oh, let the harps break forth in sound!
And saints and angels sing before you.	Our joy be all with music crowned,

The harps and cymbals all unite.
Of one pearl each shining portal,
Where, dwelling with the choir immortal,
We gather round your dazzling light.
No eye has seen, no ear
Has yet been trained to hear.
What joy is ours!
Crescendos rise; your halls resound;
Hosannas blend in cosmic sound.

Our voices gaily blending!
For Christ goes with us all the way—
Today, tomorrow, ev'ry day!
His love is never ending!
Sing out! Ring out!
Jubilation!
Exultation!
Tell the story!
Great is he, the King of glory!

This ecstasy is all the more remarkable when it is realized that these hymns were written during a time of plague. Times of suffering have often brought forth great devotional poetry. This was certainly true of the period of the Thirty Years' War. The sufferings of war caused Johann Heermann (1585–1647) to contemplate the sufferings of Christ in *Herzliebster Jesu* (*LBW* #123).

Ah, holy Jesus, how has thou offended
That man to judge thee hath in hate pretended?
By foes derided, by thine own rejected,
O must afflicted.

Who was the guilty? Who brought this upon thee?
Alas, my treason, Jesus, hath undone thee.
'Twas I, Lord Jesus, I it was denied thee;
I crucified thee.

Another hymn growing out of the experience of bloodshed and pestilence of the war was Martin Rinkart's (1586–1649) "Now thank we all our God" (*LBW* #533), which has been called the "Lutheran Te Deum." It has been thought that the hymn was written to celebrate the end of the war with the signing of the Peace of Westfalia in 1648. But in Rinkart's own manuscript it seems that the hymn was written to be sung as a table grace by his children. It is worth noting that many of the hymns which have come to be sung in public worship originated in domestic devotions. This particular hymn has come into widespread use in English-language hymnals through the translation of Catherine Winkworth (1829–78), who translated many of the German chorales into English.

Heerman and Rinkart were pastors, but lay persons were also writing devotional hymns which eventually secured a place in public worship. One of the most noteworthy lay hymnwriters was Johann Franck (1618–77), a lawyer who became mayor of Guben in Brandenburg in 1661. To him we are indebted for one of the finest communion hymns, "Soul, adorn yourself with gladness" (*Schmücke dich*, LBW #224), and the great hymn of comfort and hope whose text served as the basis of J.S. Bach's unaccompanied funeral motet, "Jesus, priceless Treasure" (*Jesu, meine Freude*, LBW #457). Franck began the long series of "Jesus hymns" which reached their culmination in the hymns of the Pietist movement.

The tunes to which many of these seventeenth century lyrics were wedded were composed by Johann Crüger (1598–1662), the cantor of St. Nicholas' Church in Berlin. In 1657, Paul Gerhardt (1607–76) became the third assistant pastor at St. Nicholas'. His contact with Crüger stimulated Gerhardt's poetic gifts, and his collaboration with the cantor helped his hymns achieve a popularity which only increased with the rise of Pietism in the latter part of the seventeenth century. Gerhardt was an orthodox Lutheran who refused to sign a pledge not to bring doctrinal discussion into his sermons. This was an act of political defiance because the expansion of Brandenburg-Prussia meant that Reformed as well as Lutheran populations were included in the electorate, and the elector's policy was to serve as head of one Protestant Church in his territories which served both traditions. The result of Gerhardt's refusal to sign the pledge meant that he was removed from his position by Elector Frederick William in 1666. He remained without a parish for some years, during which his wife and son died (three of his children had died earlier). In 1669 he was appointed archdeacon of Lübben, and lived there with a sister-in-law and a sole surviving son in a somewhat unsympathetic parish until his death in 1676.

It is not surprising that a person with Gerhardt's poetic sensibilities, living through the Thirty Years' War and considerable personal misery, would write hymns in a more subjective mood than what had been written previously. His one hundred and twenty-three hymns express a confidence in God's love that gives them an emotional warmth often lacking in earlier Lutheran hymns. This is especially evident in his Advent hymn, "O Lord, how shall I meet you?" (*LBW* #23), and even more so in "Jesus, thy boundless love to me" (*LBW* #336), which was translated into English by John Wesley. This latter hymn fervently petitions the indwelling of the love of Christ in the soul.

> Oh, grant that nothing in my soul
> May dwell, but thy pure love alone;
> Oh, may thy love possess me whole,
> My joy, my treasure, and my crown!
> All coldness from my heart remove;
> May ev'ry act, word, thought, be love.

It is not surprising that the poet who could express such sentiments found a congenial spirit in St. Bernard of Clairvaux, and he added verses to a hymn attributed to St. Bernard, "O sacred Head, now wounded" (*LBW* #116, 117). With Gerhardt we reach the high point of classical Lutheran hymnody.

DEVOTIONAL LITERATURE

Many of these hymns were not originally written for church services, but for family devotion. They found a use in public worship especially under the influence of Pietism, which was looking for a more personal expression of the relationship between God and man. We have seen that Nicolai's two great chorales were appended to a book of meditations, written to comfort people during a time of plague, entitled *Mirror of Joy*. The most important devotional books of the post-Reformation period were the *Books on True Christianity*, by Johann Arndt (1555–1621).[78] It was in Arndt's writings especially that the Augustinian mystical tradition represented by St. Bernard and Johann Tauler first came back into Lutheranism in full force. The Lutheran prayer for divine grace is fused with the mystical yearning for union with God in the depths of the soul.

Arndt's influence on Lutheran piety was such that he has been called "the father of Lutheran pietism."[79] He fused justification with sanctification in such a way that "justification by faith" became the principle of a transformation of the human soul by the indwelling of Christ. Arndt lifted up the concern to see the evidence of justification in Christian life which was put into programmatic form by Philip Jacob Spener (1635–1705), whose most famous work, *Pia Desideria* (1675), was originally published as a preface to an edition of Arndt's popular sermons on the appointed Gospel readings for the church year (the 1615 *Postil*).[80] The Orthodox school condemned Arndt and Spener for undermining Baptism as a means of grace, and therefore also undermining the believer's assurance of salvation by confusing justification and sanctification. This school held instead the view of "forensic" or juridical justification, that the sinner is declared justified before God for Christ's sake.

This does not mean that the Orthodox theologians had no concern for the spiritual life. The greatest of the Orthodox theologians, Johann Gerhard (1582–1637), complained about the need for personal reform and spiritual renewal and wrote a devotional book that was less influential than Arndt's but still important in the history of Lutheran spirituality: *Meditationes sacrae* (1606). Gerhard was able to restore the Pauline "Christ in us" mysticism, so prominent in the Greek fathers whom he read, without compromising the "Christ for us" emphasis of the Orthodox school. The idea of "Christ in us" and our incorporation into him is especially emphasized in Gerhard's meditations on the fruits of Holy Communion.

> What can be more intimately united to the Lord than His own human nature, which He hath taken in his incarnation, into fellowship with the adorable Trinity, and thus made the treasury of all the blessings that heaven has to bestow? What is so intimately joined to Him as His own body and blood? With this truly heavenly food He refreshes our souls, who are miserable worms of dust before Him, and makes us partakers of His own nature; why then shall we not enjoy His gracious favor?[81]

Both Arndt and Gerhard contributed significantly to a genre of literature that gained in popularity during the seventeenth century and has continued to nurture the spiritual growth of countless Christians. Devotional literature in the form of books of meditations is not unique to Lutheranism, but such materials have been very important in Lutheran spirituality. The twentieth century especially has seen the mass publication of inexpensive, serialized devotional booklets, of which the Methodist publication, *The Upper Room*, is one of the most successful. Lutheran counterparts include *Portals of Prayer*, published under the auspices of the Lutheran Church—Missouri Synod, and *The Word in Season*, published by the Board of Publication of the Lutheran Church in America. The format of these booklets includes a brief Bible reading, a meditation on it, a prayer, and a thought for the day. As Kenneth F. Korby has written, "One could multiply almost endlessly the number of such 'devotional booklets,' nurturers and shapers of the prayer life of many people. To my knowledge no serious liturgical, pastoral, and theological study has been made of these widely used materials. Such a study would surely be in the interest of and of service to the renewal of liturgical prayer."[82]

FOLK PIETY

No presentation on Lutheran spirituality would be complete without noting the indigenization of Lutheran faith and practice in the cultures of whole groups of people. This began to happen in Germany with the spread of the Reformation as a popular movement, aided by the use of the Catechism and the singing of hymns. Luther himself was something of a folk hero, hailed as the Saxon Hus and the German Hercules. The indigenization of Lutheranism occurred at a slower pace in Scandinavia, where the decision to embrace the Reformation was more of a political and economic move than a popular one. As the Swedish literary figure, Vilhelm Moberg, has written in *A History of the Swedish People*, II: "So Sweden officially became an Evangelical Lutheran kingdom, with its own state Church, but a great deal of time was to pass before people were transformed spiritually from Catholics to Protestants. Here was no question of a spontaneous conversion; and it is quite possible that, but for Gustav Vasa's monetary straits, the Swedes would have remained Catholics to this day."[83]

Yet Sweden did become a Lutheran nation after several decades of preaching, catechizing, legislating, and worshiping according to an evangelical mass-order. By the seventeenth century Lutheranism was solidly rooted in the Scandinavian kingdoms and their territories, and in Finland (which Sweden had lost to Russia in 1809). The development of a genuine folk piety in these northern countries was possible by the nineteenth century because of the spurt in hymn-writing. In Sweden we may note the contribution of Johan Olof Wallin (1779–1839), who became archbishop of Uppsala in 1837, but whose lasting fame rests on his poetry and hymns. As early as 1807 he began to publish collections of old and new hymns, and between 1811 and 1819 he edited a revision of the Swedish hymnal, which included some one hundred and thirty hymns written by Wallin himself and nearly two hundred others revised or translated by him. The sense of collective feeling in his poetry is perhaps best expressed in "We worship You, O God of might" (*LBW* #432). A warmer expression of confidence in the transcendent God is expressed by Caroline V. Sandell Berg (1832–1903) in the perennially popular, "Children of the Heavenly Father" (*LBW* #474). The great nineteenth century Norwegian hymnwriter was Magnus Brostrup Landstad (1802–1880), who also published collections of folk literature. Folk piety was deepened in Norway by the controversial career of the lay preacher, Hans Nielsen Hauge (1771–1824), and in Finland by the similar career of the lay preacher, Pauvo Routsalainen (1777–1852). Pietist leaders in Sweden included Henrik Schartau (1757–1825), who laid great stress on the church's worship and whose catechetical lectures drew great crowds, and Carl Olof Rosenius (1816–68), who stressed a theology of "objective justification" which he personalized by an emphasis on Bible study and soul-searching. Scandinavian immigrants to America in the nineteenth century brought this intensely pietistic spirituality with them.

The great champion of folk piety and folk church in Denmark was Nikolai Frederik Severin Grundtvig (1783–1872). Grundtvig was brought from rationalism to a living faith through a typical pietist conversion. But unlike some others whose conversion experience led them to the margins of the church, Grundtvig rediscovered the church as the teacher of the faith and the sacraments as the necessary nourishment of faith. He occasioned controversy over his attacks on those who treated Christianity as a philosophical idea rather than as an historical revelation handed down through a living succession in the sacramental tradition. This delayed ecclesiastical advancement until the end of his life when he was made a bishop without a diocese. Much of his career was spent as chaplain of a home for aged women. He developed the view that the church must be the educator not only of individuals but of whole Christian peoples. His involvement in the whole life of his people was expressed in his research into Nordic mythology, his poetry, and his authorship of over a thousand hymns. Grundtvig's view of the church's involvement in the whole life of a people is most succinctly expressed in "Built on a Rock" (*LBW* #365).

> Built on a rock the Church shall stand,
> Even when steeples are falling;
> Crumbled have spires in ev'ry land,
> Bells still are chiming and calling—-
> Calling the young and old to rest,
> Calling the souls of those distressed,
> Longing for life everlasting.

DISCIPLESHIP AND CROSS-BEARING

While Grundtvig was cultivating the kind of folk piety that has given Lutheranism a sturdiness that comes from the merger of religious and ethnic identity, a younger contemporary was attacking the very concept of culture Christianity. Søren Aabye Kierkegaard (1813–1855), the father of modern existentialism, was opposed to the National Church because it institutionalized and killed the essential spirit of Christianity. With a revolutionary view of truth, Kierkegaard held that truth is not something to be determined by detached reflection, but rather by experience of life with all its risks. Christianity ought not so much comfort people as challenge them to search their hearts and come to know themselves as they really are before God. As he wrote in *The Sickness Unto Death*,

> There is so much said now about people being offended at Christianity because it is so dark and gloomy, offended at it because it is so severe, etc. It is now high time to explain that the real reason why man is offended at Christianity is because it is too high, because its goal is not man's goal, because it would make of a man something so extraordinary that he is unable to get it into his head. A perfectly simple psychological investigation of what offense is will explain this, and at the same time it will show how infinitely silly their behavior has been who defended Christianity by taking away the offense.[84]

Kierkegaard's "attack upon Christendom" was based on the fact that the church, which Christ commissioned to preach the scandal of the cross, was parading itself in the world as a power to be reckoned with. The church has, in fact, betrayed Christianity. The "betrayal of Christianity" depends on an enormous hoax, namely, "the maxim that one becomes a Christian as a child, that if one is rightly to become a Christian, one must be such from infancy." Thus "Christendom is from generation to generation a society of non-Christians."[85]

The nineteenth century was not prepared for Kierkegaard's attack on culture Christianity, and it was not until the twentieth century with its catastrophes of world wars and totalitarian states that Kierkegaard could be truly appreciated. Only in the twentieth century has it occurred to some that to be a Christian in the biblical sense is to be taken out of the problemless world of the bourgeoisie and thrust into the dark night of suffering with Christ. Christendom is Christianity without the cross; it operates precisely with what Luther castigated: a theology of glory. Kierkegaard applied what he had learned from the tradition of Luther in an area where Luther had not applied his own theology: the area of church and society. Midway through the twentieth century, the German pastor and theologian, Dietrich Bonhoeffer, applied the same corrective: grace is not "cheap," but "costly." The cost is "discipleship" and following the way of the cross. This *imitatio Christi* was not a reappropriation of medieval piety, but an application of the gospel of justification to the twentieth century. For that gospel holds up the cross of Christ—the symbol of defeat and failure—as inimical to every form of Christian triumphalism. It constitutes a challenge to a society founded on the notion of limitless human progress; and it also speaks a word of consolation to those who experience the limitations of human perfection.

Lutheranism has not exerted much of an influence on North American society. It may be that Lutherans are only now in a position to exert some influence as they reappropriate and apply what is central to their own tradition of spirituality in the context of the experience of limitation and failure which North American society is facing for the first time in its history.[86] Not insignificantly, the recovery of the theology of the cross is coming not only from European thinkers but also from the first original Christian theology from Japan, the *Theology of the Pain of God*, by Kazoh Kitamori. With fresh insight into the gospel of the cross, Kitamori shows that God loves the objects of his wrath, that he searches out those who spurn him. There is both a mystical dimension and an ethical power in this theology. "We become united with the pain of God through our pain, and we are united with God through the joined pains."[87] "For those of us who follow the Lord of the cross by bearing our cross and follow the pain of God by suffering pain, ethics must also be determined by the love of the cross—the pain of God . . . . We must love the unloveable . . . ."[88] Lutheran spirituality based on the theology of the cross is a spirituality come of age in a "world come of age."

NOTES

1. These confessional documents include the Apostles', Nicene, and Athanasian Creeds; the Augsburg Confession (1530); the Apology of the Augsburg Confession (1531); the Smalcald Articles (1537), the Small Catechism (1529); the Large Catechism (1529), and the Formula of Concord (1577). See *The Book of Concord*, ed. and trans. by Theodore G. Tappert in collaboration with Jaroslav Pelikan, Robert H. Fischer, and Arthur C. Piepkorn (Philadelphia: Fortress, 1959). Hereafter cited as Tappert.

2. See Jaroslav Pelikan, *Obedient Rebel. Catholic Substance and Protestant Principal in Luther's Reformation* (New York: Harper and Row, 1964), especially Part One: "Critical Reverence towards Tradition." As an example of Lutheranism's commitment to the catholic and apostolic tradition see Martin Chemnitz, *Examination of the Council of Trent* (1565–73), Part I, trans. by Fred Kramer (St. Louis: Concordia, 1971), "Concerning Traditions," pp. 217–307. See also Peter Fraenkel, *Testimonia Patrum. The Function of the Patristic Argument in the Theology of Philip Melanchthon* (Geneva, 1961).

3. See *Interpreters of Luther. Essays in Honor of Wilhelm Pauck*, ed. by Jaroslav Pelikan (Philadelphia: Fortress, 1968).

4. Many of the older Catholic interpretations of Luther suffer from a view which sees the reformer as an ossified Occamite. Thus Heinrich Denifle, *Luther und Luthertum; in der ersten entwickelung*, II vols. (Mainz: Kirchheim, 1904, 1909); Joseph Lortz, *Die Reformation in Deutschland* III vols. (Freiburg: Herder, 1939–40); and Louis Bouyer, *The Spirit and Form of Protestantism*, trans. by A. V. Littledale (Westminster, Md.: Newman Press, 1956). A more balanced and insightful reading of Luther in relation to late Medieval renewal movements is provided by John P. Dolan, *History of the Reformation* (New York and Toronto: A Mentor-Omega Book, 1965).

5. Louis Bouyer, *Introduction to Spirituality*, trans. by Mary Perkins Ryan (Collegeville: Liturgical Press, 1961), p. 287.

6. See Louis Bouyer, *History of Christian Spirituality*, I. *The Spirituality of the New Testament and the Fathers* (New York, Tournai, Paris, Rome: Desclee, 1963), pp. 71ff, 79ff.

7. Roland Bainton, *Here I Stand* (New York and Nashville: Abingdon-Cokesbury, 1950), p. 25.

8. *Luthers Werke*. Weimar Kritsche Gesamtausgabe [hereafter cited as *WA*, followed by volume and page numbers] 38:143; quoted in Gordon Rupp, *The Righteousness of God. Luther Studies* (London: Hodder and Stoughton, 1953), p. 103.

9. *Luther's Works*. American edition, ed. by Jaroslav Pelikan and Helmut T. Lehmann (St. Louis: Concordia and Philadelphia: Fortress) [hereafter cited as *LW*, followed by volume and page numbers] 31:358–9.

10. *LW* 21:157.

11. *LW* 21:162.

12. Dietrich Bonhoeffer, *The Cost of Discipleship*, Eng. trans. (New York: Macmillan, 1963), pp. 189–90.

13. *LW* 51:99.

14. *WA* 44:819; quoted in Rupp, p. 104.

15. *WA* 5:79; quoted in Rupp, p.107.

16. *LW* 34:337.

17. Erich Vogelsang, "Luther und die Mystik," *Luther-Jahrbuch 1937*, pp. 32–54.

18. *Theologia Germanica of Martin Luther*, ed. by Bengt Hoffman (New York: Paulist, 1980).

19. *Luther's Works*. Second Philadelphia Edition, XXXI: 75.

20. See Steven E. Ozment, *Homo Spiritualis. A Comparative Study of the Anthropology of Johannes Tauler, Jean Gerson and Martin Luther (1509–1516) in the Context of Their Theological Thought* (Leiden: E.J. Brill, 1969).

21. See Bengt Hägglund, *The Background of Luther's Doctrine of Justification in Late Medieval Theology* (Philadelphia: Fortress Facet Books, 1971), pp. 4ff.

22. Bengt R. Hoffman, *Luther and the Mystics* (Minneapolis: Augsburg, 1976), p. 15.

23. *LW* 31:50

24. *LW* 31:52

25. *LW* 31:53.

26. *LW* 31:55–56.

27. *LW* 31:63–64.

28. *LW* 31:298.

29. *LW* 31:349.

30. *LW* 31:351.

31. See Eric W. Gritsch and Robert W. Jenson, *Lutheranism. The Theological Movement and Its Confessional Writings* (Philadelphia: Fortress, 1976), pp. 70ff, 91ff.

32. See Bard Thompson, *Liturgies of the Western Church* (Cleveland: World Publishing Company, 1961), for the mass-liturgies of Luther, Zwingli, Bucer, Calvin, Cranmer, and Knox.

33. See *LW* 53: *Liturgy and Hymns*.

34. See Luther D. Reed, *The Lutheran Liturgy*, 2nd ed. (Philadelphia: Fortress, 1959), pp. 88ff. It should be noted that in the sixteenth century, and for several centuries afterward, Norway

was a part of Denmark and Finland was a part of Sweden, both politically and ecclesiastically, and therefore liturgically as well.

35. See Heinrich Bornkamm, *Das Wort Gottes bei Luther* (München, 1933).

36. Quoted in Bainton, pp. 354–55.

37. *LW* 36:340.

38. Quoted in Hermann Sasse, *This Is My Body* (Minneapolis: Augsburg, 1959), pp. 252–53.

39. *Formula of Concord*, Solid Declaration VII; Tappert, p. 575.

40. See Wilhelm Stählin, *The Mystery of God*, trans. by R. Birch Hoyle (St. Louis: Concordia, 1964), pp. 23ff, 68ff.

41. *LW* 53:28.

42. *LW* 53:82.

43. *LW* 38:316.

44. Tappert, p. 591.

45. *Lutheran Book of Worship* (Minneapolis: Augsburg and Philadelphia; Board of Publication of the Lutheran Church in America, 1978), #215 [hereafter cited as *LBW*]. (Hymns are designated by the sign #.) It should be noted that Luther adapted this hymn from a Corpus Christi *Leise* that was sung by the congregation between verses of the Latin sequence, *Lauda Sion Salvatorem*, which was sung by the choir during the Corpus Christi procession. See Ulrich Leupold, *LW* 53:252.

46. Louis Bouyer, *Eucharist*, trans. by Charles U. Quinn (Notre Dame, Ind.: University of Notre Dame Press, 1968), pp. 396–97.

47. See Reed, pp. 140ff.

48. Arthur Carl Piepkorn, *Profiles in Belief*, II (San Francisco: Harper and Row, 1978), 97–98.

49. *WA* 2:716; quoted in William H. Lazareth, *Luther on the Christian Home* (Philadelphia: Muhlenberg Press, 1960), p. 91.

50. *LW* 35:98.

51. *LW* 35:99.

52. *LW* 35:100.

53. Martin Luther, *Three Treatises* (Philadelphia: Muhlenberg Press, 1947), p. 14.

54. *Ibid.*, p. 192.

55. *Ibid.*, p. 230.

56. *Ibid.*, p. 231.

57. Piepkorn, II, 86–87.

58. Lazareth, p. 96.

59. Preserved Smith and Charles Jacobs, eds., *Luther's Correspondence and Other Contemporary Letters*, II (Philadelphia: Lutheran Publication Society, 1918), p. 50.

60. *Three Treatises*, p. 251.

61. Tappert, p. 359.

62. *Ibid.*, p. 342.

63. *Ibid.*

64. *Ibid.*, p. 345.

65. *Ibid.*, p. 346.

66. *Ibid.*, p. 348.

67. *Ibid.*, p. 351.

68. *Ibid.*, p. 459.

69. *Ibid.*, p. 352.

70. *Ibid.*, pp. 352–53.

71. See Friedrich Heiler, *Prayer*, trans. and ed. by Samuel McComb (New York: Oxford University Press, 1958), pp. 236–37.

72. See Arthur Carl Piepkorn, "Benedicite and Gratias," *Response* 5/3 (1964), 139–43.

73. Tappert, p. 249.

74. See the Chorale Service specifications in *LBW*, p. 120.

75. See Friedrich Blume, *Protestant Church Music*, Eng. trans. (New York: W.W. Norton and Co., 1974), pp. 14ff, and Carl F. Schalk, "German Hymnody," in Marilyn Kay Stulken, *Hymnal Companion to the Lutheran Book of Worship* (Philadelphia: Fortress, 1981), pp. 19ff.

76. See F. Ernest Stoeffler, *The Rise of Evangelical Pietism* (Leiden: E.J. Brill, 1965), pp. 197f.

77. For commentary on these and other hymns from the Reformation period and the Age of Orthodoxy, as well as hymns of the Pietist and Rationalist periods, and Scandinavian hymnody, see E.E. Ryden, *The Story of our Hymns* (Rock Island: Augustana Book Concern, 1930).

78. See Johann Arndt, *True Christianity*, trans. with an Introduction by Peter Erb (New York: Paulist Press, 1979).

79. Stoeffler, p. 202.

80. Philip Jacob Spener, *Pia Desideria*, trans, with an Introduction by Theodore G. Tappert (Philadelphia: Fortress Press, 1964).

81. Johann Gerhard, *Sacred Meditations*, trans. by C. W. Heisler (Philadelphia: Lutheran Publication Society, 1896), p. 105.

82. Kenneth F. Korby, "Prayer: Pre-Reformation to the Present," in *Christians at Prayer*, ed. by John Gallen (Notre Dame: University of Notre Dame Press, 1977), pp. 128–9.

83. Vilhelm Moberg, *A History of the Swedish People: From Renaissance to Revolution*, trans. by Paul Britten Austin (New York: Pantheon Books, 1973), p. 169.

84. Søren Kierkegaard, *Fear and Trembling* and *The Sickness Unto Death*, trans. by Walter Lowrie (Princeton University Press, 1941, 1954), p. 214.

85. Søren Kierkegaard, *Attack Upon Christendom*, trans. by Walter Lowrie (Beacon Press, 1944), p. 212.

86. See Douglas John Hall, *Lighten Our Darkness: Toward an Indigenous Theology of the Cross* (Philadelphia: The Westminster Press, 1976).

87. Kazoh Kitamori, *Theology of the Pain of God* (Richmond: John Knox Press, 1954), p. 79.

88. *Ibid.*, p. 93.

Howard G. Hageman
REFORMED SPIRITUALITY

THE SPIRITUALITY OF ZWINGLI

It is difficult, if not impossible, to discuss Reformed spirituality as a single concept. It might be supposed that Reformed spirituality and the spirituality of John Calvin would turn out to be the same, but that is hardly the case. Since Calvin was a second generation reformer, there was a Reformed spirituality in existence before him which his own brand of spirituality was never able completely to replace. Furthermore in the late seventeenth and early eighteenth centuries there were spiritual developments in the Reformed tradition which deeply influenced Reformed piety and took it in quite a different direction from Calvin's understanding.

By common consent, the primary mover in what was to become the Reformed tradition was Ulrich Zwingli (1484–1531). Almost an exact contemporary of Luther's, he came at the question of reformation in a very different way which made it virtually impossible for the two reformers to understand each other when finally they met at Marburg in 1529. A parish priest (though never a member of a religious order), Zwingli was greatly influenced by the Erasmian point of view. His emphasis therefore was much more on a reconstruction of dogma in the light of the best New Testament scholarship than on any inner experience.

Deeply distrustful of anything that could detract from the central position of the Word, Zwingli would gladly have dispensed with everything in the liturgy except preaching. As it was he did away with all forms of church music and reduced public prayer to the barest minimum.[1] His emphasis on the primacy of the Word led him to relegate the eucharist to a quarterly celebration the only purpose of which was to remind the faithful of the atoning death of Christ, though there are some signs that he had begun to rethink his position before his tragic death on the field of battle in 1531.

The piety of a Zwinglian Protestant, therefore, was extremely Biblical. God's Word was the sole source and sustainer of the new life so that familiarity with it was absolutely essential. To facilitate that familiarity, he instituted a week-day service called the *prophesying*, which to Zwingli was as important (if not more so) than the Sunday liturgy. In it the faithful offered their comments on a passage of Scripture while the clergy listened and were silent. It was a kind of adult Bible class in which the members of the congregation shared their understanding of the Word with each other.

But the prophesyings were not intended to be a liturgical exercise for their own sakes, but to be instruments to strengthen the faithful in the Word. Zwingli's own confession here is significant.

> I came at length to trust in no words so much as those which proceeded (from the Bible). And when miserable mortals . . . tried to palm off their own works as God's, I looked to see whether any means could be found in which one could detect whether the works of man or of God were the better, especially as I saw not a few straining every nerve to make the simple-minded accept their own views as divine even though they were at variance with or in direct opposition to the words of God.[2]

It was the same Biblical impulse that led Zwingli at the beginning of Lent in 1519 to abandon the use of the lectionary to preach consecutively on Matthew's gospel with the Greek text in front of him on the pulpit. Roland Bainton has described the excitement of a young member of the congregation, Thomas Platter, who spent every night studying Greek and Hebrew with sand in his mouth so "that the gritting against his teeth might keep him awake."[3]

Although Zwingli's understanding of the eucharist might seem to rob it of all mystery, in the eucharistic liturgy which one of his colleagues, John Oecolampadius, provided for the congregation in Basel, however, the spirituality of this point of view comes through clearly.

> The Shepherd hath died for the lambs; the innocent hath suffered for the sinners, the Head for the members. By ineffable love, the High Priest hath sacrificed himself to the Father as a burnt offering on our behalf, and with his blood hath sufficiently secured and sealed our union with God the Father. Therefore let us hold these benefits in an everlasting and lively remembrance. His blood touches our heart! Now we wish to live and aspire unto Christ and not to ourselves, thus to be incorporated with him as members, redeemed and purified by his blood. Wherefore we remember with thanksgiving the benefit of his body and blood, even as he hath willed us to recall by the holiest of all services—his Supper.[4]

That quotation from Oecolampadius indicates the spiritual possibilities in an understanding of the eucharist that has often been dismissed as a "bare and naked sign."

By centering so strongly on the Word and drastically removing everything that might be used to seduce people from it, Zwingli developed a spirituality which had two principal foci. For one thing, Zwingli's insistence on the centrality of Scripture developed a piety that was largely inward. It was never his intention to see the value of the Bible as merely intellectual knowledge; it was to penetrate the soul of the believer and take possession of it. Jacques de Senarclens has described Zwingli's intention in this way.

> (According to Zwingli) the source of the conflicts of the time is found in ignorance. And since all human teaching is vain unless God inwardly enlightens and draws us, both individually and corporately we must pray fervently that God may cause the light of his Word to shine and that he may draw us by his grace, poor and ignorant that we are.[5]

Already in the quotation from de Senarclens a second Zwinglian emphasis is noticeable. The root of our trouble is *ignorance* which only a knowledge of Scripture can correct. Implicit in the Zwinglian point of view is an emphasis on knowledge which is not without an intellectual cast. In order to be delivered from our misery, we need a right knowledge, and that right knowledge can only be one which is derived from the Word of God.

These two tendencies, one toward inwardness and the other toward knowledge, easily became distorted in later Zwinglian piety into an inner subjectivity and a rational approach to the faith. While certainly the original teaching of Zwingli intended no such results, there can be no question that they began to appear in those areas in the Reformed tradition where a Zwinglian piety prevailed. Indeed, it could be argued that New England Puritanism, for example, despite all of its protestations of loyalty to John Calvin, was basically Zwinglian in its approach. The same could be said for large areas of Dutch Protestantism as well.

Louis Bouyer, no friend of the Zwinglian spirituality, has been quick to point out the excesses and distortions to which it led.

> The first of them was the opposition between the inner and the outer. . . . The outer, whether it meant Church-as-institution, the sacraments or ascetic practices was automatically reduced to the role of being no more than an expression (always suspect and dangerous at that) of the inner, or else was condemned outright as materialistic and idolatrous. . . .
>
> It was a religion so reasonable that it was latent rationalism—in spite of seeing itself as a child of the Gospel—and was in fact no more than the last fruit of a scholasticism that had become impenetrable to the Christian mystery, before eliminating religion itself in a free-thought faintly tinged by mystical moralism.
>
> Sincere and moving as piety toward Christ may have been in these Christians who were so biblical in desire but so platonizing and rationalizing in fact, it was a piety that did no more than color with religious emotion and tenderness what otherwise would have been a mere intellectualist ethic.[6]

Bouyer's judgment may seem harsh, but it is interesting to compare it with what Calvin had to say about Zwingli's views on the eucharist. They were those of a *homo profanus*, which perhaps can best be translated as a *secular person*. But whether in their pristine or their distorted form, Zwinglian ideas were the com-

mon ones in the Swiss Protestantism to which Calvin came in
1536. The fact that Zwingli had died a martyr's death in 1531
gave his piety an even greater sanctity in the eyes of the Zwinglian
faithful. Liturgically, eucharistically, theologically and spiritually,
all of the Reformed churches in both German and French speaking Switzerland were Zwinglian when Calvin came to them.

As we shall see, the spirituality of Calvin was something very
different, but it had to be imposed not on a *tabula rasa*, but on a
spiritual pattern which had already been set for almost twenty
years and was sanctified with the memory of a great spiritual
hero. That fact has given Reformed spirituality a dual character
which it has had from its very beginning. William Farel's Neucha-
tel liturgy, which was in use in Geneva when Calvin came, contains the following instruction to the preacher.

> After the prayer, the preacher commences by taking some
> text of the Holy Scripture, which he reads as clearly as did
> our Lord in Nazareth, and having read it, he expounds word
> for word without skipping, using scriptural passages to clarify
> the subject which he is explaining. He does not depart from
> Holy Scripture lest the pure Word of God be obscured by the
> filth of men, but bears the Word faithfully and speaks only
> the Word of God. And having expounded his text as simply
> as possible and without deviating from Scripture, as God gives
> grace he exhorts and admonishes the hearers, in keeping with
> the text, to depart from all sin and error, superstition and
> vanity, and return wholly to God.[7]

Or listen to the clear Zwinglian tone in the following passage
from Farel's eucharistic liturgy.

> . . . our blessed Savior has abundantly expressed his very great
> love, by giving his life for us, washing and purging us by his
> blood. Thus, before he suffered, he instituted his holy Supper
> in that last meal which he held in this mortal life and which
> he said he deeply desired. It was his will that in memory of his
> profound love in which he gave his body for us on the cross
> and spent his blood for the remission of our sins, we should
> partake of the same bread and drink of the same cup, without
> any discrimination, even as he died for all men without dis-
> crimination. And he bade all men to take, eat and drink in his
> Supper.[8]

THE SPIRITUALITY OF CALVIN

Such was the spiritual climate in Geneva to which John Calvin came as a young lawyer of twenty-seven in 1536. He has been so modest about his conversion to the evangelical faith that it is not possible to say where he belonged, but it seems reasonable to suppose that he thought of himself as a Lutheran. Doubtless there were many aspects of spirituality which in 1536 he had not yet thought through. It is equally possible that the Zwinglian spirituality of Geneva forced him to consider many questions that were new to him. There is some evidence that as early as 1537 he was already expressing some dissatisfaction with the spiritual situation as he found it in Geneva.

As is well known, Calvin was expelled from Geneva in 1538 and spent his next four years in Strasbourg as minister of the congregation of French refugees there, working under the supervision of Martin Bucer. This pastoral experience under the guidance of a man who was dedicated to finding some kind of common ground between Zwinglian and Lutheran was deeply significant for the growth of Calvin's ideas of spirituality. When he returned to Geneva in 1542, though he had to make some compromises, it was with some well defined ideas about the meaning of spirituality, and it is to these that we shall now turn our attention.

The spirituality of John Calvin is seldom examined. Most of us would feel at home in considering the theology of John Calvin and would almost at once find ourselves wrestling with predestination, the sovereignty of God and all the other theological headlines which have come to be associated with the great reformer's name. But the spirituality of Calvin is something about which it is much harder to get a conversation started, so closely has his name become associated with what we all know as Calvinism.

Wilhelm Niesel, surely one of the best of the modern interpreters of Calvin, has said that the real center of Calvinism as a living faith is not predestination or the eternal decrees. The real center is the *unio mystica*, the union of Christ with the believer. Mingling his own language with that of Calvin, Niesel says:

> For Calvin . . . that joining together of Head and members, that indwelling of Christ in our hearts—in short, that mystical

union is fundamental. We do not, therefore, contemplate him outside ourselves from afar in order that his righteousness may be imputed to us, but because we put on Christ and are engrafted into his body—in short because he deigns to make us one with him. For this reason, we glory that we have fellowship with him.[9]

All of this is to say that Calvin would not have analyzed the various stages of Christian experience as we tend to, conversion, justification, sanctification, etc. Calvin begins with Jesus Christ and our union with him and makes that the starting point from which all of his gifts and benefits come. To quote Niesel once more:

The distinctive thing in this teaching is that he (Calvin) first of all lays the foundation, by speaking of our union with Christ, next he deals with the gift of sanctification and only then develops his doctrine of justification.[10]

If we wish to discuss the spirituality of Calvin, therefore, this must be our starting point, the mystical union with Christ. (That should provide no difficulty for those who accept the Heidelberg Catechism as a faithful witness to the gospel. For it is obviously the starting point of that document as well. The celebrated first question begins with the affirmation that we belong totally to our faithful Savior, Jesus Christ.) The relationship is not of our choosing or devising, but one which he has created. But it is the basic reality from which all other spiritual benefits are derived. "Not only," writes Calvin, "does Christ cleave to us by an indivisible bond of fellowship, but with a wonderful communion, day by day, he grows more and more into one body with us until he becomes completely one with us."[11]

There can be no question but that this living relationship begins with baptism. Certainly baptism does not create the relationship; baptism is simply the sign and seal of our acceptance and forgiveness in Christ. But that fact must not lead us to separate the sign from the thing signified. As Calvin says, "baptism assures us that we are so united to Christ himself that we become sharers in all his blessings."[12] But the new relationship which has been initiated in baptism now has an entire lifetime in which to grow and develop. We shall consider that growth and develop-

ment first and then consider the means which Calvin saw as assist-
ing them.

Before moving to a consideration of these questions, however, we must notice the extent to which American Reformed
Christianity has shifted the basis of spirituality from that held by
Calvin. For him it was the saving act of God in Christ, signed and
sealed by the sacrament of baptism. For a large number in the
Reformed Churches today, it is the sign of the decision of the
converted person. That shift has had all kinds of consequences
for understanding church and sacraments and is fundamental for
the concept of the Christian life.

But now let us return to consider the meaning of growth and
development and the means which assist them.

(a) It is well known that the Lutheran reformation found
itself extremely vulnerable at the point of the relation between
faith and works. Even though Luther tried to find a place for
good works as the fruit of faith, by his heavy emphasis on *justification by faith* alone, he was always open to the charge, which his
Roman Catholic opponents did not hesitate to make, that his
point of view made all good works unnecessary.

It is much more difficult to make that charge against Calvin.
Indeed, Louis Bouyer, the Roman Catholic historian of spirituality, had this to say:

> Calvin, on the other hand, while also maintaining that justi-
> fication precedes, and is hence independent of any possible
> works that man may do, added that a faith that did not pro-
> duce both external works and the progressive sanctification
> of our whole being was but an appearance of faith and there-
> fore would not have justified us.[13]

(The third section of the Heidelberg Catechism is a good evidence of Calvin's understanding of this point. The second section
which deals with our redemption is not complete without the
third which deals really with our sanctification.) No one can
belong to Christ and not be involved in the style of life which his
new relationship demands.

One of the great demands of that new way of life is ethical.
From the Calvinist perspective, we have not been redeemed from
the law, but made able to obey the law. Calvin never wearies in

reminding us that the assurance of our belonging to Christ is to be found not only in our own inward feelings, but in the manner of our outward lives. He would, I think, have been baffled by the later attempt to distinguish between *mysticum* and *practicum*. While valuing the importance of the *mysticum*, he would certainly have maintained that any *mysticum* which did not result in *practicum* was specious. Not even in his liturgical composition will he let us forget that we have been fed at the Table so that we may be more effective agents of the gospel in the world.

We must stress the fact that when Calvin uses the words *justification* and *sanctification*, he does not use them sequentially, as is often the case in many contemporary discussions, nor does he place one above the other as is often done. He sees them rather as dual gifts that come from our relationship with Christ. B.A. Gerrish has put it this way:

> The benefits of Christ, according to Calvin, are ours only as a result of this secret communion that we have with Christ himself. In the *Institutes* he distinguishes two *graces* we receive from Christ; reconciliation (or justification) and sanctification. Neither of the two is given precedence as the supposed center of Evangelical theology, since both look away to the christological point of reference above them. The dominant motif is the *real presence* of Christ with the Christian as the head of the body.[14]

From the time of his baptism on, therefore, the believer through the indwelling of Christ is not only made right with God but is continually enabled to grow into the grace and likeness of his Lord. His being made right with God and his growth into Christ are therefore closely interdependent. Bouyer is right; for Calvin there is no being made right with God that is not accompanied by growth in grace; and obviously no growth in grace is possible for those who are not right with God. The locus in which this all takes place is the Church, which is the next topic we must consider in our consideration of Calvin's spirituality.

(b) It might be well to begin our consideration of the Church in Calvin's spirituality by reminding ourselves of the most famous statement he ever made about it. "We cannot have God as our Father if we do not have the Church as our mother." Indeed

Book IV of the *Institutes* begins with a chapter heading, "The True Church with which as Mother of all the godly we must keep unity." Once again the grudging praise which Louis Bouyer gives to Calvin's ecclesiology is worth quoting.

> Nothing is more revealing of Calvin's neo-Catholic reaction than the space he allotted to the Church in the successive editions of his *Institutes*—from a few pages to a quarter of the work. But still more important is the formal reappearance of a Church that is the mother of believers because the mother of their faith, a Church that is neither the invisible ultra-Augustinian Church of Luther in his first phase, nor the merely religious organization handed over to the supposedly Christian state and depending on its authority alone, such as Luther set up later to combat sectarian anarchy.
>
> . . . The Calvinist Church had a structure of its own independent of the state, whether Christian or not, and on Calvin's express word it proceeded from the divine will as affirmed in the New Testament.[15]

Niesel has some words which provide a helpful commentary on Bouyer's last point.

> Reformed theology treated with great breadth the doctrine of the Church as a living organically articulated community without losing sight of the individual and with no thought of establishing principles for an authoritarian church, but offering guidance for the assembly of God's people to the praise of God's glory in a world which though lost has been placed under God's promise. . . . Calvin spent his whole life serving this true gathering of God's people in many places, and created the necessary conditions to ensure that the tumults of the Counter-Reformation could not suppress again what had so recently been born of God's Word and Spirit. In the Reformed countries, the Jesuits found not just preaching stations, but witnessing and active congregations with well-ordered ministries and firmly bound together as their Synods showed.[16]

In a word, in Calvin's thinking the Church precedes the individual and not the other way around as has become so popular in contemporary spirituality. It is into the Church that we are brought by baptism and it is in the context of the Church that we grow up into Christ by the use of the means of grace. That is why Calvin can agree with Cyprian that "outside the Church there is no salvation." To be sure, God in his sovereignty is not bound to the Church, but we are.

Calvin is not unaware of the invisible nature of the true Church but he does not give it the exaggerated importance which it has in so many pietist ecclesiologies. Calvin's understanding of the invisible Church is firmly rooted in his understanding of election. The Lord alone knows who are his. But that in no way lessens our obligation to be part of the visible Church since God has willed that she be our mother. We have the promise that where two or three are gathered in my Name, I am in the midst of them, and that promise cannot fail.

This seems to be a good place to observe that our common view of spirituality often suggests the lonely pious individual striving to become more like Christ. That image has little or no place in the spirituality of Calvin. While I am sure that he engaged in private prayer, Calvin has surprisingly little to say on the subject. The Christian joins in the prayers of the people of God on the Lord's Day and in daily services in the Church. But by himself he is not at home praying; he is out in the world engaging in obedient ethical activity. To be sure that ethical activity is nourished and supported by his life in the Church; but, as Abraham Kuyper has reminded us in his classic Stone Lectures on Calvinism, Calvin had a total view of the necessity of self-consciously penetrating the domain of politics, science and art as well as the domain of religion.

B.A. Gerrish has a nice comparison between Luther and Calvin here.

> (Luther) preached the Word, slept, and drank his beer; and while he did nothing more, the Word did it all. With Calvin things were quite different. As he lay on his deathbed, he fell to reminiscing about the course of his life and remarked: "When I first arrived in this church, there was almost nothing. They were preaching and that is all. . . . There was reformation."[17]

It is in the Church, therefore, and not in the private closet that Christian growth takes place—and there always as the gift of God in Christ and not as the result of human effort and striving. Certainly any tendency to asceticism as an agent of spiritual growth would have been condemned by Calvin as pure Pelagianism.

(c) Within the Church the primary agent of spiritual growth is for Calvin the preaching of the Word. Indeed, his not so friendly critic, Louis Bouyer, expresses no little surprise at this point.

> (The new life) was a life that the Holy Spirit created within us, yes, but the only gift of the Spirit that Calvin seemed willing to enlarge on was the gift of understanding the Scriptures.[18]

Bouyer's criticism is somewhat exaggerated, but even taken at face value, it really misses what Calvin believed about the preaching of the Word. The Franch Oratorian is thinking of preaching as commentary on the gospel, the traditional Roman Catholic approach to the question. For Calvin, however, the phrase which contemporary Roman Catholicism uses would have been highly congenial—the real presence of Christ in his Word.

So far from being a mere commentary on the gospel, for Calvin the reading and preaching of the Word is the way in which Christ comes to us and shares himself with us, enlarging our understanding, strengthening our commitment, deepening our assurance. So totally did Calvin see the reading and preaching of the Word as a single indissoluble event (and not one a commentary on the other) that his Liturgy contains no provision for the reading of the Word; it simply assumes that reading and preaching will be a single act.

Because the Word is the instrument through which Christ is given to us, it stands at the very center of the life of the Church and at the very center of the life and growth of the Christian. Listen to part of the prayer which Calvin suggested should be used before the Word on Sunday.

> As we look into the face of the Son, Jesus Christ, our Lord, whom (God) has appointed Mediator between himself and us,

let us beseech him in whom is all fulness or wisdom and light
to vouchsafe to guide us by his Holy Spirit into the true
understanding of his holy doctrine, making it productive in
us of all the fruits of righteousness.[19]

Let me attempt to exegete that prayer as to what it says about
preaching. I see in it four themes which I should like to discuss
briefly.

1. Preaching is the real presence of Christ in his Word. In it,
"we look into the face of Jesus Christ our Lord." It is not a speaking about Christ; it is an event in which Christ himself comes to
us and offers himself to us in all of his fullness.

2. This presence of Christ in his Word is effected by the Holy
Spirit. It is the power of the Spirit that makes Christ who is at the
right hand of God present with us in an effective way.

3. As a result of this confrontation with the living Christ, our
understanding of him and his saving presence is enlarged. Our
grasp of his gifts to us is increased and strengthened and we perceive more sharply and more meaningfully what he means to us.
BUT . . .

4. This increase in knowledge and understanding is not (as it
so often became in later Calvinism) merely a head trip as if there
were virtue in knowing more about the doctrine. It is functional,
enabling us to be more productive of the fruits of righteousness.
This, indeed, is the final purpose for which Christ gave himself to
us in his Word.

I have done that small piece of exegesis because when we
come to consider the eucharist in Calvin's spirituality, we shall
have occasion to notice how closely his understanding of it parallels his understanding of preaching.

I do not think that in his understanding of the reading and
preaching of the Word there is any basic difference between Calvin and Luther. The only significant difference is the way in which
Calvin so definitely links it with our style of life in the world. One
suspects that for Luther the assurance of forgiveness would have
been the final result of the real presence of Christ in his word,
whereas for Calvin it is definitely the empowering for a righteous
life.

(d) At this point, I should like to inset a brief consideration of the importance of the liturgy in the spirituality of John Calvin. We often pass by the fact that he composed a liturgy for his congregation in Strasbourg, revising it later for use in Geneva, but even more by the fact that he discouraged any attempts to tinker or tamper with it. Whatever we may think of the liturgical quality of his *Form of Prayers*, Calvin thought it had an important role to play in the life of the Church since liturgy is more than preaching (here he definitely parted company with Zwingli) but also includes prayer, praise and the celebration of the eucharist.

One wonders what Calvin would have to say about many of the liturgical vapidities in the Reformed Churches today. "Those who introduce newly invented methods of worshiping really worship and adore the creature of their own distempered imaginations," wrote Calvin. And while he did not claim final excellence for his own liturgy, he was strongly in favor of one from which ministers should not be allowed to vary. Such a fixed liturgy, he wrote, would limit "the capricious giddiness and levity of such as effect innovations."[20]

In making such observations Calvin was seeking to defend the act of worship against certain destructive tendencies which he saw at work in his own time and which have certainly blossomed like a rose in ours. Briefly put, Calvin wanted to guard worship from becoming a massaging of our own feelings. The real purpose of worship, as he never wearied of saying, is to glorify God. That must put adoration as the central theme of liturgical activity. But, as Calvin also repeatedly said, the real way to glorify God is to obey him. Liturgical activity has that as a closely related purpose—the enabling of the people of God to give him glory in secular service.

Hence one of the most dramatic shifts which Calvin made in traditional liturgical usage—the use of the Law as an act of thanksgiving after the announcement of forgiveness. The Calvinist *Gloria in Excelsis* is the Ten Commandments. I think that that substitution speaks volumes about the Calvinist idea of spirituality. Here is almost the last word of Calvin's *Liturgy*, the end of the prayer of thanksgiving after communion. Notice how it echoes the same theme we have noted.

Now grant us this other benefit: that thou wilt never allow us to forget these things; but having them imprinted on our

hearts, we may grow and increase daily in the faith which is at
work in every good deed. Thus may we order and pursue all
our life to the exaltation of thy glory and the edification of
our neighbor.[21]

Though I have never found any reference to it in Calvin, he
must have considered another factor in his insistence on the value
of a virtually unaltered weekly liturgy. I refer to the fact that
through constant repetition its language became part of the wor-
shiper's piety. Whether or not that had been Calvin's intention,
it certainly took place in churches which took his liturgical ideas
seriously. My favorite illustration is the case of Marycke Popinga,
a five year old moppet, who startled the congregation of the
Dutch Reformed Church in New York in 1698 by perfectly reciting the Sunday prayer before the sermon, as the domine said,
"with energy and manly confidence." So moved was the congregation, according to the domine, that when Marycke had finished,
they said the prayer together "not without tears." Could there be
a better indication of the way in which repeated usage makes
liturgical language part of individual piety and spirituality?[22]

(e) At this point we have to look at a last aspect of Calvin's
understanding of spirituality, his idea of the eucharist. We all
know that the place of the eucharist in the life of the Church was
one of Calvin's greatest frustrations. Down to the end of his life
he protested against the infrequency of its celebration, but all in
vain. Never was he able to celebrate it oftener than monthly in
Strasbourg, while all during his years in Geneva a quarterly celebration was the rule.

If Calvin could have spoken about the "real presence of
Christ in his Word," he certainly would not have hesitated to
speak about the "real presence of Christ in his Supper." For to
him the Supper was only another form, though an important
form, of the Word, another means by which Christ comes to
share himself with his people. If preaching is the *audible* form of
the Word, the eucharist is the *visible* form. But we need both
forms of the Word really to be involved in the wholeness of the
gospel.

Despite the fact that Calvin's ideas of the eucharist are contained in almost evey Reformed confession, we have largely forgotten the depth of his belief in the real presence and the impor-

tance which he assigned to the eucharist in his ideas of spirituality. B.A. Gerrish has put it in this way.

> Once the idea of Christ's living presence, effected through the Word of God, has been presented as the heart of Calvin's gospel, his doctrine of the eucharistic presence is already half stated. The role he assigns to the Lord's Supper in the life of the church is traced to the fact that communion with Christ is not wholly perfect from the very first, but subject to growth, vicissitudes and impediments. He does not think of "receiving Christ" as a crisis decision, but rather as a magnitude subject to variation. . . . The very nature of its symbolism suggests to Calvin that the Lord's Supper is a matter of nourishing, sustaining and increasing a communion with Christ to which the Word and baptism have initiated us.[23]

Gerrish lists seven characteristics of Calvin's understanding of the eucharist which I should like to mention, reducing them to six, although my comments on each one will be much briefer than his.

1. The eucharist is a gift, not a good work. For the Roman Catholic of his time it was a good work, a sacrifice presented by man to God. But it was no less a good work for the Zwinglian who saw in the eucharist only a thankful recollection of Christ's death and recommitment to the Christian community.

2. The gift is Jesus Christ himself. We have already commented on this sufficiently in our discussion of the preaching of the Word.

3. The gift is given through the signs. Again this is aimed at both Roman Catholics and Zwinglians, though in different ways. In medieval Catholicism, the sign became absorbed in the thing signified, while for Zwingli the sign is only a sign.

4. The gift is given by the power of the Holy Spirit—an entire essay could be written on the pneumatology of the eucharist in Calvin's thinking. It is enough to notice here that the gift is not received by the recitation of a formula but by the presence of the Holy Spirit.

5. The gift is given to all who communicate but it is received only by those who have faith. (I have combined Gerrish's fifth and sixth propositions in that statement.)

6. The gift evokes gratitude. We have already noticed this theme in our brief discussion of Calvin's thanksgiving after communion.[24]

No lovelier description of what the eucharist meant to the spirituality of Calvin can be found than in this little confession in the fourth book of the *Institutes*.

> In his sacred supper Christ bids me take, eat and drink his holy body and blood under the symbols of bread and wine. I do not doubt that he himself truly presents them and that I receive them.

It is unfortunate that this very deep faith in the real presence of Christ in the eucharist became obscured in all of the sixteenth century controversies about the mode of the presence, controversies in which Calvin was often an active participant. In those controversies, it is evident that Calvin often felt the limitations of the vocabulary with which he had to work. He was caught up in the dichotomy between body and spirit which was the way in which the sixteenth century thought. He was also limited by the naively geographical way in which Christ was located at the right hand of God, as was the case with all the reformers. Gerrish suggests that in his struggles with a limited vocabulary, Calvin was "moving toward a fresh conception of the substance of Christ's body as precisely its force or power, so that the substance is present, albeit in a nondimensional way."[25] But to enter into that kind of discussion is not only outside our topic, but spoils the air of mystery with which Calvin always viewed the eucharist. I prefer to close this part of the discussion with words taken from Calvin's own eucharistic liturgy.

> Above all therefore, let us believe those promises which Jesus Christ who is the unfailing truth has spoken with his own lips. He is truly willing to make us partakers of his body and blood in order that we may possess him wholly and in such wise that we may live in him and he in us.[26]

What was the spirituality of John Calvin? Once we have been received into God's new people by baptism, we are given everything that Jesus Christ is and has and are enabled to appropriate it in increasing measure by sharing Christ in the preaching of his Word, in the receiving of his Supper, in the liturgical life of his body, the Church. From the power and the strength which we receive in these ways, we are enabled and expected for obedient service to God in the world which is under his promise.

REFORMED SPIRITUALITY AFTER CALVIN

The spirituality of Calvin was by no means accepted in the entire Reformed tradition. Coming, as it did, into a situation already dominated by Zwinglian piety, Calvinist spirituality was never as widely accepted as Calvinist theology or church order. Louis Bouyer has claimed that Calvin had only limited success in trying to convert the Reformed churches to his point of view.

> It is because these churches were later to adopt the practical organization put into effect by Calvin that they are persistently and misleadingly called *Calvinist*. . . . The *Reformed* churches as a whole, and leaving aside the Presbyterian synodal organization and some minority groups of Scottish and Dutch theologians, have always felt the greatest repugnance for the theological theses that properly belonged to Calvinism. It was Zwingli who so excellently expressed the basic mentality of *Reformed* churchmen . . . even if we cannot strictly call them his disciples.[27]

One of the places where the spirituality of Calvin flourished was in seventeenth century Scotland among a group known as the Aberdeen Doctors. Although their loyalty to the Stuart regime had forced them to accept a modified form of episcopacy, the Aberdeen Doctors remained loyal to Calvinist spirituality. G.D. Henderson, the best historian of religion in seventeenth century Scotland, has pointed out the surprising way in which the Aberdeen Doctors and their successors remained loyal Calvinists in spite of their acceptance of episcopacy.

> The great mass of the clergy . . . continued in the Calvinistic faith which had been generally characteristic of Scotland for over a century. Even Robert Leighton, the saintly Bishop of Dunblane and Archbishop of Glasgow, was a Calvinist.[28]

The most celebrated of the later Aberdeen Doctors was Henry Scougal, whose little devotional manual, *The Life of God in the Soul of Man* (which had a great influence on John Wesley), is his most famous work. In a sermon of preparation for the Holy Sacrament, he had this to say about the eucharist.

> This Sacrament doth not only represent a wonder that is past, but exhibits a new. The bread and wine that are received are not bare and empty signs to put us in mind of the death and sufferings of Christ. Our Savior calls them his body and blood and such, without question they are, to all spiritual purposes and advantages.
>   . . . These words of our Savior are spirit and life, are to be understood in a spiritual and vital sense; but though these elements be not changed in their nature and substance, yet they undergo a mighty change as to their efficacy and use.[29]

Those interested in tracing the survival of Calvin's spirituality in that of the Aberdeen Doctors will first of all take note of the fact that the very title of Scougal's devotional manual, *The Life of God in the Soul of Man*, is an echo of the Calvinist insistence that the *unio mystica* is central to the Christian faith. What is more, the quotation from his sermon on the eucharist clearly indicates his rejection of the Zwinglian understanding of that sacrament in favor of Calvin's. When he wrote that the "elements undergo a mighty change as to their efficacy and use," he was almost quoting Calvin himself.

Another area in which Calvinist spirituality flourished, as it did in northeast Scotland, was in Puritan New England. Since the spirituality of Puritanism is to be considered elsewhere in this book, we shall not study it in detail here. It is sufficient to point out that Charles Hambrick-Stowe in his definitive work *The Practice of Piety* has pointed out that Puritan piety contained two contradictory strains, one anti-sacramental while the other was much in the spirit of Calvin.

> One thrust of Puritan piety led to sacramental iconoclasm; at the same time the orthodox displayed "a burst of fascination with eucharistic devotional material and sacramental piety."
>   . . . In their public worship New Englanders maintained a doctrine of the real presence that differed little from Calvin.[30]

In his discussion of the Puritan understanding of the eucharist as a vital part of spirituality, Hambrick-Stowe cites a number of New England divines, including such well-known names as John Cotton, Thomas Hooker, Thomas Shepherd and Increase Mather. He also has an extended discussion of the eucharistic poetry of Edward Taylor, the pastor of Westfield. His description of some questions from John Cotton's Catechism, *Milk for Babes*, is filled with echoes of Calvin's spirituality.

> "What is done for you in baptism?" The answer that came back was "the pardon and cleansing of my sins since I am washed not only with water but with the blood and Spirit of Christ." Baptism led "to my ingrafting into Christ and my rising out of affliction and also . . . my resurrection from the dead at the last day. . . ."
>
> Cotton's reply to the same question concerning the Lord's Supper was that the broken bread and the poured wine were "a sign and seal of my receiving the body of Christ broken for me and of his blood shed for me, and thereby of my growth in Christ, of the pardon and healing of my sins, the fellowship of his Spirit, of my strengthening and quickening in grace, and of my sitting together with Christ on his throne of glory at the Last Judgment."[31]

There was one significant American attempt in the nineteenth century to restore the spirituality of John Calvin to its rightful place in the Reformed tradition. The so-called Mercersburg movement took place in the German Reformed Church from about 1845 to 1870. Its leaders were the two theologians from the Seminary in Mercersburg, Pennsylvania, John Williamson Nevin and Philip Schaff. Theirs was a serious effort to take Calvin's ideas of church, ministry, liturgy and sacraments and translate them into nineteenth century terms.

It says much about the validity of Bouyer's assertion about the minority position of Calvinist spirituality within the Reformed churches (quoted earlier in this essay) that when Charles Hodge, the distinguished Princeton Presbyterian theologian read Nevin's *Mystical Presence* which bears the clear subtitle *A Vindication of the Calvinistic Doctrine of the Eucharist*, he expressed both surprise and horror at the discovery that Calvin could have written such stuff.

He tried to argue that when it comes to Sacraments, Zwingli is the responsible Reformed authority.

The same thing happened to Schaff's *Principle of Protestantism* which appeared at about the same time. Because Philip Schaff had asserted that the Reformation was derived from medieval Catholicism, he was tried for heresy by the Classis of Philadelphia. We can be grateful that at that trial the charge was dismissed, but the fact that it could have been brought in the first place indicates how little understanding of Calvinist spirituality there was at that time. In fact, when the Dutch Reformed Church read the Mercersburg theologians, it broke off relations with its German Reformed sister on the grounds that it did not wish to consort with a body so afflicted with "Romanizing tendencies."

Today all that has been forgotten and there is general recognition of the significant contribution which Mercersburg, and especially John W. Nevin, made to the restoration of a largely forgotten area of Calvinist theology and spirituality. Indeed, there is general agreement that Mercersburg theology was one of the most important developments in the history of the American Church.[32]

One of the most important ways in which Calvinist spirituality was threatened in both Europe and America was by the rise of evangelical pietism. Since Pietism is a subject which will be fully discussed in another chapter of this book, there is no need for an extensive discussion here. But it must be noted that with its heavy emphasis on the individual Pietism completely altered traditional Calvinist spirituality. In the Reformed churches on the continent, Pietism seems to have been more churchly in its spirituality. It sought to revitalize the life of the Church by a new emphasis on catechization, pastoral visitation, an interest in missions and the use of hymns as well as psalms in the Sunday liturgy.

But in America the situation was quite different. For one thing, after the American Revolution, the whole model of American life changed from the old pattern of social community to the self-reliant individualist. Social historians, Rowland Berthoff and John Murrin, have this description of what happened.

Freshly released from bonds of social community as well as of feudal lordship, the new democratic individualism harked

back to . . . the yeoman freeholder, a figure most typical of
the back country settlements of Pennsylvania, the new Southwest and northern New England. Increasingly, he would be
taken as the archetype of the American everywhere . . . self-
reliant, honest and independent.[33]

Berthoff and Murrin also have pointed out that the rise of the
rugged individualist as the American model replaced older
models such as the tightly knit community of a New England vil-
lage or the patronal society of the Hudson Valley.

Once the model of the "rugged individualist" began to pre-
dominate, especially on the American frontier, Calvinist spirituality was doomed. It had already been struggling with the new
individualism of the Great Awakening in the new light vs. old light
controversies that wracked the Congregational, Presbyterian and
Reformed Churches in the colonies. But once the success of the
new republic had crowned the self-reliant individual as *the* American pattern, then the new measures of a Charles Finney, as well
as the camp meetings and revivals of Baptist and Methodist origin, became the new effective pattern. In what they felt was the
only way to survive, traditional Reformed churches tried to adopt
Baptist and Methodist spirituality to their own needs. The results
are still with us today.

It could be a fitting comment to say that while the spirituality
of evangelical pietism probably is still dominant in American
Reformed churches today, the closing half of this century has
seen a renewal of Calvinist spirituality as a result of the ecumenical movement. When Reformed Churches which had largely
abandoned their traditional Calvinist stance found themselves in
dialogue with other Christian traditions, there was at first a good
deal of foundering with questions such as baptism, eucharist and
ministry. So widely had evangelical pietist spirituality spread in
Reformed circles that many were unaware of their own tradition
and thought only in terms of the individual believer and his
response to the gospel. In many instances, it came as a surprise
to learn that there was in the Reformed tradition a carefully articulated churchly spirituality involving liturgy, sacraments and
ministry.

It was just this uncertainty that led to the rediscovery and renewal of Calvinist spirituality within the Reformed tradition. With the Mercersburg movement as the pioneer, there has in recent years been a serious effort in Reformed circles to update Calvin's ideas, trying to free them from the concepts and terminology in which they had been locked for many years. Most recently, the World Council's Lima Document on *Baptism, Eucharist and Ministry* has challenged many Reformed thinkers to critique it from a Calvinist point of view.

A final word must be said about something which pervades all genuine Reformed spirituality whether of the Zwinglian, Calvinist or Pietist variety. Since Reformed thinking has always emphasized that the Christian life begins with the election of God in Christ, its stress has always fallen on the divine rather than the human activity. While Calvin has always been known as the theologian of election and predestination, the survival of that idea has been not so much a theological proposition as a "sweet and comforting assurance" to the Christian in his spiritual pilgrimage.

However much Zwingli and Calvin may have differed at other points, they were at one in basing all spirituality on the divine choice and activity. Reformed tradition has always seen the church in Roland Bainton's words as

> . . . the body of the elect, a band of the chosen of the Lord, calling no man sovereign save under God, not worrying about salvation, sustained by the assurance of the unshakable decree, committed not to the enjoyment of the delights of life but only to the illustration of the honor of the sovereign God . . . .[34]

The important thing to notice in Bainton's description is the phrase *not worrying about salvation*. Because salvation was the irreversible decision of a sovereign Lord, there was no point in asking questions about one's status or in being concerned about the state of one's spiritual health. One of the leading Calvinists of the nineteenth century, Herman Friederich Kohlbrügge, urged his congregation in Elberfeld, Germany, not to ask whether or not they possessed the gifts of the Spirit, but to remember that they had a gracious Father. That is the authentic Reformed spiritual voice whether spoken in Zurich, Geneva or Elberfeld.

Steven Ozment has a splendid summary of Reformed spirituality, including a quotation from Calvin himself.

Man's fallenness obsessed Calvin both in his teaching and his ministry. A large part of the *Institutes of the Christian Religion* is a sad hymn to what man could have been "if Adam had remained upright". A still greater part of the *Institutes* celebrates Christ's redemption of mankind and the possibility for true Christians to recover, gradually and partially, Adam's original righteousness. Calvin believed nothing so much as that "our religion . . . must enter into our heart and pass into our daily living and so transform us into itself that it may not be unfruitful for us". Anything less, for himself or for the citizens of Geneva, was . . . a religion of the tongue and mind, a piety of faith alone.[35]

NOTES

1. Bard Thompson, ed., *Liturgies of the Western Church* (Collins, Cleveland and New York, 1962), pp. 147–48.

2. Steven Ozment, quoted in *The Age of Reform* (Yale, New Haven, 1980), pp. 323–24.

3. Cf. Roland Bainton, *The Reformation of the Sixteenth Century* (The Beacon Press, Boston, 1952), pp. 82–83.

4. Thompson *op. cit.*, p. 214.

5. Jacques de Senarclens, *Heirs of the Reformation* (Westminster, Philadelphia, 1958), p. 90.

6. Louis Bouyer, *A History of Christian Spirituality*, Vol. III (Seabury, New York, 1982), pp. 82–83.

7. Thompson, *op. cit.*, p. 216.

8. *Ibid.*, p. 219.

9. Wilhelm Niesel, *Reformed Symbolics* (Oliver and Boyd, Edinburgh, 1962), p. 182.

10. *Ibid.*, p. 192.

11. *Ibid.*, p. 185.

12. *Ibid.*, p. 268.

13. Bouyer, *op. cit.*, p. 86.

14. B.A. Gerrish, *The Old Protestantism and the New* (Chicago University, Chicago, 1982).

15. Bouyer, *op. cit.*, p. 91.

16. Niesel, *op. cit.*, p. 254–55.

17. Gerrish, *op. cit.*, p. 258.

18. Bouyer, *op. cit.*, p. 86.

19. Thompson, *op. cit.*, p. 209.

20. *Ibid.*, p. 195

21. *Ibid.*, p. 208.

22. J.B. Lyons, *Ecclesiastical Records of the State of New York*, Albany, New York, Vol. II, p. 1240.

23. Gerrish, *op. cit.*, pp. 111–12.

24. *Ibid.*, pp. 112–15.

25. *Ibid.*, p. 117.

26. Thompson, *op. cit.*, p. 207.

27. Bouyer, *op. cit.*, p. 78.

28. G.D. Henderson, *Religious Life in Seventeenth Century Scotland* (University Press, Cambridge, 1937), p. 92.

29. Marion Lochhead, *Episcopal Scotland in the Nineteenth Century* (London, John Murray, 1966), p. 27.

30. Charles Hambrick-Stowe, *The Practice of Piety* (University of North Carolina Press, Chapel Hill, N.C., 1982), p. 125.

31. *Ibid.*, pp. 123–24.

32. For a full discussion of the Mercersburg movement in general and of John W. Nevin in particular, see *Romanticism in American Theology* by James H. Nichols and *Tradition and the Modern World: Reformed Theology in Nineteenth Century* by Brian A. Gerrish.

33. *Essays on the American Revolution* (University of North Carolina Press, Chapel Hill, N.C., 1982), p. 276.

34. Bainton, *op. cit.*, p. 122.

35. Ozment, *op. cit.*, p. 380.

Peter C. Erb

ANABAPTIST SPIRITUALITY

There is a custom, now over four hundred years old, to use the term "the Reformation" to designate the religious movement which arose in opposition to Catholicism following the publication of Luther's Ninety-Five Theses in 1517. More often it is referred to as "the Protestant Reformation" and is used to include the reforms of the Swiss under Zwingli in Zurich, of Calvin in Geneva, of the Anglicans in England. Such use of the term, however, raises serious problems; a more suitable way of understanding the religious ferment of the early sixteenth century is to categorize the various reforming groups of the period under three headings. There was first the reform which began within the Catholic Church itself and was underway by the end of the fifteenth century; this movement grew rapidly after 1517 and is thereafter often referred to as the Counter-Reformation. A second reform was carried out under the direction of the political authorities in protest against Catholicism, and it is this that we generally refer to as Protestantism.

The first two "reformations" have been much discussed, but there existed alongside these two a third group of reformers which have only recently received close attention. In their theology and spirituality, the disparate members of this group fall somewhere between Catholicism on the one side and Protestantism on the other. They are today generally referred to as "Radical Reformers." The members of the Radical Reformation (described also as "the Left Wing of the Reformation"), were not so much "radicals" in the modern sense of the word (i.e. revolutionary), as "radicals" in their search to reestablish Christianity according to its "roots" (radices). Among these, the only ones which have a significant continuation into the twentieth century are the Anabaptists, the ancestors of the Mennonites, the Amish, and the Hutterites; in a sense the Baptists are their spiritual stepchildren.

The word "Anabaptist" means "rebaptizer" and was used to designate those persons who from the mid 1520s in Germany and the Lowlands insisted that true Christians must make a conscious, responsible, adult choice to unite by baptism with a visible community of similarly-minded Christians. As a result they opposed the practice of infant baptism and, in the formative period, persons who wished to join with them were therefore rebaptized. The term "Anabaptist" comes from the Greek words *ana* (again) and *baptizein* (to baptize) and is parallel to the German word *Wiedertaeufer* (again-baptizer). From the time of the inception of the movement until the early years of the twentieth century, however, the Anabaptist movement had to suffer less complimentary designations, most popular among which was *Schwaermer* (analogous to the English word *swarmers*, as in "a *swarm* of insects"). Nor was the attack upon them a matter of mere rhetoric; the earliest Anabaptists were persecuted and martyred, and this in spite of their clearly announced refusal to bear arms and their emphasis on practical acts of love toward their fellow human beings.

Any discussion of Anabaptist spirituality raises problems because of the problem of the definition of spirituality itself, because the theme has not been extensively studied in regard to the Anabaptists, and because of the problems inherent in any classification of the Anabaptists themselves. The definition of spirituality provided by traditional writers on the subject relates the term primarily to prayer. Prayer is discussed by the Anabaptists, but in almost all cases the subject is treated generally within a broader framework. To limit the use of the term to prayer and to the devotional and mystical lives would inevitably give a limited and false picture of the Anabaptist tradition. For the purposes of this chapter, therefore, I use the term spirituality more in terms of piety generally, that is, I understand it as the form in and through which the Christian life of a particular individual or group is manifested; spirituality is the form of a specific faith commitment.

Because of the assiduous work of Mennonite scholars from the beginning of this century and the extensive studies of many others following the Second World War, the negative image once held concerning all the religious groups in the early sixteenth century who did not fit the Catholic, Lutheran or Calvinist categories is now almost a thing of the past. But numerous questions remain regarding the relationship of the Anabaptists to their medieval heritage and to other Reformation traditions, their specific origins, their theology, and their spirituality.

Great help was offered to answering many of these questions in 1962 when the Harvard historian George H. Williams published his encyclopedic outline of the Anabaptists and other groups like them under the title, *The Radical Reformation*.[1] His work was made possible by that of many scholars before him (in particular Harold S. Bender and those responsible for the publication of *The Mennonite Encyclopedia* in 1959[2]), and his argument needed to be revised in some respects as later studies were to show, but Williams' volume did help students of the period to bring some order into an era which looked to all approaching it with only the brief guides then available like a crazy-quilt pattern.

Williams made several attempts at categorizing the various groups which comprised the Radical Reformation and on the basis of his work the movement can be conveniently classified into four groups: Revolutionaries, Anabaptists, Mystical Spiritualists and Rationalists.[3] Although Mennonite scholars in particular have tended to emphasize the differences between these various groups, recent studies have pointed out that such differentiation ought not be be overstressed.[4] Some Anabaptists found themselves close to Mystical Spiritualists and others to some of the theological emphases of the Revolutionaries; moreover, a great number of divisions can be found among the Anabaptist communities in themselves.

THE RADICAL SETTING

The mapping of Radical Protestantism is extremely complex; the mobility of its major figures increases the difficulty in classifying its various geographical and theological species. The Revolutionaries, men like Thomas Muentzer (1488?–1525), Andreas Bodenstein von Karlstadt (1480?–1541), Melchior Hofmann

(1495–1543?) and Hofmann's militant disciples who set up a theocracy at the city of Münster, resided at various points across Europe from Prague to the Atlantic and from Switzerland to the Baltic.[5] Their peace-loving Spiritualist colleagues, Sebastian Franck (1499–1542) and Caspar Schwenckfeld von Ossig (1489?–1561), traveled lesser distances—for the most part between Augsburg and Strassburg—but the extent of their itinerancy within these regions must not be overlooked. Henry Niclaes (1501–1580?) and David Joris (1501?–1556), both Dutch Spiritualists, followed a similar pattern.[6]

The numerous pacifistic Anabaptists were located in seven main areas: Switzerland and the German areas to the north [The Swiss Brethren under Conrad Grebel (1498–1526), Felix Mantz (c. 1498–1527), Michael Sattler (c. 1490–1527) and their associate Balthasar Hubmaier (1480?–1528)]; southern Germany and Austria [Hans Denck (c. 1500–1527), Ludwig Haetzer (c. 1500–1529), Hans Hut (d. 1527) and Pilgram Marpeck (d. 1556)]; central Germany, the Netherlands, and northern Germany [Menno Simons (c. 1496–1561), and Dirk Philipps (1564–1568)]; England, northern Italy and eastern Europe [Jacob Hutter (d. 1536)].[7] The Italian, Swiss and eastern regions also gave birth to rationalistic and often anti-Trinitarian radicals such as Michael Servetus (1515–1563), Bernardine Ochino (1487–1567) and Faustus Socinius (1539–1604). With these the French Humanist radical Sebastian Castellio (1515–1563) may also be grouped.[8]

The difficulties with such divisions are obvious: Hofmann was not a revolutionary although one wing of his followers was; Menno Simons is Hofmann's decendant; Muentzer and Karlstadt have much in common with the Spiritualists as, to a lesser extent, does Denck; Schwenckfeld and Franck are radically opposed on a number of central issues. The classification is, nevertheless, useful if one is aware of the fluidity of theological principles and motifs with respect to the groups involved. In general, Revolutionaries were those who sought to bring about the Kingdom of God by social upheaval;[9] Anabaptists, those who saw the Kingdom in brotherhoods of committed, that is, voluntarily baptized and therefore rebaptized, believers;[10] Spiritualists, those who drew a sharp distinction between natural and spiritual realms and maintained that only the latter was a possible basis for the establishment of the Kingdom. Spiritualists neglected, as a result, formal ecclesiastical structures, such as church, sacraments, the words of Scripture, creeds and symbolic books.[11] Of the four groups of radicals noted the Revolutionaries and the Anabaptists were concerned with objective social structures, the Mystical Spiritualists and the Rationalists more with questions of individual piety and theological matters.

By 1535 the revolutionary wing of the Radical Reformation was effectively stopped and died shortly thereafter.[12] The other radical traditions continued. There is evidence of a continuity of Italian rationalism in the work of John Milton.[13] The Anabaptists consolidated under the name Mennonite by the late sixteenth century and, despite their divisiveness, spread across north Germany to Prussia and eventually to Russia. The Swiss and South German groups spread into the Palatinate, Alsace and Lorraine, and eventually emigrated in part to America.[14] The Schwenckfelders, although unorganized and small, retained a vigorous intellectual tradition in southwest Germany until the Thirty Years War—their most significant author here was Daniel Sudermann (1555–1631)—and in Silesia until the end of the eighteenth century.[15]

The divisions among the Anabaptists themselves were both of a geographical and of a theological nature. For our present purposes we will discuss Anabaptism as it arose in three major geographic areas: the Zurich region of Switzerland and the German territories immediately to its north; south Germany; and the lowlands, in particular the Dutch-speaking areas and north Germany. First evidences of the movement occur in Zurich in the mid-1520s, and it is still a matter of debate whether the movement began here and then spread to the rest of Europe or whether we are dealing with a number of movements which began in different ways in different areas and only later unified themselves.[16]

THE SWISS BRETHREN

Early in 1525, a small group of Christians gathered under the leadership of Conrad Grebel and Felix Mantz in Zurich. Both men had opposed Ulrich Zwingli, the chief reformer in the city, on the issue of infant baptism. The story of the beginning of the new religious community, referred to as the Swiss Brethren, is told by an approving chronicler as follows:

> And it came to pass that they were gathered together until fear began to come over them; yea, they were pressed in their hearts. Thereupon they began to bow their knees to the Most High God in heaven and called upon him as the knower of hearts, implored him to enable them to do his divine will and to manifest his mercy toward them. For flesh and blood and human forwardness did not drive them, since they well knew what they would have to bear and suffer on account of it. After the prayer George Cajacob arose and asked Conrad to baptise him, for the sake of God, with the true Christian baptism upon his faith and knowledge. And when he knelt down with that request and desire, Conrad baptised him, since at that time there was no ordained deacon to perform such work. After that was done the others similarly asked George to baptise them, which he also did upon their request. Thus they together gave themselves to the name of the Lord in the high fear of God. Each confirmed the other in the service of the Gospel, and they began to teach and keep the faith. Therewith began the separation from the world and its evil works.[17]

These emphases on baptism and particularly on "separation from the world and its works" are the keys to understanding the thought of the Swiss Brethren, and they lie at the root of a letter written by Grebel to Thomas Muentzer in September of 1524.[18] What is evident from the first lines of the letter is Grebel's egalitarian view of the church. He addresses Muentzer "without title" and requests that the latter return answer to him "like a brother." Grebel clearly accepts Muentzer as a member of the brotherhood of the redeemed, and for that reason he writes, admonishing him to change his ways in regard to certain liturgical reforms which, Grebel believes, are in opposition to the Scriptures and the ideal that the church is a voluntary body of committed believers. Jesus Christ, God's son, "offers himself as one master and head of all who would be saved and bids (them) be brethren by the one common word given to all."

Christ it is, according to Grebel, who has moved the Swiss to contact Muentzer "to make friendship and brotherhood with him." Grebel's description of Christ as "master" and "head" and his designation of the body of Christ as comprising those "who *would be* saved" emphasizes his concern with the role of "works" in the Christian life. Christ, he states, is the "master and the one who makes holy." Earlier Christians, Grebel feels, fell away from the true faith, and even with the Reformation there are many who want "to be saved by superficial faith, without fruits of faith, without baptism of trial and probation, without love and hope, without right Christian practices."

Grebel and his associates "daily beseech God earnestly with constant groaning to be brought out of this destruction of Godly life and out of human abominations to the true faith and divine practice." Their prayer is not primarily for individual wants but for the establishment of a new order in which the practice of baptism and the Lord's Supper might be consistent with "what may be found in pure and clear Scripture," and thereby supporting the function of the church as it is understood by the Swiss Brethren. That church will be known, Grebel believes, by its fruits of faith, among which will be the baptism of trial and probation, a baptism of blood, which follows the baptism of water and is a mark of the true church as certainly as the pure and proper celebration of the Supper is.

The Supper is especially important for Grebel because, when properly practiced, it reflects all that the Christian life is: a union of believers in faith and mutual love in which each believer "calls to mind Christ's body and blood, the covenant of the cross," and expresses a willingness "to live and suffer for the sake of Christ and the brethren." The true fellowship reflected in the practice of the Supper must be kept pure and separate from the realm of the anti-christ where the two ordinances of baptism and the Supper are practiced in an idolatrous "priestly" fashion. Persons not maintaining true fellowship must not be allowed to participate: "If one is found who will not live the brotherly life, he eats unto condemnation . . . and dishonours love which is the inner bond." The Supper provides bread, "simply bread, yet if faith and brotherly love precede it, it is to be received with joy, since when it is used in the church it is to show us that we are truely one bread and one body and that we are and wish to be true brethren with one another."

Separation from the world will inevitably result in suffering, the Swiss Brethren believed, and their position was supported by the many Anabaptists who wrote on the subject of martyrdom and faced the practical implications of their martyr theology with bravery. In the early church the experience of martyrdom, of physically dying to self and living to Christ (a second baptism or baptism of blood), was transformed by the desert fathers and the monastic movement into an act of separating oneself from the world and living in a hermitage or cell, totally committed unto Christ. The monk's second baptism is an entrance into the cloister and thereby a dying unto self, living among brethren for Christ alone. The Anabaptist movement had much in common with this monastic ideal. They too upheld the ideal of community, required obedience to the brotherhood, and spoke of entrance into it as a second (re-)baptism. Because of their changed circumstances they very often experienced this second baptism not metaphorically as did their monastic pregenitors, but physically.[19]

That many Anabaptists overemphasized the extent of the persecution is likely, but its ferocity must not be understressed.

> Finding that the customary method of individual trials and sentences was proving totally inadequate to stem the (Anabaptist) tide, the authorities resorted to the desperate expedient of sending out through the land companies of armed executioners. . . . The atrocious application of the policy was made in Swabia where the original four-hundred special police of 1528 sent against the Anabaptists proved too small a force and had to be increased to one thousand. An imperial provost-marshall, Berthold Aichele, served as chief administrator of this bloody program . . . until he finally broke down. . . . The count of Alzey in the Palatinate, after three hundred and fifty Anabaptists had been executed there, was heard to exclaim, "What shall I do; the more I kill, the greater becomes their number."[20]

Having undergone experiences such as these, it is not surprising that the theme of martyrdom should have been a major one in the piety not only of the sixteenth century Anabaptists but their descendants down to the twentieth century as well.

MICHAEL SATTLER AND HIS "SCHOOL"

Perhaps best known of all the Anabaptist martyrs is Michael Sattler. Sattler was a native of Stauffen in Breisgau, had entered the Benedictine monastary of St. Peter in the Black Forest, and was prior there in the 1520s when he came into contact with Reformation ideas. By March of 1525 he was a member of the young Anabaptist community in Zurich. His defense of Anabaptist ideals resulted in his imprisonment and then in his expulsion from the city. He traveled to Strasbourg, was a central figure at the Anabaptist conference at Schleitheim in 1527 and was martyred shortly thereafter.

Three contemporary reports of his trial and martyrdom have been preserved, the most interesting an account of Klaus von Groveneck.[21] In the preface to his piece von Groveneck comments on Sattler's death with eschatological and dualistic images. So separate must true believers remain from false ones, he insists, that the death of men like Sattler who follow the ideal to its fullest cannot but be expected. Martyrdom is the result of a life lived totally to Christ in expectation of the last days.

> Since in these last most dangerous times, when (thanks be to God) the light of divine truth has gone out, and shines so brightly that it makes manifest the abominable error of the anti-christ and shines into the thick darkness of false doctrine, and thereby takes away from the enemy of man's salvation that which he has seized, destroys his kingdom, and [since] the kingdom of Christ is gaining ground, now the strong warrior . . . becomes active, readies himself for defense, uses all his evil ruses, creates sects and division which he lets be decorated . . . so beautifully that . . . the elect servants of God might be seduced.[22]

The purpose of presenting the lives of martyrs in a time such as this is edifactory.

> It seemed good to us to make known in print this authentic and wonderful story . . . so that many might see how God so marvelously deals with His saints here, and tests them as gold through fire, that is, with manifold temptation and testing . . . so that everyone might use and strengthen his faith, might not

let himself be turned away from the bright and clear Word of God by any kinds of miraculous signs or seemingly wonderful doctrine, but should hold fast thereto with solid faith, until God lets him see into all truth.[23]

Martyr acts are a category of spiritual literature, not historical or polemical exercises but admonitions, consolations for a people who have separated themselves from the world in a freely chosen act of baptism, and who continue to separate themselves in celebrating the Lord's Supper, that archetypal act by which their community is united as one bread and body and poured out as one blood.

It is important to emphasize the eschatological setting in which von Groveneck places his account, for if one does not do so, the radical dualism of Sattler's own works can be badly misconstrued. Three extant compositions can be confidently ascribed to Sattler: a letter to Capito and Bucer, a letter to the church at Horb where he was imprisoned in 1527, and the first "confession" of the Anabaptists, the 1527 "Brotherly Union of Schleitheim."[24] All insist on a clear separation of true and false believers, of church and world, and at times are almost Manichaean in that insistence. In his letter to Capito and Bucer, for example,[25] Sattler lists twenty statements which hinder him from agreeing with the Strasbourg reformers. Each supports an ecclesiological dualism: the true church is made up of believers in Christ who are reconciled to the Father, incorporated by baptism into Christ, "foreknown" by Christ and "minded" like him, and despised by the world over which the devil rules. Flesh is set against spirit, the children of light against the children of darkness, those who trust the Father against those who trust weapons, those who trust heavenly citizenship against those whose primary allegiance is the earthly state, those who "practice in deed the testimony of Christ" against those who only mouth the words of religion. "In sum there is nothing in common between Christ and Beliel."

Likewise in the Schleitheim confession Sattler writes:

We have been united concerning the separation which shall take place concerning the evil and the wickedness which the devil has planted in the world simply in this: that we have no fellowship with them, and do not run with them in the confession of their abominations. So it is; since all who have not entered into the obedience of faith and have not united themselves with God so that they will to do his will, are a great abomination before God, therefore nothing else can or really will spring or grow forth from them than abominable things. Now there is nothing else in the world and all creation than good or evil, believing and unbelieving, darkness and light, the world and those who are out of the world, God's temple and idols, Christ and Beliel, and none will have part with the other.[26]

Such language must, however, be read in its context. When Sattler makes a statement such as "there is nothing else in the world *and all creation* than good or evil," he is not a Manichaean. He is simply speaking of the separation that "shall take place" in the final days, days in which he believes he is writing. His dualism is eschatological, not cosmological; he is concerned with the end of time, not with the nature of reality. The purpose of Sattler's dualistic language is to admonish those to whom he is writing to "go out from Babylon and the earthly Egypt [so] that we shall not be partakers in their torment and suffering which the Lord shall bring upon them," as he points out immediately after the section quoted above. What is to be shunned is the abomination, the false Christians who appear to be what they are not and are therefore treacherous, leading individuals to believe that they are in Christ when in fact they are worshiping the anti-christ.

The same eschatological concern is clear in the twenty points Sattler makes in the letter to the Strasbourg reformers.[27] The first of these speak of an incorporation into Christ by rebaptism, and the last direct attention to the Father in heaven and the citizenship of heaven as known by all the saints at the end of time. Very similar patterns can also be seen in two texts from the Sattler "school." In the treatise "On Two Kinds of Obedience," the author closes his discussion with a description of the fall of Babylon, and the eschatological concern is primary in the piece "On False Prophets or the Anti-Christ."[28]

Just as there is a danger of misreading Sattler's comments on separation as Manichaean, so too one can mistake his discussions of baptism as individualistic and Pelagian. But any emphasis he places on the importance of individual activity is mitigated by other comments he adds on the importance of the individual in community. What is immediately evident, for example, on reading his letter to the Strasbourg reformers is the significance the community of believers has for him.[29] His is a spirituality not developed from individualistic principles, but from a social perspective. The letter is divided into three parts, a first discussing the background to the impasse now established between Sattler on the one side, and Capito and Bucer on the other, a second which establishes the dualism between the followers of Christ and the people disposed to the "world," and a third which speaks to the practical politics of religious disagreement. What is under specific discussion are differing interpretations regarding "baptism, the Lord's Supper, force or the sword, the oath, the ban, and all the commandments of God."

In the introduction to the letter Sattler addresses his theological opponents as "dear brothers in God," a phrase which he uses consistently when he speaks to them, and endeavors to outline the nature of the differences which divide them. All his discussions, both with those who disagree with him and with those who agree with him, have been carried out in community. He points out that he has "recently spoke[n]" with the Strasbourg reformers "in brotherly admonition and friendliness" and that they answered in exactly the same manner. Moreover, the understanding he has reached "out of Scripture, namely out of the New Testament" regarding the topics under discussion was not reached on an individualistic basis, but "together with my brothers and sisters."

These comments must not be considered rhetorical; Sattler takes up the basis for them elsewhere in his writing. They are not an attempt to soften his opponents' position with the guise of friendliness. The crisis for Sattler may well be, not the specific theological matters at hand but the fact that within the body of Christ there is a division among believers. It is especially interesting to note that he designates Scripture as the New and not the Old Testament, and that he insists on a hermenutics in community—the interpretation of Scripture must be carried out with a "hermeneutics of good-will" and not of "suspicion."

As a result, Sattler is particularly troubled by the use made among Capito, Bucer and their colleagues of 1 Timothy 1. He agrees with them that it is clear from the early part of the chapter (he seems to be referring specifically to the first five verses) "that love is the end of the commandment, wherefore it is necessary that all of the commandments of God be guided by the same." But on the basis of the passage the Strasbourgers have seemingly admonished Sattler and his associates to maintain "moderation and friendliness" and not to press their theological points, particularly their dualist requirements for church membership. They have probably emphasized 1 Timothy 1:4–5, charging that Sattler and his associates are occupying themselves with "myths and endless genealogies . . . speculations rather than divine edification, for love [as] the end of the commandment." Sattler interprets the closing statement of verse 5, however, not as requiring some individuals to give up divisive theological matters not held by the majority, but with the responsibility noted in verse 3 to "charge" those who are teaching falsely "not to speak any different doctrine" because as verse 5 indicates "the end of the commandment is charity from a pure heart and a good conscience and a faith which is not feigned." In other words the Strasbourgers as interpreted by Sattler read "end" to mean "purpose" and define the *purpose* of the commandment as an *attitude* of love, moderation and friendliness, whereas Sattler and his colleagues understand "end" to mean "goal" and interpret the verse as indicating that the *goal* of the commandment is to bring about *love itself* manifested in a pure heart, good conscience and a faith which is not the pretense of idolatrous "priestly" practice.

In particular Sattler maintains this position in regard to the practice of baptism, the Supper, the ban, the use of force, and the oath. All five of these "acts" must be consistent with the ideal of "divine edification" mentioned in 1 Timothy 1:4 which will build up love itself, not simply of love as moderation or a willingness to accept differences within a community but love as pure heart, good conscience and non-fictive faith freely chosen in baptism, manifested in the celebration of the Supper, kept pure by banning those who are not pure from attending the Supper, separated from worldly force and responsible to a heavenly government, not an earthly one. It is a love expressed and nurtured by a pure community, a love which is, as a whole and in community, Christ's love, and not simply an individual *expression* of love.

The broad attention given to the pacifism of contemporary North American Mennonites, the direct descendants of the Anabaptists, has resulted in an overinterpretation of passages in the writings of Sattler and other Anabaptists which speak of the use of the sword.[30] Sattler's "pacifism" is not that of his contemporary Mennonite offspring who understand it for the most part in the context of a love ethic *commanded* by Christ and supported by proof-texts selected from the synoptic Gospels (turning the other cheek, loving enemies, etc.). It is rather an ecclesiological dualism which explains his position.

In the Schleitheim Confession the first reference to the use of the sword occurs in an ecclesiological context and the evil against which a Christian is "not to resist" (Mt 5:39) so as "to protect friends . . . against enemies" is an evil which seeks to force conformity with the world, which refuses to allow believers to remain separate from the world. A little later in the same work Sattler is willing to allow the use of the sword outside the religious community (outside the perfection of Christ), but he believes that true Christians are never outside the perfection of Christ and therefore can never be in the situation of using the sword or of serving as a magistrate since this is the realm of the world and not that of the church to which the believer is fully committed. The same argument seems to explain his insistence that a Christian not use an oath; the use of the oath is required in a world which is only pretending (fictive faith) to be committed to the Father and the Christian must not participate in such an exercise.

Before one leaps too quickly to point out to Sattler that he is inconsistent in his stance and that his dualism means that he is allowing one morality for the world and another for the community of believers, one must attempt to interpret his thought within the eschatological framework so important to him. Sattler is living in the last days, when Church and world are being separated unto the final judgment and the decision to be baptized is the choice of Christ over anti-christ. Each individual must be certain that he or she is on the right side since Christ is coming soon and will take only those in the community back to himself. The rest will be destroyed. Sattler is not attempting to work out the details of a morality and a social and political theory which require a separation of church and state in a secularized society. For him there will very shortly no longer be a world in which the sword is used to maintain a semblance of order and insofar as the sword does maintain order, that is, in respect to the functioning of the world, it is an indication of God's grace, even though it will soon no longer be needed.

An important element in the description of any spirituality is a description of its worship practices, but little is known of early Anabaptist worship. What is known must be gleaned from a congregational order attached to the Schleitheim Confession.[31] The words "congregational order" which describe this piece refer not to the order of worship but to the order of all gatherings of believers, every one of which is "worship." All rules of order are shaped by two principles: all gatherings must be formed "according to the command of the Lord and the teachings of his apostles [i.e., as found in the New Testament]" and according to the new commandment of love for one another so that love and unity may always be maintained. The primary purpose of gatherings is edification, the support of the faith. All brothers and sisters are to "meet at least three or four times a week." They are to "exercise themselves in the teaching of Christ and his apostles and heartily to exhort one another to remain faithful to the Lord as they have pledged." When together, they are to read a passage of scripture and one is to explain it to the others. None are to act frivolously and each is to admonish the other of the error of his or her actions. There is to be a common fund so that the poor will not be in need (related to this, gluttony is to be avoided).

Whenever there is a gathering the Supper is to be celebrated. Once again, the Supper and the images of community and of willingness to die are the central themes treated and the themes which mark the tone of Anabaptist spirituality.

> The Lord's Supper . . . proclaim[s] the death of the Lord, and thereby warn[s] each one to commemorate, how Christ gave his life for us, and shed his blood for us, that we might also be willing to give our body and life for Christ's sake which means for the sake of the brothers.[32]

ON GRACE AND FREE WILL: BALTHASAR HUBMAIER

At the center of almost every discussion in the sixteenth century is the question of the relationship between grace and free will. In 1525, for example, Luther opposed Erasmus' *Freedom of the Will* with his own *Bondage of the Will,* and in his conclusion points to what he considers the central question. "You have not wearied me," he writes to Erasmus, "with those extraneous issues about the papacy, purgatory, indulgences and such like—trifles rather than issues— . . . you and you alone have been the hinge on which all turns—you sought the jugular."[33]

It was this doctrine of grace which for Luther and others was the "standing or falling" article of the Protestant Reformation and it was for this reason that Luther attacked the Anabaptists so fiercely. For him they were simply monks in another costume, people who denied God's grace with their emphasis on works, and who belied the significance of faith by requiring that all true believers "freely choose" to be rebaptized. As Luther saw it such baptism was not a gift of grace but a human work on which one relied to one's own destruction. In an important sense Luther was correct: the Anabaptists were not Protestants and, although they were not Roman Catholics either, there was much in their doctrine of grace which reflected earlier medieval positions.

For medieval Catholics the model of grace was medicinal— each human being is sick unto death, and unless a physician comes, death will be inevitable. Christ comes as the physician bodily (the Church is the body of Christ) and provides the medicine. His act of coming and the medicine is grace. If the patient uses the medicine regularly and follows the physician's advice, he or she will return slowly to health. In this model change takes place; people become better. There is an imitation of Christ.

For Protestants on the other hand, the model was a forensic or legal one. Each individual has committed a crime and deserves the death penalty. The individual comes before God the judge who pronounces her or him free of the penalty. After the pronouncement the person is saved from death (*justus,* justified before the law), but remains as guilty (a sinner, *peccator*) of the crime as before the court appearance (in Luther's oft-repeated phrase: *simul justus et peccator*). No change occurs. Such a person cannot for a moment pretend that he or she has gained justification in any sense—it has simply been granted. The person is always guilty and deserving of death. He or she does not become better; there can be a "following" of Christ but no "imitation" as the Protestant German translations of the work by Thomas a Kempis indicate (*Nachfolgung Christi,* not *Imitatio Christi*).

These two different models were paralleled by radically different views of the human person. For medieval Catholics each person is good, made in the "image and likeness" of God. Made in God's image, each person has a good intellect which seeks to know God as the highest truth and a will which desires to love God as the highest good. But in the fall of Adam the "likeness" of God or sanctifying grace was lost. It is returned in baptism, penance, and the other sacraments. Without it one can do nothing. One's will and intellect seek the highest but inevitably choose a lesser good and worship it in place of the greater. For Protestants there is no distinction between image and likeness. When the likeness was lost, the image was lost with it. Human beings are thus nothing in Adam and must be fully recreated in Christ.

Once such an approach has been established in both the Protestant and Catholic case, the reading each gives to the Bible is different. Protestant attention has generally been directed to Ephesians 2:8 (By grace are you saved through faith [*fide sola*] and that not of yourselves lest any man should boast), whereas Roman Catholics have emphasized Galatians 5:6 (In Jesus Christ neither circumcision nor uncircumcision counts for anything, but faith which works by love [*fide charitate formata*]). In the Sattlerian treatise "On the Satisfaction of Christ" interestingly, the classic Protestant passage from Ephesians 2 is not used but the Galatians 5 passage with its emphasis on faith working through love is.[34]

In a sense the Anabaptists were trying to find a middle way between the two extremes. If one is saved solely by grace, how is it possible for that grace to come through faith formed by love since the love which forms it is an act of the human will. In the early church the grace-free will dichotomy was simply accepted as a mystery in the same way the mystery of the Trinity is accepted. God cannot logically be both three *and* one and one cannot logically be redeemed both by grace *and* free will. In the western church little concern has been given to the illogic of the doctrine of the Trinity, but from the time of Augustine great energy has been expended attempting to explain the relationship of grace and free will.[35]

For the church before the time of Augustine and to some extent for the eastern church after him, the mystery was simply allowed to stand with little discussion. For the western church, however, and particularly for the western church of the sixteenth century, the question took on an importance because of its effect on spirituality. For Luther the problem was to provide pastoral care for badly or falsely catechized people who realized they could not do enough to merit salvation from a righteous God. As much as the Anabaptists and most other radicals with them agreed with Luther's pastoral insight regarding freely given grace, they felt that his teaching had not resulted in a true reformation of the church. From their point of view the doctrine of grace by faith alone was a principle which supported libertinism and they returned therefore, as best they could, to teaching a mystery which upheld both sides of the paradox: grace *and* free will; faith *and* works.

One of the most striking treatises on the theme of the grace and free will was written by Balthasar Hubmaier.[36] Hubmaier was a graduate of the University of Freiburg, a priest, prorector of the university and pastor at Regensburg and Waldshut in Breisgau. There in the early 1520s he was attracted to the Swiss Reformers and carried on discussions with Zwingli. In 1525 he had joined with the Swiss Brethren and for the next three years until his martyrdom in 1528 he wrote extensively in defense of the movement, although in a non-Anabaptist scholastic style. The marks of scholastic method are clear in his *On the Free Will,* a relatively short work in four parts which he completed in 1527.[37] He begins the piece with an outline of his doctrine of man, "a corporal and rational creature," as he sees him, "made up of body, spirit and soul." Each of these human aspects has a will, "the will of the flesh which does not want to suffer; the will of the soul is willing to suffer and yet, on account of the flesh, is also unwilling; the will of the spirit is glad to suffer." Even in a treatise on the will, martyrdom and suffering is a central theme. Before the fall, flesh, soul and spirit were all good. The will of the flesh given by God to the first man could choose disobedience and did so, bringing upon itself death. "But the Spirit of man remained utterly upright and intact, before, during and after the fall, for it took part, neither by counsel nor by action, yea it did not in any way consent to or approve of the eating of the forbidden fruit by the flesh." The will of the soul was caught between the flesh and the spirit. It was "maimed" and "wounded" to such a degree that it could not choose good or reject evil since it had lost the knowledge of both.

The situation of fallen man is radically changed with restoration through Christ.

> The flesh is still worthless and good for nought . . . [b]ut the spirit is happy, willing, ready for all good. The soul, sad and anxious, standing between the spirit and the flesh, knows not what to do, is blind and uncomprehending as to heavenly things, in its natural powers. But because it has been awakened by the word of God, jolted, warned and led . . . through his comforting word . . . [and] enlightened through the Holy Spirit, thereby the soul comes again to know what is good and what is evil. It has recovered its lost freedom. It can now freely and willingly be obedient to the spirit and can will and choose the good.[38]

Under no circumstances will Hubmaier accept a radical predestinarian stance. Following the vocabulary of the scholastics he makes a distinction between the absolute and the revealed will of God. According to neither of these wills, Hubmaier insists, does God wish "to harden, blind or damn anyone save those who of their own evil and of their own choice wish to be hardened, blinded and damned." God draws, but man can choose, and as a result it is expected that those who are of God will turn from their evil ways and live a life of love for God and others.

THE MYSTICAL ELEMENT
IN ANABAPTISM: HANS DENCK

A similar position on the subject of grace and free will is upheld by Hans Denck [39] but in his work the scholastic vocabulary of Hubmaier is exchanged for a language and rhetoric influenced by the mysticism of the late middle ages. A Bavarian, Denck was a graduate of the University of Ingolstadt and rector of a school in Nürnberg. It was there in January of 1525 that he ran into major difficulties with the authorities because of his religious position and was banished. By June of that year he was at St. Gall, meeting with the Anabaptists. For the next several years he traveled throughout South Germany and in 1527 went to Basel, made a "recantation" to Oecolampadius who was leading the Reformation in that city. He died of the plague in November of that year.

Denck took up the question of grace and free will in his *Whether God Is the Cause of Evil?* written when he was at Augsburg in 1526.[40] Working from a theological model which is very close to that of the late medieval mystics, Denck insists that "salvation is *in* us but not *of* us just as God is in all creatures but not for that reason from them." There is an eternal word in every human heart and that word one must not deny. Denck's position does not deny the importance of the physical incarnation of Christ or the importance of the Scriptures, however, "The word was in human beings that it might divinize them. . . . [It] had, however, to become man in Jesus for this reason that people both in the spirit and in the flesh, from within and without, behind and before, and in all places might have testimony." The divine is thus active within and outside of man; man depends on it for salvation, yet at the same time there is an expectation that one must respond to the word which is in one.

In his treatise Denck is not concerned either with the fall or with original sin, and with these two topics deemphasized he can easily support his doctrine of adult baptism, having as a result no need to develop an explanation for the salvation of unbaptized children who, with the word of God in them, were given over if they died before they were baptized, to the mercy and love of God.

The love of God is the subject of what is perhaps Denck's finest work, *On True Love.*[41] Love, he tells us in the beginning of this work, is "a spiritual power by which one becomes united or desires to become united with another." Like the late medieval mystics again Denck develops this theme, pointing out that the lover "forgets himself" and is willing to die for the sake of a beloved. If such love is pure, it will extend out of its groundless source beyond the individual and the specific beloved to all persons and beyond them into eternity. Love hates itself, as it were, for the sake of the beloved. Love is a spark from God which cannot be grasped by flesh and blood, and blessedness increases to the degree that this love is loved.

Such love was incarnated in the human being, Jesus of Nazareth:

> And it pleased the eternal love that a man in whom love was manifested in its highest form, would be called a saviour of his people. It was not that Christ needed humanity to save someone, but God was so completely united in him in love that all the acts of God were considered the acts of the man, and all the suffering of this man were considered the suffering of God.[42]

The love of man for God and of God for man cannot be better demonstrated than in the person of Christ. "Whoever desires to learn and to grasp love, can achieve his goal no more simply than through this Jesus Christ." Those who live under the law are servants, but those who live under love are the children of God. The law in itself was not evil nor was following it evil, but those who know love in Christ have found a more perfect fuller law.

It is at this point that Denck raises the question of baptism. It is seen as analogous to circumcision but in typical Anabaptist style Denck avoids the implication of a full analogy, thereby necessitating a belief in infant baptism.

> The new law is an adoption so that all who are under it can be brought under it by no human means, but only by merciful God, a faithful father; they are drawn into the abyss of their souls and born therein and he thus gives them to know his dearest will, love itself as presented by Christ Jesus. . . .

> And in a similar way, the mark of the covenant, baptism, is to be given to and not cast off by only those who are called by the power of God through the knowledge of true love and who desire and endeavor to follow it.[43]

The question of works is to be understood in the context of the new birth. "The one who does not love has no need for works [practices] in themselves, but the one who has and understands love will practice works as Jesus did." However, the question naturally arises, if the old works have been set aside, why should one insist on new ones: baptism and the Supper? Their only purpose, says Denck, differing from the rigorism of Sattler and the Swiss, is for "a confession and memorial to that to which one is called, namely to God away from the world, and [as] an indicator that the ones so called will serve God all their lives in holiness and righteousness." What Denck does is make baptism and the Supper into symbols, placing less emphasis on their actual practice than the Swiss Brethren do. Baptism occurs only once since it is a symbol of the fact that the new covenant occurs only once in Christ, and the Supper is taken repeatedly to symbolize the unending and repeated need to practice and live daily in the new covenant. Even the opposition to infant baptism is based on the implications of its symbolic significance:

> Infant baptism is wrong because the first and most important concern of the message of Jesus Christ is that men be taught and that they be made disciples whose chief responsibility is to seek the kingdom of God. . . . If someone baptises a person before that person is a disciple, the act signifies that baptism is more necessary than teaching and knowledge.[44]

Similar symbolic arguments are developed to oppose the swearing of oaths and the use of weapons. The Sermon on the Mount's admonishments against swearing are tied by Denck to the admonition to be perfect, even as "your Father is perfect." If one were as perfect as the Father, one could swear, but on earth we are all en route to perfection and therefore cannot do so without committing the sin of hypocrisy. If we swear we are indicating that we have reached perfection. The use of defensive weapons is opposed first because it indicates that the loyalty of the one who uses them is to an earthly kingdom and not to a heavenly one. On this topic Denck is much less dualistic than his Swiss co-believers.

Denck closes his treatise *On True Love* with a brief comment on his intention in the work. "Everything which I have written,"

he states, "has flowed from the perfect love of Christ so that anyone who has the spirit of the Lord can understand it. . . . Anyone
who understands it and teaches something other than it teaches
is truly an antichrist; anyone who does not understand it does not
yet understand the Lord Christ." What Denck is here doing is
distinguishing between the spirit of a text and the letter. The
spirit of a text which arises from the spirit of Christ can be
grasped by the true Christian who lives in the spirit of Christ but
it cannot be understood by those who live only in flesh and blood
and it will not be properly interpreted by an anti-christ who clings
only to the words.

Denck's hemeneutics, as here reflected, is close to that of the
mystical spiritualists: like them he makes a distinction between the
spirit and the letter and parallels his distinction with the distinction between the body and the soul in the person. Like the Swiss,
he too is dualistic, but whereas the Swiss upheld an ecclesiological
dualism distinguishing between the church and the world,
Denck's dualism is "anthropological." An ecclesiological dualism
allows the letter of the scripture to be primary, and tends to lit-
eralism in its hermeneutics, whereas the "anthropological" dualism of Denck supports a "spiritual" or symbolic reading of the
text of scripture, of all Christian literature, and of major Christian themes such as baptism, the Supper and the Church itself.
These are to be understood by the "true," "inner" Christian , but
not by those who merely follow external practices.

This spiritual interpretation (in the German sense, both
geistlich and geistich) allows Denck in his Order of God[45] to distinguish the Schriftsgelehrten from the Geistesgelehrten, and to
describe the latter as those who live outside of the world. But for
him those outside of the world are those who live in their hearts,
in the inner man. The two ways of life are understood primarily
in an anthropological sense of the inner man, and good works are
not reflected primarily in human actions but in the unity of the
human will and God's will. Like the medieval mystics Denck insists
that the free will is the will which is tied to the will of God and
the will in bondage is the will which acts unto itself. The search
for external peace is therefore a search which leads to destruction. What is important is the search for inner peace, for a unity
in diversity like the unity in diversity in the trinity itself.

PILGRAM MARPECK AND
SOUTH-GERMAN ANABAPTISM

Midway between the position maintained by Denck and that of the Swiss is the South-German Anabaptist Pilgram Marpeck.[46] Among the most significant of the Anabaptist theologians, Marpeck carried on a debate with mystical spiritualism and maintained a continual critique of the Swiss Anabaptists. It is easiest to begin reflection on the nature of his spirituality by contrasting it with that of the spiritualist Caspar Schwenckfeld von Ossig.[47]

Schwenckfeld was a Silesian nobleman and counselor of the Duke of Liegnitz in the 1520s, but his position on the sacrament and his spiritualistic division of spirit and letter, spiritual church from physical church, Creator from creation caused his duke embarrassment and Schwenckfeld went into self-exile in 1529 to avoid further difficulties. He traveled to Strasbourg and when he arrived there, he might well have been greeted by Pilgram Marpeck, then director of forestry in that city. Marpeck was an Anabaptist, but, despite his theology, was retained in the service of the city until 1532 because of his engineering ability. His skill as an engineer brought him to Augsburg in the 1540s, where he remained for the rest of his life. In Strasbourg he and Schwenckfeld were seemingly on friendly terms, but on Marpeck's arrival in Augsburg, antagonisms flared into theological war. In 1540 Schwenckfeld fled to Justingen near Ulm and but a few miles to the west of Augsburg. From this place, he moved out on pastoral visits to conventicles of fellow believers in Ulm and Augsburg, and he made an inevitable impact on Anabaptist groups in the area.

Marpeck came to their defense with the publication of his *Admonition* in 1542.[48] Neither man understood the other. Marpeck possibly saw Schwenckfeld in light of Sebastian Franck's teaching which moved toward individualistic pantheism, and Schwenckfeld, because of earlier experiences with seventh-day Judaizing Anabaptists in Silesia, viewed Marpeck according to their premises, with which the Augsburg Anabaptists had little in common.

Both Marpeck and Schwenckfeld painted their pictures of religious reality from differing perspectives, and thus they found it difficult to evaluate properly their opponents' point of view in any particular doctrine. Marpeck was fully the Anabaptist; he interpreted all doctrine with the life of Jesus of Nazareth in mind. Schwenckfeld, on the other hand, although not rejecting the importance of Jesus' earthly career, centered his interest on the glorified Christ at the right hand of the Father. Marpeck tended to be concerned with the concrete manifestation of the divine, and thus with the physical structure of the church: the act of baptism, the role of the brotherhood in including or excluding members from the Lord's Supper, and the literal words of Scripture. Schwenckfeld mistrusted such emphases, fearing that they could lead to trust in created things and away from the guidance of the Spirit. For him, the spirit of the Scriptures had priority; it, and not the text, spoke to the individual heart. The inner washing of baptism and the inner renewal available in the Lord's Supper were considered to be of most importance in his theology, not the rites associated with them, nor the patterned structures of organized Christianity.

Marpeck strongly upheld a doctrine of man's free will, and Schwenckfeld countered his position with an emphasis on God's elective role in salvation. Whereas Schwenckfeld saw man as soul and body, and tended to concern himself with the soul first, Marpeck looked to the physical, whole man comprised of body, soul, and spirit. Finally, the two men disagreed on the Christian's relationship to the state: Schwenckfeld insisted that the Christian might serve in public office, but Marpeck separated church and world into distinct categories which were to some extent mutually exclusive.

One must take care, however, not to overemphasize the differences between the two men. Schwenckfeld did support the establishment of conventicles of believers, and he did emphasize the reading of the Scriptures. On the other hand, Marpeck was the first to realize that the literal words of the biblical text were not of final concern. In this he was opposed to the more literalistic approach of the Swiss Brethren, and he had much in common with his contemporary, Denck.[49]

Each of the Anabaptists discussed to this point reflects a strand of late medieval spirituality. Sattler's spirituality is similar to that of the late medieval Benedictines and Denck can be profitably discussed in the context of the popular Eckhartian tradition of the late fifteenth—early sixteenth centuries. Marpeck can perhaps be best characterized as a spiritual descendant of the conventualar Franciscans, and in his opposition to Schwenckfeld the coventualar opposition to the Franciscan spirituals is reflected. In his opposition to the Swiss the spirituality of men like Bonaventure is reflected.

In his *Clear Refutation* of 1531[50] Marpeck begins his attack on the spiritualists whom he describes as erring spirits in their refusal to use any outward ceremonies. Against their belief that the apostolic succession ended with the apostles themselves, Marpeck insists that the succession has continued in the true church planted in the hearts of believers. For Marpeck the church thus retains its authority through the ages.

How seriously Marpeck had taken the threat of spiritualism can be noted by his *Clear and Useful Instruction*[51] which he seems to have written at approximately the same time as the 1531 piece already noted. The fact that he makes use of the word *stillstand* (used by Schwenckfeld to support the cessation of the practice of the Lord's Supper until all religious disputation was ended) in this text is an indication that Marpeck already had the teachings of Schwenckfeld in mind and that he already perceived the threat of spiritualism for the incipient Anabaptist movement. One may note as well the attachment to this work on those who despise the humanity of Christ and those who pretend to be new prophets and hide behind the image of Cornelius who although he was not baptized still prayed and practiced Christian works; the section seems directed against the spiritualists.

In 1531, when he began to write against Schwenckfeld, Marpeck was also embroiled in a debate with the Swiss Brethren. His *Judgement and Decision*[52] to them indicates that he wishes to continue relationships with them, and as a result he defends himself against the charges they have laid against him in a way which more clearly indicates his view of how the Christian is to relate to his immediate brethren than does the work against Schwenckfeld which becomes increasingly more polemical. He makes some comments on the Gospel of all creatures, pointing out to the Swiss that the spirit of Christ was given to all creatures before the advent of Christ; such a doctrine would of necessity force the

Swiss to soften their ecclesiological dualism and their rigorous insistence that some are in the church and others are not. As a result Marpeck cannot accept the Swiss use of the ban; in place of this he counsels patience and forebearance, and develops a notion of progress in the Christian life.

Perhaps nowhere is Anabaptist spirituality reflected as clearly as in Marpeck's letters. These include, in addition to the *Judgement and Decision* already discussed, a number addressed to individuals and other, more topical pieces on the church, libertarianism, sin, the lowliness and humanity of Christ, love and servanthood.[53] Each of these is written not with a concern to establish a direct dogmatic point but to encourage a fitting spirituality.

Two such letters, for example, treat the nature of the church. The first of these was written to the faithful in Wuerttemberg in 1544.[54] In it Marpeck distinguishes in the style of the Swiss Brethren between the church of Christ and that of Hagar, between the true church and the false. Those who are the offspring of Hagar are not fed "with the milk of love, but with lifeless water, kept in a little barrel." They are not to be believed. They are children "without God the Father and the Holy Spirit, without the seed of the living Word." But beyond these few comments all parallels between Marpeck and the Swiss end. His treatment is of a wholly different tone than that of the Swiss Brethren. The letter is not a description of the two churches, but is primarily a discussion of the Church of Christ, emphasizing love, which Marpeck believes is central in any treatment of the church. His letter begins with words reminiscent of Denck and of the late medieval mystics. Marpeck then goes on to explain in greater detail the nature of this love.

My dear ones, loved in God the Father through Jesus Christ: This love is the true source from which all love flows. For this love, which is the one love and the one God, flows from the heavenly Father in Christ and from Christ in the Father. In the Holy Spirit this love brings about the unity of all faithful hearts. She is a bond and an inseparable unity, an eternal beginning stretching from the highest height. She takes to herself the influx of whatever is loved and may in truth be loved. In particular, love, which is God in all, is the observer

of that which she herself has created and formed in the likeness of her image. In Him, according to her manner and her
nature, which is essence itself, love has an eternal likeness.
She is eternally loved again by man. When she lives in the new
heaven and the new earth as a holy city, the new Jerusalem,
her form, will be fully seen in Him. Prepared as a bride for
her husband, she will come down out of heaven from God,
Himself the essence of love. A dwelling of God, she will be
the most beautiful of all. She shows herself to her bridegroom
and husband, and she is the banner above all. She is the seal
imprinted on hearts of all the faithful and she is the pledge
for eternal security, victory, and conquest against all hate and
enmity.[55]

The clothes love wears are the virtues which must be worn
unspotted (note the emphasis on works), but they are not made
by the individual; they are given by the Father (by his grace). The
mystery of the church, however, is not seen clearly on earth. It is
only seen with the eyes of the flesh. Following this Marpeck goes
on to offer his readers further glimpses of the Bride's adornment
using images chosen primarily from the Song of Songs. The faithful are those "kissed by the mouth of God"; they are "fed by her
breasts filled as those breasts are by the Holy Spirit."

The unadulterated milk flows out of her body. Without deceit
or wrong, the mother, the true Sara, bears her children to the
Father. And her breasts are loved. The children of the mother
are all eager for her milk, and suck from her breasts to their
hearts' content.[56]

This spiritualist interpretation of the church is carried further by Marpeck in his letter on the inner church.[57] In it he begins
by discussing the knowledge which is given to the faithful.

I, along with many others who testify to it through faith, have
had only a glimpse of her form. This glimpse has created great
longing in our hearts to see her again, fully and as she really
is. Perhaps we, with all who desire it, may get another glimpse
of her, and see her form, so that our hearts may be more

eager with desire to seek her and see her form. Then, we, too, may be clothed with her apparel, and please her with fervent service.[58]

They are raised and nourished, and grow and increase, in the discipline which the mother applies to them. Thus, they live in neither sin nor in the filth of their carnal nature. Rather, when they reach their mature adulthood in Christ, their bridegroom, they are taught and instructed in the discipline of the Holy Spirit. Then, possessed with wisdom, understanding, and perception, they are given over to the Father, who receives them as heirs of the eternal inheritance and kingdom with Christ.

What more joyous thing can we experience than to confess to one another that we know that Christ Jesus is in the Father and God the Father is in Christ, and remains so eternally. Indeed, we know, recognize, and also feel that Christ is in us and we in Christ, and remain so eternally. Moreover, we know and recognize that the dwelling of God the Father and His Christ is built in our hearts. Now, in this time, they have made a dwelling, and dwell in us. Indeed, we also know and recognize the fruit and work of the Son, which the Father works in the Son and the Son in us, whereby we remain in His Word. The fruit is perfect love. We recognize therein that the Father and the Son have made their dwelling in us, and live in us.[59]

The church community will, Marpeck expects, reflect this love, but Marpeck's initial interest is not in discussing this matter fully. Rather he goes on to spiritualize almost all aspects of the physical nature of the church and the ways in which that love manifests itself. "The one place of worship is above" where true worshipers worship in spirit and in truth. The only place where such worship can be done is in hearts of men.

Because the Jerusalem which is above is only built by Jesus Christ in the Spirit, the heart is in the inner and only temple. In this Jerusalem is the place of worship, namely, in Spirit and in truth. The hearts of men, the hearts of the true believers, are also the inner choir and sanctuary, into which no one can enter except our High Priest; to Him alone the choir and the sanctuary have been dedicated by God the Father, who is able to search the heart, thoughts, and soul. This choir and sanctuary is known only by the High Priest, Christ; in it He prays to the Father for the sins of men. Only his High Priest, Christ Jesus, can see how the inner choir and the sanctuary are shepherded and formed. This church is seen only by the Spirit, and only in the spirit, through the High Priest Christ, is there forgiveness and remission of sins. That is the inner church of Christ.[60]

Marpeck does not simply stop with such a statement, however. To do so would be for him to come very close to accepting Schwenckfeld's position, as he understands it. Rather, he insists:

In collaboration with the Holy Spirit, this inner church of the Holy Spirit is also directed to perform external works, to be a light before the world. It witnesses inwardly between God and man, but it is also formed externally, and testifies in love shown toward the neighbor. According to the measure of the internal working of the Holy Spirit, which leads to the external forgiveness of sin and the improvement of the external man, teaching, baptism, and the Lord's Supper show love toward all men. In this manner, the Spirit, mind, and will of the Father are revealed by the external man, Jesus Christ; they are revealed bodily, by word and work, in the same form as the internal working of God the Father.[61]

This "communion of the saints means that, through Jesus Christ, remission of sins is available." The fact of remission means that sins have a reality and must be properly discerned and punished. The task of such discernment is given to the saints.[62]

With such an emphasis on the concrete nature of the church Marpeck has returned, as it were, to a position in keeping with the Swiss Brethren. Any act of discipline, however, which is enacted by the church must be carried out within the context of the lowliness and humanity of Christ. These latter themes Marpeck emphasizes in great detail in other letters. The humility of Christ and all his true followers is marked by patience.

Therefore, as the Lord says, we must arm and prepare our souls with patience for we will need patience if we wish to

preserve the treasures and the true rod of our high priest
Aaron which, together with the golden bucket, blossomed in
our souls.[63]

With such patience love grows, and such love is the true
bread of heaven, Marpeck writes, in a tone remarkably similar to
that of his great opponent Schwenckfeld.

> In the loving hearts of the faithful is the true bread from
> heaven, which the Father gave us from heaven and which has
> given us life, kept for a perpetual remembrance. This bread
> [is] His broken or prepared flesh and blood, given up for our
> life. The pure flesh and blood of the virgin Mary prepared this
> flesh and blood for us, and this heavenly bread, which the
> Word made flesh, raises us from death to life. It is true food
> and drink, given for our life; it nourishes and preserves our
> souls. The true bread of remembrance belongs in the golden
> bucket, and this bread is kept locked in the ark of the New
> Testament. In all patience, united with gentleness, humility,
> and surrender, our High Priest has locked the treasures in the
> ark.[64]

Here and elsewhere what strikes the reader of Marpeck again
and again are the parallels in rhetoric between Marpeck and the
late medieval mystics. In his treatment of the lowliness of Christ,
for example, Marpeck compares Christ and the ark of the covenant in ways which remind one of the treatment in the *Spiritual
Tabernacle* of Jan van Ruusbroec,[65] and in Marpeck's description
of the fruits of repentance,[66] his enumeration and discussion is
not in any way out of keeping with the enumerations of earlier
writers. At numerous places in his work there are striking parallels in his allegory and that of Bernard of Clairvaux.[67]

It is in his later work, however, *On the Love of God in Christ,*[68]
that Marpeck brings to the summit his treatement of love, the
church, and the patient bearing required of the true followers of
Christ. In this work he expands, as it were, the earlier medieval
spiritual treatment of love. No more clearly is this reflected than
in a section in which he distinguishes between the love which is
God himself and the love which is poured out on individuals.

For in Christ the fullness of Godhead dwells bodily; in us, in this time, it is only in part. Love is our teacher through the Holy Spirit that only in this time we should be led and directed by her, and learn of her. We remain seated at the feet of Christ with Magdalene, who loved much and therefore received much forgiveness and remission according to the Word of the Lord. But that is love only for our benefit and salvation. But in Christ love is complete since He sought and accepted no benefit for Himself which could have caused or initiated love. He is the fullness of everything eternally. In the creatures love is awakened and given for the benefit [of the creatures] to the praise of God. For complete love has no defect. But men, in whom she already dwells, are full of weakness; there she is full of patience. . . . Love is conciliatory. Love suffers all things, endures all things, and bears all things.[67]

It is in the context of such love that Marpeck takes up his discussion of the state and violence. Like his Anabaptist co-believers he takes up the topic in an eschatological context.[68] And like his Anabaptist co-believers as well, he opposes the use of weapons primarily because his experience of their use is in forcing individuals to choose a particular religious option.[69]

One would expect that at this point Marpeck would go on to treat martyrdom, the need for true Christians to suffer the violence of a godless world, to bear the cross of Christ even unto death but he does not. Rather he spiritualizes the theme, speaking of the "sorrow of human corruption." Yet, as he puts it, believers do not ask to be released from physical suffering but rather from sin, the root of that suffering. The world experiences the cross as torment; believers recognize it as the destruction of sin.[70] The two crosses are to be distinguished as heaven and earth are, and those who do live in the heavenly aspect must follow the example of him who

with gentle patience, love and truth overcame evil with all goodness, love, faithfulness, truth, and mercy, and [for evil] returned passionate intercession for His enemies, and surrendered His human life and eternal bliss on the cross in unbroken patience, a submissive and silent Lamb of sacrifice for the sins of man and his salvation. This is the universally hallowed cross of Christ by which in the innocence of Christ all the followers of Christ overcome, and through which they have free access in and to God, provided their hearts do not accuse them in guilt.[71]

MENNO SIMONS AND THE DUTCH ANABAPTISTS

There is a significant change in tone between Swiss and South German Anabaptists, but an even greater difference between these two groups and their Dutch co-believers. Nor is the distinction merely one of language and social or political environment. Although the Dutch Anabaptist, Menno Simons,[72] was writing at the same time as was Marpeck, he represents in a real way another generation of Anabaptism. Marpeck wrote in the context of late medieval piety reflecting on the new religious options in the framework of a theology still shaped by the tone and emphasis of an earlier world. For Menno the world had radically changed; his spiritual sources were not those of the late middle ages but those of Christian Humanists like Erasmus, who marked a clear division between themselves and medieval life.

Moreover, Menno's first major work was written five years after the promulgation of the Augsburg Confession, in a world of warring religious positions. His polemical tone is a mark of the new era, and it reflects itself not only in the way Menno addresses Lutherans, Catholics and Calvinists, but also in the way he separates himself from persons such as the radical Anabaptists of Muenster who on first glance belong to his camp. His world is a world of correct doctrine and, as a result, of a confrontational attitude.

Thus Menno's dualism was exacerbated, not softened (as was Marpeck's) by his spiritualism, and although, like Marpeck, Menno has the gift for meditational writing, the tone of his work is often marred by his excessive polemicism. Among the early Anabaptists for example, there are few devotional passages more beautiful than sections of Menno's meditation on Psalm 25.[72] Note for example his reflections on Psalm 25:8:

Good and upright is the Lord: therefore will he teach sinners in the way. O Lord of hosts, although I have walked so unrighteously before Thee from my youth that I am ashamed to lift my eyes to Thee in heaven, nevertheless I appear at Thy mercy seat, for I know that Thou art merciful and kind and desirest not the death of the sinner, but that he may repent and live. [Thy servants were many.] Diligently they reproved sin; Thy grace they heralded forth. The right way they taught. Thy sharp piercing sword was in their mouth; their light shone as the golden candlestick; they were as blossoming olive trees, as a sweet smell of costly perfume, yea, as the glorious mountain planted with roses and lilies.[73]

But the beauty of such passages are covered over by Menno's continual and bitter harangues against "God's" enemies in the text itself and above all in the introduction to the piece: "It appears dear readers that I am being loaded down with slanders and lies behind my back."[74] Although he explains that he has chosen "not [an] argumentative nor a rhetorical form" to oppose his enemies, but "the form of prayer," the violence of his opening words sets the tone for all which follows and makes his meditation, at the best, sound spiritually arrogant and, at the worst, hypocritical.

Menno was ordained a priest in 1524 seven years after Luther posted his ninety-five theses. Yet he already had serious doubts about the doctrine of transubstantiation. During the period he must have come into contact with the revolutionary Hofmannites, and in 1531 he heard of the martyrdom of one of their number for being rebaptized. The execution led Menno to consider closely the question of infant baptism and raised doubts in his mind regarding the validity of such an initiation. These doubts were intensified after the destruction of a pro-Münsterite force near his home. In the battle a Peter Simons (perhaps his brother) was slain. The collapse of Münster several months later increased his concern and study; and after having endeavored to use his priestly position as a basis on which to build a reform program, he finally resigned in 1536.[75]

The whole Hofmannite cause had been deeply disillusioned by the revolutionary wing at Münster. In the ensuing fragmentation, it was Menno who drew together the broken members of the conservative wing, welding them into the movement which would take his name. For the rest of his life, he worked indefatigably toward this goal in Holland and north Germany. So significant was his work that by some twenty years after his death all other Anabaptist groups in south Germany were being designated "Mennonists."

Menno came to lay great emphasis on defining the community, an emphasis which increased as he grew older. The responsibility of the members of the brotherhood, one for the other, was highly important for him, and it resulted in his stern endorsement of the use of excommunication and shunning. His sternness in this regard led to a break in the community he had done so much to draw together. In 1557 the Waterlanders in Holland separated from his supporters, and the issues lived on to plague the Mennonite community in 1693, when Jacob Amann led his followers to form the separated communities of the Amannsch or Amish Mennonites.[76]

Menno's dubious heritage has troubled his spiritual descendants to the present day, but one must be careful to interpret this concern in the proper setting, to regard it with his seriousness. The use of the ban and the shunning of those who were excommunicated were defined as discipline, guidance. The direction of wayward members was held to be highly important, for if one truly loved one's brothers, one could not allow a brother to stray morally or theologically. If, after personal consultation and discussion of the problem among a few members, the difficulty was not resolved because of the stubbornness of the erring member, the final act of excommunication and shunning was taken. It was theoretically an act of love, done with heavy heart, both to renew the lost follower and to purify the body of Christ. The tragedy was that it was often based on narrow theological differences, petty moral casuistry, and strong personality conflicts. In practice, it often missed the point at which it was directed.

Menno's concern with community, its purity and cohesiveness, may have owed something to his Christology, which he inherited from Melchior Hofmann. Hofmann taught a doctrine of Christ's celestial flesh which held that Christ had brought his flesh down with him into the Virgin. Menno changed the teaching to a degree, attempting to cleanse it of its most blatantly unorthodox aspects. Christ, he taught, became flesh in Mary but did not take flesh of her. For Menno Simons, Christ's flesh was divine; it was of a nature different from ours. Thus, when he heard the church described as the body of Christ, and when he spoke of the bread of communion as the body of Christ, both doctrines had a different tone for him than they did for Luther. When one considers this aspect of his doctrine of Christ, one can more easily understand the seriousness with which he regarded the church (for it was described as a special, celestial body) and the Supper (for its emblems were those of a peculiar food, Christ's flesh), and one can more properly understand why he emphasized the need for the ban so strongly. Members of the celestial flesh, he must have believed at a very deep level, are to be particularly pure, to be properly part of that body. Participation in the Supper must be the action of the pure because of its celestial associations. All the impure must be forbidden to attend.

For Menno, unlike the earlier Anabaptists, the expectation of the coming end was a doctrine rather than an existential reality and his discussions of the church-state division are, as a result, different from those of the "earlier" group. In his situation, the doctrine that the sword and political power could be used to extend a religious position had been used not against the Anabaptist cause but to support it, by believers who considered themselves to be Anabaptists themselves. Menno's rejection of the use of the sword, as a result, plays a more significant role in his developed theology than it does in that of the earlier writers.

But not only is the work of Menno distinguished from the Anabaptists such as the Swiss who wrote before him; it also marks the direction that theology would take in the century following his death; and there are a striking number of themes in it which remind the reader of those the Pietists would hold a century later and which would become central to the thought of all Mennonites. No better can these be seen than in the concluding section to Menno's *True Christian Faith* (1541).[77] In this work he writes that the "righteous must live out their faith" by repudiation of past sins and repentance for them, and by the experience and knowledge of the new birth. That new birth must be tested.

> The Word of the Lord teaches as follows: Verily, verily, I say
> unto thee, Except a man be born again, he cannot see the
> kingdom of God. And, verily I say unto you, Except ye be con-

verted and become as little children, ye shall not enter into
the kingdom of heaven. Test yourself with these. If you are
born of the pure seed of the holy Word, the nature of the
seed must be in you. And if you have become like little children in malice, then pride, unchastity, avarice, hatred, and
envy no longer reside in you, for the innocent children know
nothing of such sins. But if you continue to live in the old
Adam and not in the new nature of Christ, and walk after the
base, impure desires of your flesh, then you prove indeed that
you are not born of God and have not His faith.[78]

But it is not enough simply to test oneself by oneself if one's
sins are to be overcome. There is also need for a "true and sincere" faith.

Test yourselves once more. If you sincerely believe these
words of Christ with the whole heart; that the Almighty Eternal Father so loved you and the whole human race that He
sent His incomprehensible, almighty, eternal Word, wisdom,
truth, and Son, by whom He created the heavens, the earth,
the sea, and the fullness thereof, His eternal glory and honor
into this vale of tears; that He let Him become a poor, sad,
and miserable man; that He permitted Him for the sake of
sins of us all to suffer and thirst, to be slandered, apprehended, beaten, crowned with thorns, crucified, and killed.[79]

THE PIETIST AWAKENING AND ANABAPTISM

Menno's concern with repentance, the new birth, devotion
and the practice of piety were themes taken up in Protestantism
in general in the late seventeenth century by the Pietists. Next to
the writings and thought of the Anabaptists of the sixteenth century, the most significant influence on the development of Anabaptist spirituality was Pietism.[80]

The Pietist awakening had its roots in the practically-oriented
reform movement among seventeenth century Lutherans and
Calvinists which opposed Protestant scholasticism and its emphasis on the acceptance of closely-worded confessional formulae.
Pietism began in Frankfurt am Main in 1675 when the chief pas-

tor of the Lutheran ministerium in the city, Phillip Jacob Spener, wrote a short introduction to a collection of sermons by Johann Arndt.[81] The piece was entitled *Pia desideria* and went through numerous editions in the next several years. By the end of the century the principles enunciated in the short work had affected almost all Protestant traditions in the German, Dutch and Scandinavian countries.

The first clear indication that the Mennonites felt the impact of Pietism is the 1702 publication of a collection of martyr stories, entitled *Golden Apples in Silver Bowls;* the volume included a collection of Pietist prayers.[82] In the years thereafter a number of volumes appeared under Mennonite authorship and support which upheld Pietist principles.

Somewhat like Menno, Pietism emphasized an experientially oriented theology, insisting that true Christians must experience a new birth, repent for their sins, actively pursue a devotional life in love for God and neighbor. Pietists met in conventicles, often twice a week, for mutual edification and support in their active search for *Gottseligkeit* (blessedness).

Perhaps the finest study done on the relationship between the Anabaptist tradition and Pietism is Robert Friedmann's *Mennonite Piety through the Centuries,*[83] which outlines the growing use of Pietist literature among Mennonites in Europe and America. Although willing to recognize the similarities between Pietism and Anabaptism, Friedmann attends primarily to the differences.

Early in the work he distinguishes between the Anabaptist concern with *Gottesfurcht* (fear of the Lord) and the Pietist concern with *Gottseligkeit*. For Friedmann this is the central difference between the two movements. He does recognize that Anabaptism had an effect on the Pietist movement in its early stages and that in the late seventeenth century it was in turn influenced by the Pietist awakening. Both movements, he points out, have an interest in the new birth and both insist on the "inner transformation of the entire man."[84] As a result both have opposed to a greater or lesser extent the idea of a general state church and of confessionalism.

But the similarities between the two movements are surface matters. Anabaptism's separatism is not, as was Pietism's, from the corrupt church, but from the world itself. Both groups do teach a doctrine of the new birth but for the Anabaptists this birth is to lead to a following of Jesus *(Nachfolge)*, if need be to death. The Pietists on the other hand understand such following not in the context of martyrdom and the cross, but more in the sense of a cross of suffering over repentance. For the Anabaptists the spirit is a creative spirit, "a molding power, whose experience is the whole of life including its outward expression. The Spirit requires an unrestricted commitment, and that means for the lover of the Gospel, discipleship, *Nachfolge.*"[85] This approach to the spirit is much different in Pietism which leans toward a concept of the inner word, inner spirit, and a mysticism.

It is always important to remember when reading a volume such as Friedmann's that he was writing at a point when Mennonites in North America were attempting to distinguish themselves from other groups and to enunciate the distinctive traits of their denomination. Thus, they differentiated between their Anabaptist forefathers and other members of the Radical Reformation such as the Revolutionaries and the Spiritualists. At the same time the growing impact of American revivalism was making itself felt in twentieth century American Mennonitism and as a result leaders like Friedmann and H. S. Bender wanted to distinguish clearly between Anabaptism and the inner directed, experiential theology of the American evangelical movement. Thus Friedmann concludes the early part of his work by pointing out that salvation is not the *Geniessen* (enjoyment) of the Pietists but the suffering of the Anabaptists:

> Redemption is not only deliverance [as the Pietists taught], but involves also a commission, a task for the reborn one. It does not mean self-righteousness, but consecration to a great work. . . . It was only after Anabaptism weakened in the later centuries of its history that it at times falsely understood the genius of its own Gospel. Man is, to be sure, everywhere and at all times involved in sin, but he is capable of fighting against it. He can make himself worthy to the extent that he is capable of fulfilling God's commission in the positive sense through deed and the giving of his life. This was the great faith of the Anabaptists, a faith which rarely any of the other groups possessed.[86]

In an important way Friedmann has properly summed up the differences between Anabaptism and Pietism and has thus laid the basis for further discussions which Mennonites must now have with the broader American evangelical movement. What is at the core of Anabaptist spirituality is an emphasis on the importance of the community; the individual is made by the group, not the group by the individual. This emphasis is marked by the Anabaptist concern with the "pure" practice of the Lord's Supper, and above all with the Anabaptist doctrine of love, which is one and the same with dying unto self for the sake of God and the other. Such dying is to be understood in light of the earlier mystical notion of dying unto self, that is, in light of a self-abnegation in all matters. The latter point must be stressed: For the Anabaptist dying unto self is an inner, spiritual dying, but it can never be separated from a physical, bodily, giving of one's own energies, resources and life for the good of other human beings. Works are not to be set aside as marks of human pride or a theology of glory so as to revel in the enjoyment of inner peace, of grace as the knowledge that one is redeemed and can do nothing to bring it about, and thereby *need* do nothing to do so.

Nevertheless, Friedmann's thesis requires serious qualifications. Major sectors in contemporary Mennonitism have been strongly influenced by the Pietist and revivalist traditions, have learned much from them, and have, perhaps, still more to learn. Simply because Anabaptist doctrines are chronologically first does not mean that they must be used to challenge and set aside the significant role Pietism has played in shaping the tradition. No religious group can deny a part of the tradition to which it owes its descent without denying the whole, regardless of how disparate the parts of the tradition are. It remains the challenge for contemporary descendants of the Anabaptists to seek a balance between the opposing sources of their spirituality.

NOTES

1. George H. Williams, *The Radical Reformation* (Philadelphia: Westminster Press, 1962). For further discussions see also Roland H. Bainton, "The Left Wing of the Reformation," *Jour-*

nal of Religion, 21 (1941), 124–134, and George H. Williams and Angel M. Mergal, eds., *Spiritual and Anabaptist Writers* (Philadelphia: Westminster Press, 1957). The fullest bibliographic information is available in Hans Hillerbrand, *A Bibliography of Anabaptism* (Elkhart, Ind.: Institute of Mennonite Studies, 1962). Note also Hans-Juergen Goertz, ed., *Profiles of Radical Reformers,* trans. by Walter Klaassen and others (Kitchener, Ont. and Scottdale, Pa.: Herald Press, 1982).

2. *The Mennonite Encyclopedia,* ed. Harold S. Bender *et al.* (1955–1959).

3. Note particularly Williams, *Reformation,* 853–857, Williams and Mergal, *Writers,* 19–35. See, as well, Reinhold Fast, *Der linke Flügel der Reformation* (Bremen: Carl Schuneman Verlag, 1962), ixff. and the introduction to James Stayer's *Anabaptists and the Sword* (Lawrence, Kan.: Coronada Press, 1973, 1–23.

4. See above all Walter Klaassen, "Spiritualization in the Reformation," *Mennonite Quarterly Review* 27 (1963), 67–77.

5. Of general interest is Gordon Rupp, *Patterns of Reformation* (London: Epworth Press, 1969). On Muentzer see Eric W. Gritsch, *Reformer Without a Church: The Life and Thought of Thomas Müntzer 1488?–1525* (Philadelphia: Fortress Press, 1967); Hans-Jurgen Goertz, *Innere und Äussere Ordnung in der Theologie Thomas Müntzers* (Leiden: E.J. Brill, 1967). On Karlstadt see Ronald J. Sider, *Andreas Bodenstein von Karlstadt: The Development of His Thought, 1517–1525* (Leiden: E.J. Brill, 1973) and biographical data in Hermann Barge, *Andreas Bodenstein von Karlstadt,* 2 Bde. (Leipzig, 1905; reprint, Nieuwkoop: B. de Graeff, 1968). On Hofmann and the Munsterites see Norman Cohen, *The Pursuit of the Millennium* (Fair Lawn, N.J.: Essential Books, 1957), 272–306.

6. For extensive bibliography on the Spiritualists see discussion and notes in my *Schwenckfeld in his Reformation Setting* (Pennsburg, Pa.: The Schwenkfelder Library, 1977). A brief dependable survey of this wing of the Radical Reformation is available in Rufus M. Jones, *Spiritual Reformers in the 16th and 17th Centuries* (New York, 1914; reprint, Boston: Beacon Press, 1959).

7. Among other works, see Harold S. Bender, *The Life and Letters of Conrad Grebel* (Goshen, Ind.: The Mennonite Historical

Society, 1950); John H. Yoder, *The Legacy of Michael Sattler* (Scottdale, Pa.: Herald Press, 1973); Torsten Bergsten, *Balthasar Hubmaier: Seine Stelling zu Reformation und Täufertum, 1521–1528* (Kassel: J.G. Oncken Verlag, 1961); Henry C. Vedder, *Balthasar Hubmaier: The Leader of the Anabaptists* (New York and London: G.P. Putnam's Sons, 1905); Alfred Coutts, *Hans Denck 1495–1527: Humanist and Heretic* (Edinburgh: MacNiven and Wallace, 1927); Ludwig Keller, *Ein Apostel der Wiedertäufer* (Leipzig: Verlag von S. Hirzel, 1882); J.F. Gerhard Goeters, *Ludwig Hätzer (ca 1500 bis 1529): Spiritualist und Antitrinitarier* (Gutersloh: C. Bertelsmann Verlag, 1957); William Klaassen and Walter Klaassen, trans. and eds., *The Writings of Pilgram Marpeck* (Kitchener, Ont. and Scottdale Pa.: Herald Press, 1978); Torsten Bergsten, *Pilgram Marpeck und seine Auseinandersetzung mit Caspar Schwenckfeld* (Upsala: Almquist und Wiksells, 1958); William Klaassen, *Covenant and Community: The Life and Writings of Pilgram Marpeck* (Grand Rapids, Mich.: William B. Eerdmanns Publishing Co., 1968); Jan. J. Kiwiet, *Pilgram Marpeck* (Kassel: J.G. Oncken Verlag, 1957); Harold S. Bender, "A Brief Biography of Menno Simons," in *The Complete Writings of Menno Simons*, trans., Leonard Verduin (Scottdale, Pa.: Herald Press, 1956), 14–29; William E. Keeny, *The Development of Dutch Anabaptist Thought and Practice from 1539–1564* (Nieuwkoop: B. de Graef, 1968); Cornelius Krahn, *Dutch Anabaptism* (The Hague: Martinus Nijhoff, 1968); Irvin B. Horst, *The Radical Brethren: Anabaptism and the English Reformation to 1558* (Nieukoop: B.xde Oraef, 1972). See also Claus-Peter Clausen, *Anabaptism: A Social History, 1525–1618* (Ithaca, N.Y.: Cornell University Press, 1972) and Franklin H. Littel, *The Anabaptist View of the Church* (Boston Mass.: Beacon Press, 1958); note as well the collection of critical texts in James M. Stayer and Werner O. Packull, *The Anabaptists and Thomas Müntzer* (Dubuque, Iowa and Toronto, Ont.: Kendall Hunt, 1980). Of special value is the collection of primary sources done by Walter Klaassen, ed., *Anabaptism in Outline: Selected Primary Sources* (Kitchener, Ont. and Scottdale, Pa.: Herald Press, 1981).

    8. On these see Williams, *Reformation*, 581–571, 615–638.

    9. Note in particular the theological sections throughout Rupp, *Patterns*.

    10. See Robert Friedmann, *The Theology of Anabaptism*

122 PROTESTANT SPIRITUAL TRADITIONS

(Scottdale, Pa.: Herald Press, 1973) and the popular but excellent work by Walter Klaassen, *Anabaptism: Neither Protestant nor Catholic* (Waterloo, Ont.: Conrad Press, 1973).

11. See Williams, *Reformation*, 254–278, 325–335.

12. Note, however, Williams, *Reformation*, 381ff. on the Batenburgers who continued revolutionary activity.

13. See Christopher Hill, "Milton the Radical," *Times Literary Supplement*, Nov. 29, 1974, 1330–1332.

14. See the popular but generally accurate C. Henry Smith, *The Story of the Mennonites* (4th ed.; Newton, Kansas: Mennonite Publication Office, 1957).

15. On the Schwenckfelders in Europe see Horst Weigelt, *Spiritualistische Tradition im Protestantismus: Die Schwenckfelder in Schlesien* (Berlin: Walter de Gruyter, 1973) [English Translation by Peter C. Erb; Pennsburg, Pa.: The Schwenkfelder Library, 1984] and Franz M. Weber, *Kaspar Schwenckfeld und seine Anhänger in den Freybergischen Herrschaften Justingen und Öpfingen (Stuttgart: W. Kohlhammer Verlag, 1962).*

16. On the nature of the debate see Stayer and Packull, *Anabaptists and Müntzer*, 61–105.

17. The selection is translated from the Hutterite *Chronical* of 1525 in Williams and Mergal, *Spiritual and Anabaptist Writers*, 43.

18. For a full translation of the letter see *ibid.*, 71ff.

19. The fullest Anabaptist martyrology is that of Thieleman Janz van Braght, *Martyrs' Mirror*. For details see the relevant sections in the *Mennonite Encyclopedia*, particularly vol 3, 517ff.

20. H.S. Bender, "The Anabaptist Vision," in Stayer and Packull, *Anabaptists and Muentzer*, 14.

21. For a full collection of all Sattler's works and works by his followers, including this martyrology see Yoder, *Legacy of Michael Sattler.*

22. *Ibid.*, 67–68.

23. *Ibid.*, 68–69.

24. Translated in *ibid.*, 28ff.

25. *Ibid.*, 18ff.

26. *Ibid.*, 37f.

27. *Ibid.*, 22–23.

28. *Ibid.*, 121ff.

29. Note *ibid.*, 22.

30. On this matter note especially Stayer, *Anabaptists and the Sword.*

31. See Yoder, Legacy, 44f.

32. *Ibid.*, 43.

33. For full discussion see Harry J. McSorely, *Luther: Right or Wrong?* (New York: Newman, 1969).

34. Yoder, *Legacy,* 108ff.

35. My discussion here owes much to McSorely, *Luther.*

36. On Hubmaier see above, n. 7.

37. For translation see Williams and Mergal, *Spiritual and Anabaptist Writers,* 112ff.

38. *Ibid.*, 127f.

39. On Denck see above, n. 7.

40. For translation see Williams and Mergal, *Spiritual and Anabaptist Writers,* 88ff.

41. For text see Hans Denck, *Schriften,* hrsg. George Baring und Walter Fellmann (3 Bde.; Güterloh: C. Bertelsmann, 1955–56), vol., 2, 76ff. All translations which follow are my own.

42. *Ibid.*, 76.

43. *Ibid.*, 80–81.

44. *Ibid.*, 81.

45. *Ibid.*, 87ff.

46. Above all see the Klassen and Klaassen edition (see above, n. 7; hereafter cited Marpeck).

47. See above, n. 6.

48. Marpeck, 159ff.

49. Klaassen, *Anabaptism in Outline,* 142.

50. Marpeck, 43ff.

51. *Ibid.*, 69ff.

52. *Ibid.*, 309ff.

53. *Ibid.*, 362ff.

54. *Ibid.*, 390ff.

55. *Ibid.*, 391.

56. *Ibid.*, 395.

57. *Ibid.*, 418ff.

58. *Ibid.*, 392.

59. *Ibid.*, 420.

60. *Ibid.,*421.

61. *Ibid.*, 422.

62. *Ibid.*, 424.

63. *Ibid.*, 447.

64. *Ibid.*

65. See Jan van Ruusbroec, *Werken,* edited by J.B. Poukens *et al.,* (Tielt: Lannoo, 1944–48), vol 2.

66. Marpeck, 484ff.

67. *Ibid.*, 532.

68. *Ibid.*, 538.

69. *Ibid.*, 539.

70. *Ibid.*, 543.

71. *Ibid.*, 547.

72. See above, n. 7.

73. Menno, *Complete Writings,* 70.

74. *Ibid.*, 65.

75. See above on the Münsterites, n. 5.

76. See above, n. 14.

77. Menno, *Complete Writings,* 321ff.

78. *Ibid.*, 393–94.

79. *Ibid.*, 395.

80. For a full outline of Pietism see my *Pietists* (New York: Paulist Press, 1983).

81. On Johann Arndt see my translation of and introduction to his *True Christianity* (New York: Paulist Press, 1981).

82. For details see Robert Friedmann, *Mennonite Piety through the Ages* (Goshen, Ind.: Mennonite Historical Society, 1949).

83. Friedmann's work was published in part for the first time in the *Mennonite Quarterly Review* prior to the Second World War and the volume itself completed for the most part in 1942.

84. *Ibid.*, 72.

85. *Ibid.*, 82.

86. *Ibid.*, 87.

Paul V. Marshall
ANGLICAN SPIRITUALITY[1]

I. THE IDEAL OF "COMPREHENSION"

"Anglicans" are those Christians whose denominational origins are the Church of England, and who remain in communion with that church and the other members of the worldwide Anglican Communion. Mainstream Anglicanism is represented in the United States by The Episcopal Church.

When Anglicans speak of spirituality, they do not mean to discuss a religious part of one's brain. Rather, Anglicans tend to define spirituality as one's way of being, as one's orientation to self, world and God.[2] The spirituality, the way of being, encouraged by Anglicanism, cannot be said to be for everybody, but that is not for want of trying.

Those words are written quite deliberately, for the spirituality of Anglicanism, taken as a whole, includes a sincere commitment to being church in which Christians of many stripes can live together. Some Christian churches have as the basis of their internal unity and fellowship with other churches a particular slant on Christian doctrine, such as "justification" or "the sovereignty of God." Others look for an experience, such as being "born again," or being "baptized in the Spirit." But it is neither denominational doctrine nor ecstatic experience that binds Anglicans together. Rather there is a commitment to being the Church, and striving to do what the Church is called to do in the world.

As far as formal creedal requirements are concerned, contemporary Anglicanism has not gone beyond acknowledging the authority of Scripture as primary Christian document, confessing the creeds of the "undivided Church" of the first centuries, and asking for maintenance of apostolic patterns of ministry, and the celebration of the two great sacraments. Each of these four points (the Chicago-Lambeth "Quadrilateral") is intentionally expressed in rather minimal terms, and together they allow great latitude.[3] This is not a confessional church: Anglicans are not told precisely how to interpret the scriptures, or how to believe the creeds. They do not have worldwide agreement on exactly what ordained ministry is and who is eligible for it. In addition to the two "sacraments of the Gospel" most make liturgical provision for four or five others. As we shall see, Anglicans of vastly different outlook live together within this framework, and a wide variety of Anglican theologies proceed from it. The one given for all Anglicans is the concept of the Church carrying on its historic mission in historic patterns of corporate life. Only from an a priori assent to the creedal claim that there in fact is a holy catholic church that prays and witnesses, does Anglican theology proceed in its inquiry. There is a built-in tolerance for the varieties of inquiry and the temporary nature of results. There is at the heart of this diversity within broadly constructed unity, in fact, patience. "It is not yet revealed what we shall be." Certainly Anglicanism has had its share of "true believers" whose ideological commitments displace their commitment to the church as community, but they have been less successful in Anglicanism than in some other churches.[4] That this is in some respects an apparent accident of history has had an effect on Anglican attitudes toward historical process and the life of the Church.

Most readers of this book are no doubt aware that the Reformation in England came later than it did on the continent, and that theological and liturgical reform came some years later than the separation of the English church from foreign authority. Almost everyone knows that Henry VIII's desire for a male heir played a catalytic role in his rejection of papal claims, and that at first nothing changed in English church life besides the shifting of ultimate ecclesiastical authority from the Roman see to the King and Parliament.[5] The fact that the separation did not come as a result of some flash of religious insight has left Anglicanism forever free (some might say forever deprived of) strong ties to any one personality or school of theology. From the time of Henry, the principal question has been, "We are responsible to be the Church, so how ought we to act?"

There were those ready with prepared answers to that question. Henry VIII's and Edward VI's Archbishop Thomas Cranmer had definite loyalities to the continental reformation. Many Englishmen had studied abroad. There were a number of strong protestant parties in England who were supported by their coreligionists in Europe. Lutherans, Calvinists, and Anabaptists were among those continental groups who had advocates in England. Under Elizabeth I occurred the "settlement" of the English Church, and the beginning of a self-conscious effort to steer a middle course with integrity. The Middle Way, the "via media" of which Anglicans speak, is not an indifference to issues, but an apprehension of the complexity and richness possible in responding to them. Neither the predominant theology nor the liturgy of Elizabeth has survived throughout the Anglican Communion, but the overall policy of as much accommodation of differing parties as possible remains the way Anglican national churches operate today.[6]

Because there was more than one sixteenth century answer to the question of how to be the Church and more than one party ready to give it, no one theological outlook has ever had complete control in Anglicanism. Certainly there have been times when a particular outlook has been dominant, but there has always been more than one point of view. This has at times led to painful consequences, and Anglicanism has experienced in each of its national churches those same struggles for power which other denominations know. The difference is that no one has ever won a permanent victory: early seventeenth century dreams for a completely Calvinistic Anglicanism, or eighteenth century visions of a church of genteel philosophers, or the nineteenth century hopes for an ultramontane baroque Anglicanism have never come true. Each has had its following, some to the present day, but no party has seen its dreams completely dominate the church. Very few of world Anglicanism's leaders would ever want them to, for Anglicanism has gained something special in the slow process of becoming a church for so many kinds of Christian.

Another result of Anglicanism's origin in diversity is that one seldom speaks of individual Anglican theologians, but rather of parties or interest groups within the Church. Anglicanism has always been a corporate enterprise, and there has grown up in

Anglicanism something of a group method in theology. In the 1960's one thinks especially of *Soundings*, the work of a group of Cambridge University dons.[7] There have been other groups of more lasting influence. As this is written the 150th anniversary of the Oxford Movement is being celebrated throughout the Anglican Communion, and one immediately thinks of *Tracts for the Times*. The tracts are a monument to group theology. One also thinks of later group publications, *Lux Mundi, Essays Catholic and Critical,* and *Anglican Evangelicalism,* just to name a few. Individual Anglicans and their parishes tend to be spoken of as belonging to one of several groups. We hear of "High," Catholic, Liberal Catholic, or Anglo-Catholic parishes, representing types within one stratum of churchmanship. There are "Low," Evangelical and "Broad" parishes representing others. But these labels are deceptive, and boundaries are always changing. The Episcopal Church even has within its ranks a group called the "Evangelical and Catholic Mission." Students of spirituality will want to note that because the Anglican experience is group-oriented and not formed by any dominant theologian, Anglicans have a heightened sense of historical process and perhaps an equally heightened tolerance for its ambiguities. "We call no man master" was the cry of seventeenth century Anglicanism, and it can definitely still be heard.

To some tastes Anglicanism's spirituality of pragmatism, of being as comprehensive a Church as possible first and asking fine theological questions later, may be quite distasteful. It may even turn out to be wrong at the Last Day. But the point for readers of this book is that implicit in that pragmatism is commitment to a kind of spirituality that deserves notice. Anglican spirituality, because of its roots in a pragmatically constituted church, is first of all corporate and liturgical; it is also in some sense eclectic; and it is, again, quite tolerant of imperfection and ambiguity both personal and institutional.

Christians of other traditions not uncommonly find Anglicanism difficult to understand. "Anglican" means English, yet most Anglicans are not English—in fact the majority are not Caucasians. The twenty-five national churches which make up the Anglican Communion are in communion with the Archbishop of Canterbury, but he has no authority outside of England and some of its missionary jursidictions. Although Anglicanism has preserved the historic pattern of Christian ministry, including a succession of bishops about which they have said and written so much, Anglican bishops have far less actual power than, for instance, their Methodist or Roman Catholic counterparts. As we have just seen, a good deal of varying terminology is employed in describing different stripes within Anglicanism.

As an inquirer got to know Anglicans, the puzzlement might deepen, for some of them would object to finding a chapter dealing with their church in a book devoted to the spiritualities of Protestantism. In the last decade the Episcopal Church in this country dropped the name "Protestant" from its official title. This action reflected the fact that some Episcopalians do not consider themselves protestant at all, and most do not consider themselves protestant in the ways that members of other denominations involved with the Reformation do. Almost all Episcopalians think of their church as part of the great catholic tradition.[8] There are, on the other hand, a minority of Episcopalians who celebrate with some intensity the heritage of the sixteenth century reformers.

Does the spirituality of the Anglican Communion or the Episcopal Church deserve treatment in this book? Put another way, are Anglicans protestant?

Regardless of how one interprets Henry VIII's political and religious intentions in terminating the authority of the Roman hierarchy in his domain, in several important respects the answer must be yes. The wide latitude given to individual pilgrimage in faith and theological inquiry, much of what Paul Tillich has called "the protestant principle," is to be found in Anglicanism, including Anglo-Catholicism.[9] There are, for instance, no official rules concerning birth control or the use of alcohol, but there is a variety of strongly held conviction on these and other ethical matters. Concepts of biblical and theological authority remain subject to revision and criticism. Ecclesiastical government is participatory: no major decisions about doctrine, discipline, worship, or money are made without the participation and consent of laity with bishops and lesser clergy. Although Anglicanism is organized and administered hierarchically, if an Anglican should say that "the church teaches" something, it would be a serious mistake to assume that one should translate that as "the hierarchy has promulgated this teaching." In its most precise form that statement would mean that the bishops, clergy, and laity have enacted something (perhaps a statement in the Book of Common Prayer or its catechism); in its least precise form it would mean that Anglicans have generally understood the testimony of Christian tradition to mean this or that.

So yes, in a guarded way Anglicanism is to be called protestant. The way is guarded because in general Anglicans feel more at home reading the patristic writers than they do Luther, and because their primary commitment is to being a Christian Church in a way comfortable to the entire sweep of the catholic tradition. It is their contention, in general, that in Anglicanism the catholic tradition has comprehended the protestant principle. "Comprehensiveness" is a term especially dear to Anglicans, and indicates their intention to live together as catholic protestants and protestant catholics. This is the view of most Anglicans, and is a fair description of how Anglicanism in fact works. It should still be remembered that at the extremes there are Anglicans who consider themselves no protestants, and also those who would claim that title without qualification. Historically, those who have left Anglicanism are those who no longer wish to be comprehended.[10] What is important for shaping the practical spirituality of the Anglican Communion is that there is a place for these extremes within it, and that in actual practice they cooperate.

II. THE BOOK OF COMMON PRAYER

All this divergence, in which Anglicanism hopes to model what a truly ecumenical church, a comprehensively Christian church, might look like, comes together in the pragmatic stance of Anglicanism: the Church takes its identity first of all in agreeing to do what the Church does. That involves organization, governance, proclamation, charitable service, and, most visibly to most Christians, worship. There has been in Anglicanism, from the days of Archbishop Cranmer on, a firm conviction that the liturgical life of the Church is its celebration and prime experience of its corporate identity and of its mission. Perhaps more

than other Christians, Anglicans are, by experience, committed
to Prosper's dictum, "Lex orandi legem statuat credendi." Properly quoted, the dictum states the conviction that the law of
prayer constitutes and shapes the law of belief. Worship is not
identical with theological inquiry, as the misquotation "lex orandi
lex credendi" would imply, but it certainly is prior to it.

Worship does come first for Anglicans, whose theologians
have historically prayed the liturgy first and only when asked,
"What does it mean to believe in a God who is worshiped with
these words and actions?" Theological inquiry is given broad
scope in Anglicanism—but always within the given of the worshiping community, the community of faith. The historical result
of this commitment to common prayer is that Anglicanism has
produced more than its proportionate share of historical liturgiologists. The seventeenth century was a period more formative
for Anglicanism than any other, including Queen Elizabeth's
"settlement" of the church in the sixteenth, and may be taken to
illustrate our point. Extreme Puritans wanted no liturgy at all.
Moderate Calvinists wanted, as did their namesake, a fixed but
flexible liturgy, while the party led by Archbishop William Laud
sought a uniform text and practice. The point for us about their
debate is that most of them, regardless of their position, were
debating the meaning of the historical evidence of the worship of
the apostolic and patristic church. They argued about ancient
texts with which beginning students of liturgy still wrestle today.
Almost none of the writers were attracted to a simplistic view of
the matter: there was but little sustained appeal to the observation that because the New Testament does not prescribe a liturgy
there ought not be one, although this was of course said, notably
in popular Puritan pamphlets. What there was among those
engaged in serious debate was a prolonged engagement over the
correct understanding of historical testimony to Christian worship, particularly that of the early fathers on matters of fixed texts
and liturgical conformity. No official Anglican liturgy has ever
claimed to be that of the early church or even of a single early
metropolitan church, but they have all claimed, rightly or
wrongly, a consonance with the worship of the first Christians.[11]
The appeal to the testimony of the fathers even remained part of
the approach of those whose consciences led them from the

Church of England at the restoration of Charles II. The Puritan Richard Baxter, in describing his *Reformed Liturgy,* claimed that while it was based solely on the Bible, he had checked it against, amid other authorities, Hamon L'Estrange's *Alliance of Divine Offices,* England's first work of mature comparative liturgiology, and a gold mine of patristic evidence for liturgical text and practice.

It is to miss one of the key issues of Anglican history to dismiss the Puritan-Laudian struggle as one over mere "style," as does one major work.[12] From the Anglican point of view, use of a fixed liturgy within the great tradition of Christian prayer is to participate in the whole religious society of one's contemporaries, and just as consciously to enter into the worship of the Church throughout the centuries. "At all times and in all places" is much more than a throwaway line in Anglican liturgy. In the sixteenth and seventeenth centuries, when Anglicanism was more self-consciously protestant, more self-consciously doing a new thing, the traditional in liturgy testified to that new thing's roots in the faith of the whole Church and the whole company of heaven.

Again, the seeming fuss about worship is not a preoccupation with the "furniture of religion," as one critic of Anglicanism put it. It proceeds from the Anglican conviction that worship shapes a religious society's self-understanding and its action, an observation that runs from Cranmer to Richard Hooker to our own day. Anglican spirituality is first of all corporate spirituality, liturgical spirituality, "prayerbook spirituality."

Here the Anglican spirit is in some discord with much contemporary Christianity and related styles of spiritual direction, to say nothing of the anthropology implicit in the life of the "me generation." When many Christians think of "spirituality" today, they think of the spiritual individual who prays, serves, and even witnesses, but who may or may not find the Church's worship relevant, or who imports to the experience of worship extremely privatized allegorical overlays. Anglicans give and receive at least as much private spiritual direction as other protestants, and they have rather more monks and nuns living lives of prayer than other churches with Reformation connections. Nonetheless, they have resisted attempts to portray the liturgy as anything other than corporate, or as the occasion of Christians having their private devotions and individual experiences together. Anglican spirituality assumes that private prayer and corporate prayer need each other, and rely on each other, but are not identical with each other.

The private devotions of Lancelot Andrewes assume that the liturgy shapes the life of the individual who prays in his closet. George Herbert's masterpiece, *The Temple,* portrays the life of the individual Christian within the very shape of sacred space and liturgical appointments, a journey from "church porch" to everlasting life. It has even been suggested that the best short introduction to Anglicanism is to read Herbert.[13] In our own day the work of Anglican poets such as Sir John Betjeman and T.S. Eliot also reflects the influence of the Church's liturgy and calendar.

In essence then, *The Book of Common Prayer* is meant to be more than a liturgical text, such as a Roman missal or the protestant section of *The Book of Worship for U.S. Forces,* although it has liturgical texts in common with each. *The Book of Common Prayer* is a rule of life. It is meant to describe, shape, and support the Anglican way of being Christian. The prayerbook has never been a clerical or monastic book, as were the missal and breviary, but from the first was intended to be the property of the laity.

The first thing to be noted about the spirituality of worship with "the prayerbook," as Anglicans habitually refer to *The Book of Common Prayer,* is that the book is there—fixed testimony to our connection with other Christians, other times, and other places. The prayerbook reminds us of the truth that John Donne, Dean of St. Paul's, urged, that none of us is an island. As intensely personal as one's experience of religion may be, in the liturgy it is linked up with, and perhaps examined by, the worship of the Church. The Church, worship, Bible and tradition become objective reality when the Anglican picks up the prayerbook.

Daniel Stevick has argued that this function of the book's existence is far from constricting individual spirituality: it rather facilitates it by expanding the personal horizon.

> The engagement mediated through such benign, generous forms can be an enlargement and a liberation. I come to church with things I want to find and express, but there my expectations meet the firm, genial *Book of Common Prayer.* It

welcomes me. It encourages and assists me in saying what I want to say. But it sets my interests alongside others in a large open movement. It may not have in mind today only what I have in mind. It asks me to say things I had not thought myself especially ready to say. Its balance addresses my onesidedness. When I am too euphoric, it reminds me of brokenness, of failure, and of the need for confession of sin. When I am in despair, it reminds me of forgiveness greater than sin and hope beyond human destructiveness. It holds before me a realism and a largeness of faith that I seldom have on my own and always need. It reminds me of deep, forgotten things. The Prayer Book reaches into my own experience, kindly, judgingly and redemptively. It does so by setting me within forms which derive from clsssic apprehensions of the Christian message. I am delivered from the necessity of finding the meaning of my own existence out of my own resources. Those great liturgical forms are mine; I revel in them. Yet they rebuke me, surprise me and extend me. Their very formedness is not oppressive, rather it is a ministry of grace.[14]

If the liturgy is to do that, and not merely serve as a take-it-or-leave-it set of props for the sermon, it becomes clear why Anglicans have been so concerned about changes in the liturgical text: the symbols being examined in the process of revision were the symbols of our very lives as Christians.

But revisions there have been. Cranmer himself, in addition to his early liturgical creations, issued two prayerbooks (those of 1549 and 1552). Among the notable revisions in England have been those of Elizabeth (1559), Charles II (1662), and the proposed book of 1928. In America there has been revision about every other generation, the latest being that of 1979.

When one looks at the trends in liturgical revision in Anglicanism, one sees the development of an Anglican consciousness in England and the United States which is less and less sectarian and more an more genuinely catholic. Each revision since 1552 has lessened the influence of the sixteenth century need to make liturgy talk doctrine, and increasingly blended accents eastern and western in its language of praise.

As each revision of the prayerbook has become less and less a vehicle for reformation doctrine and more an expression of praise in harmony with the broad Christian tradition, the role of the liturgical text in Anglican spirituality has become clearer. In the 1979 *Book of Common Prayer* of the Episcopal Church, there are three eucharistic rites. The first is couched in the language of the Cranmerian tradition. The second, in contemporary English, uses the common English translations of traditional texts now familiar to most Christians in this country. The third is, at first glance, not a liturgy at all, but an outline for an informal celebration. Worshipers are directed to gather in the Lord's name, proclaim the word, pray for the church and world, greet each other, and celebrate the sacred meal.

It is this third rite which best illustrates what the other two rites are also intended to do. They all serve to describe and make possible the liturgical action, what the Church does when it worships. The word *actio* is hardly new to liturgical language, of course, having been once applied to the most sacred moments of the medieval western liturgy, but in considering the spirituality of Anglican liturgy it must be used in a broader sense. The liturgy is not perceived as a document to be read, but as a script or a musical score, which comes to life when performed. The script is not a monologue and the score is not a solo: the liturgy is designed to make possible the ensemble playing, the coordinated *actio* of the Christian assembly.

To enter into the liturgy not as spectator or even as meditator on the mysteries, but as a member of a cast or a player in an ensemble shapes the Christian's perception of self and of the Church. A good play is ruined when actors upstage each other, and a string quartet loses its magic when one player continually dominates the performance. Even the most improvised jazz requires agreement as to when each player will take what my grandfather used to call his "lick" at the principal theme. The point is that the 1979 *Book of Common Prayer* assumes that what we do in liturgy models what the Church is in the world: a coordinated body with different ministries all working to make Christ's presence a reality. The role of the more conspicuous members of the assembly is to make possible the worship of the whole body.

The role of the prayerbook is to insure that the action takes place. No matter which of the vastly different texts of the three rites is employed, the same things happen in the same order, and as the assembly celebrates the mystery of Christ it acts out its own identity. What the liturgy's external circumstances will be is not prescribed: all that is required to celebrate the eucharist is a congregation, a presbyter or bishop, bread and wine, a table, and a table cloth. This means that Anglicans of different tastes on a given Sunday morning may appear at first glance at buildings, vestments, and liturgical choreography to be from different liturgical galaxies, but they are in fact doing the same thing. The diversity that has resulted from the historical effort to accommodate as many groups as possible has resulted in the theological perception of the Church as a body in which people working in different ways and looking quite different can serve the same ends.

The value placed on the corporate and liturgical is an essential element of Anglican spirituality. It presupposes a life of private prayer, but one responsive to the corporate life of the church. Again Stevik speaks the mind of the prayerbook:

> Unless I have a life of private prayer, my participation in corporate prayer will be limited. I will not bring much to it nor derive much from it. But if private prayer is my sole or dominating form of prayer, I shall develop a privatized, self-enclosed spiritual experience. I cannot know or express myself truly apart from the strong bonds which unite me with others.[15]

The great Anglican thinker F.D. Maurice put it somewhat more succinctly: "When you are most alone you must still, if you would pray, be in the midst of a family; you must call upon a Father; you must not dare to say *my* but *our* Father."[16] This emphasis on the corporate also means that spiritual direction means something a bit special in Anglicanism. Within the liturgical setting of Anglican culture, spiritual direction, or "spiritual friendship," as it is coming to be called, is not primarily a transaction between two otherwise isolated individuals, who somehow employ the "worship experience" as a resource for personal growth. Nor is it understood as an alternative to psychotherapy. Rather, spiritual direction is emerging as a unique activity which happens between members of the Church with reference to the individual's life within the total body. With its provisions for Christian initiation, Sunday eucharist, reconciliation of penitents, daily morning and evening prayer, and services for the crisis moments of life, the prayerbook becomes chief spiritual director, and Anglican manuals of spiritual direction assume that director and directee are already caught up in this way of life and wish to further understand and apply it.

This insight is now a common one, and was perhaps best expressed early in our century by the Englishwoman Evelyn Underhill, whose books are currently being reissued. Underhill was a keen student of the history of worship and mysticism, and some of the analysis in her *Worship* (repr. 1982) remains unsurpassed. Just the title of one of her books explains a great deal about the spirituality of the member of the liturgical assembly. She called it *Practical Mysticism for Normal People*. Anglicanism does not set out to be the Zen of Christianity, nor does it seek to make miniature monks and nuns of those not called to the religious life. It rather looks to build the entire Church, strengthening and coordinating all of its members. We shall return to Underhill later to consider method in spirituality, but here the point is the practicality and the "ordinariness" of what the prayerbook intends: referral of the whole of life to God. Accordingly, Marion Hatchett titled his work on Anglican liturgy *Sanctifying Life, Time and Space* (New York, 1976), and Charles Price and Louis Weil introduce the prayerbook to lay audiences under the title *Liturgy for Living* (New York, 1979).

This means that Anglicans, along with most protestants, seldom use the word "vocation" to mean a call to some readily identifiable church work. Each member of the liturgical assembly is dismissed by the deacon to go and do what God has given to be done in every area of life. From beginning to end the prayerbook baptismal service makes it clear that every Christian is called to follow Christ throughout life's journey, and under any circumstances. The same thought is present at the celebration of the eucharist. Eucharistic Prayer "C" includes the following at the conclusion of its supplicatory section:

> Open our eyes to see your hand at work in the world about us. Deliver us from the presumption of coming to this Table for solace only, and not for strength; for pardon only and not

for renewal. Let the grace of this Holy Communion make us
one body, one spirit in Christ, that we may worthily serve the
world in his name.[17]

The prayer is meant to be complementary in spirit to Cranmer's
well-known "Prayer of Humble Access," still in use and much
loved in Anglicanism. There the petition begins "We do not presume to come to this Thy table trusting in our own righteousness," and goes on to appeal to the mercy of God and the cleasing
effects of salvation upon the soul. In Prayer "C" is added the
growing apprehension of the fact that one is baptized and communicated within a Church which has the mission of representing
Christ to the world. The combination of these two prayers of the
type liturgiologists call "prayers for fruitful communion" makes
clear the relationship of worship to the rest of life. Worship does
indeed refresh and comfort, especially at the eucharistic feast,
but the Christian life the prayerbook seeks to build is more than
refreshment and comfort, it is always discipleship and sometimes
it is crucifixion. The liturgy points us to this reality and prepares
us for it in the words and acts of its celebration.

III. A SAMPLING OF ANGLICAN SPIRITUALITY

In the previous sections we have looked at Anglicanism in
general, as well as examining its corporate and liturgical spirituality. We now turn to a sampling of those persons, books, and
movements which have been significant in the development of the
several strata within the Anglican tradition. The subjects selected
do not tell the whole story, of course, and are not necessarily an
Anglican Hall of Fame. Each has been chosen to illustrate an
important aspect of Anglican spirituality.

A word of warning. Anglicanism is not a crazy quilt of theologies. Its various parties and movements are best seen as coop-
erating contributors in its attempt to be the Church in its fullness.
The Dean of Durham, Peter Baelz, addressed this issue in *The
Times* of London:

If Anglicanism is to make its special contribution to the coming great church, it must recognize that its catholic, evangel-

ical, and liberal traditions are interdependent and not mutually exclusive; moreover, such interdependence is not merely the oucome of the contingencies of history but represents a specific and important understanding both of the nature of God Himself and the manner of His self-revelation.[18]

That being the case, the following sections must not be read as a sampler of Anglicanisms, but as samples of how Anglicanism's self-perception developed.

The subjects chosen date from the seventeenth century and onward. They achieved their significance after Cranmer had established the prayerbook as the center of Anglican life. They postdate the Elizabethan Richard Hooker's monumental *Of the Laws of Ecclesiastical Polity* (1594–1597), which outlined a theology of the church, its right to existence as part of a Christian society, and the value of participation in its life. After Cranmer, Hooker and others of their century had laid the foundations, the Anglican tradition took flight.

George Herbert (1593–1633): Ambiguity and Acceptance

Bishop Neill has already been cited on Herbert's value as an introduction to Anglican thought. In some sense the twentieth century has discovered Herbert, but it was Samuel Taylor Coleridge who wrote of this poet priest, "I find more substantial comfort . . . in pious George Herbert . . . than in all the poetry [I have read] since [I read] the poems of Milton. . . . The stanzas are especially effecting to me, because the folly of over-valuing myself . . . is *not* the sin or danger that besets me—but a tendency to self-contempt, a sense of utter disproportionateness of all I can call *me*, to the promises of the Gospel—*this* is my sore temptation. . . . The promises I say: not the *threats*." Of all those poets whom Johnson labeled "metaphysical," Herbert stands out as the one whose only subject and source of inspiration was his religious faith.

It is a commonplace now to note that Herbert was a man in conflict: he has been variously described as a confused aristocrat, an ambitious upper-class twit, a saintly pastor, a servant to the needy, a major Christian poet, and a saint. It was a very unusual

thing for a man of his background to rusticate as a country parson, to be sure, and Herbert was aware of the contradictions
present in his life. He now is commemorated in the calendar of
the Episcopal Church, perhaps not in spite of, but because of his
apprehension of that conflict.

Herbert was very forthright in calling his collection of poems
"a picture" of his "many Spiritual Conflicts." For the purposes
of an exposition of Anglican spirituality, it is a very good thing
that there is no way to arrange them in chronological order, so
as to suggest that he passed from those conflicts to a tidily nailed
down spiritual life at some one moment. In fact, in "The Tem-
per" he expresses an awareness of his changing feelings:

> How should I praise thee, Lord! how should my rymes
>   Gladly engrave thy love in steel,
>   If what my soul doth feel sometimes,
>   My soul might ever feel!

It does seem that whatever peace Herbert had with himself—for he may well have been *all* of the things he has been
called—came not so much from solving his conflicts and arrang-
ing everything tidily, but from transcending them. Like many of
the gentry of his time he contained within him both the fop and
the slave of duty. His description of the perfect priest in *The
Country Parson* is a curious mixture. On the one hand the parson
is to be a vessel of grace, sharing with his people "the comforts"
he had himself found in the gospel. On the other, he is to be what
we now often call a compulsive worker, perhaps enjoying those
comforts far too little.

Herbert was aware of his conflicts, as he tells us. "Love," one
of his most quoted works, describes his apprehension of a grace
beyond his drivenness.

> Love bade me welcome: yet my soul drew back,
>   Guilty of dust and sin.
> But quick-eyed Love, observing me grow slack
>   From my first entrance in,
> Drew nearer to me, sweetly questioning,
>   If I lack'd anything.

ANGLICAN SPIRITUALITY 141

A guest, I answer'd, worthy to be here:
    Love said, You shall be he.
I the unkind, ungrateful? Ah my dear,
    I cannot look on thee.
Love took my hand, and smiling did reply,
    Who made the eyes but I?

Truth, Lord, but I have marr'd them: let my shame
    Go where it doth deserve.
And know you not, says Love, who bore the blame?
    My dear, then I will serve.
You must sit down, says Love, and taste my meat:
    So I did sit and eat.

Allowing God to love and serve him as he was was an obstacle
for Herbert; letting God disregard Herbert's own standards for
himself and for God was one of his greatest life tasks. With that
surrender to an uncontrollable love, upon which even his best
spiritual gyrations could not get hooks, there came to Herbert the
peace which let him become in some measure what he wanted to
be, one who lived God's will and served his people.

Besides the great gifts his writings have given the Church as
hymns and devotional liturature, these poems which Herbert
chose to say were the result of his experience offer something
even to the people who are not much interested in literature, or
who have had the seventeenth century simply thrust upon them.
It is an important part of Anglican spirituality.

Because of the ambiguities of their institutional history, and
because of the observations of many of their spiritual parents,
Anglicans are particularly aware that each Christian is a paradox,
a mystery, an unfinished creation. We find ourselves to be both
loving and rejecting, trusting and fearful, gracious and punitive,
evangelical and legalistic, strong and yet in great and deep pain.

Perhaps because of its roots in English culture, Anglicanism
has, as did Herbert, something of a moralistic leaning. There is
therefore a constant need to accept personal and institutional
struggle, to internalize and treat ourselves with the "comprehensiveness" which we profess toward others. There is also in Anglicanism a pronounced interest in depth psychology, particularly

the work of Jung, and a concomitant temptation to over-analyze, over-psychologize.

In "The Collar" Herbert rages against his own imperfections and those of his surroundings, deciding to "go abroad" in search of the one spiritual trick that would make him whole, healthy, virtuous, effective: both important *and* servant—all the things Herbert wanted to be.

> But as I raved and grew more fierce and wilde
>   at every word
> Methoughts I heard one calling, *childe!*
>   and I reply'd *My Lord.*

There came moments for Herbert when he had to stop the introspection, stop the moralizing, and accept himself and accept the fact that that self was accepted. Herbert was well-known to take pride in his good looks and the manner of his dress. Even his devoted biographer Walton indicates this. One day while walking to Salisbury "he saw a poor man, with a poorer horse. . . ." When the horse collapsed, Herbert came to the man's aid, and so arrived at the party for which he was headed late, and with his clothing in enough disarray to subject him to comment.

So he told them what he had done, and when prodded about why he the dandy did not avoid helping, and so keep his clothes clean, he went into a long analysis of his duty to be compassionate, his fear of a bad conscience, and the paradox of his genuine concern for the man whilst worrying about his clothes. But after describing his struggle and his thanks for how it turned out, Herbert abruptly terminated the conversation with: "And now let's tune our instruments."

Even a poet of the "school of Donne" could only deal with so much introspection, so much analysis, so much spiritual discipline. Remembering that voice who had called him "child" and remembering the "love" which had seated and served him, Herbert was finally content to be no more than he was that day: he left his scrupulosity behind, and tuned his instrument for play.

What Anglicanism sets out to be, a Church in the world for others, is an ambitious program, especially considering the small numbers who are attracted to it in western countries. There are things about ourselves, our church, and our task in the world which may well never be mastered. In the likes of Herbert Anglicans are reminded that we can be crushed if we do not stop to tune our instruments, to take time off from moral earnestness, and to celebrate the word that called us "child." So we are back to the liturgy, where we take time to tell Jesus' story, to sing Herbert's songs, and to join him and angels and archangels, and all the curious company of heaven, that is, all the company of those contradictory selves whom Love has served, and who from time to time stepped from their confusion, came, sat, and ate, and then cried, "My Lord."

The Evangelical and Catholic Movements

The concern for personal peace and holy life expressed by the Laudian George Herbert was heard again, with different accents, in the Evangelical movement of the eighteenth and nineteenth centuries.

To be an evangelical Anglican does not, strictly speaking, necessarily mean that one is "low church," although many evangelicals have resisted the enrichment of the church's liturgical life in the last century. In fact, one of the most successful liturgical organizations in Anglicanism is under the direction of evangelicals.[19] Nor are all Evangelicals anti-clerical or anti-church. In a group closely related to the Evangelicals, Wesley's devotion to the eucharist and his deathbed plea to his fellow Methodists not to leave the Anglican church are too well known to require exposition here. Within the mainstream of the movement, Charles Simeon (1759–1836) chose not to criticize the prayerbook, but rather those who refused to let the power of the liturgy transform their hearts.

Evangelicalism within Anglicanism was born in the eighteenth century and was concerned primarily with personal conversion. Evangelical preaching stressed the fallenness of humanity and its restoration in Christ. William Romaine (1714–1795) set out the Evangelical message on the need for conversion succinctly:

A sinner will never seek after nor desire Christ farther than he feels his guilt and his misery; nor will he receive Christ by faith, till all other methods of saving himself fail; nor will he live upon Christ's fullness farther than he has an abiding sense of his own want of him.[20]

It might be thought that the movement represented a retrograde element in Anglican thought. In the abstract it is a step backward from concentration on the doctrine of the Church and life in the spirit to unending attention paid to the first step of Christian experience, conversion to Christ. However, Evangelicalism, like the later Catholic movement, was a response to a tendency to forget the fact that Christianity is not just another department of the general culture, and that it has a great deal to say about how life is to be transformed.

The reality of religious faith was not keenly felt in Georgian and early Victorian England, and it was not unheard of for clergymen to be more enthusiastic about riding to the hounds than searching the scriptures. Nor were church people particularly quick to meet the needs of a new class in England, the urban and industrial poor. Consequently, along with its intense effort to convict of sin and urge acceptance of salvation in Christ, Evangelicalism brought with it renewed emphasis on patterns of contemporary personal living conformed to Christ's own life. This desire to be like Christ, coupled with a strong sense of God's constant judgment, led evangelicals to work in areas of social action which still present challenges to the church. Some critics have argued that Evangelicalism contained traces of unanglican spiritual selfishness, personal religion become the whole pie. This is not quite fair. Although some of its language and images arguably were not from mainstream Anglicanism or the patristic period, Evangelicalism combined its interest in personal salvation with the classic Anglican quest to be the Church, and in fact expanded Anglican vision of a ministry which does transform culture.

In this regard Evangelicals are best remembered for pioneer efforts in education, for Wilberforce's achieving the abolition of slavery in Britain, and for the first protective labor laws in an industrialized society under Shaftesbury.

At their worst Evangelicals could solace the poor by pointing to the brief time of suffering life offered and the immense joys of heaven. But, like many Anglicans of other stripes, they could and did appreciate the ambiguities of their own position. Hannah More noted the tendency of her fellow Evangelicals to reduce the imitation of Christ to the cultivation of manners and maintenance of the social status quo. She wrote that while faith is not intended "to be a substitute for a useful life," it is not unnecessary and remains a constant call to reexamine life and its relationship to God. Her perception of her colleagues' concern with living a morally good life led her to argue what should have been obvious to an Evangelical audience, that the gospel "clearly proves that morality is not the whole of religion."[21]

Evangelicals are usually thought of as those Anglicans most concerned to talk of individual salvation. They are remembered for their part in early missionary work, and for serving as the constant reminder within Anglicanism of the authority of the Bible. The Evangelicals' very insistence on constant reexamination of the individual soul's relationship to God became the force that kept them active as agents for change in society—and then enabled them to turn neatly around with the reminder not to confuse that work with the whole of Christianity.

Evangelicalism perhaps best illustrates the point Dean Baelz strove to make in his letter to *The Times*, that Anglicans of different stripes are interdependent. Much of the Catholic movement's piety comes from Evangelical earnestness, and the work and theology of social reform done by other parties in the Church spring from a movement with which they do not consciously identify.

A great misconception arises when Anglo-Catholicism is mentioned. The early leaders of the Oxford Movement would be greatly perplexed at the extent to which the Catholic movement has become associated in the common mind with elaborate religious ritual or a taste for the arcane. It was holiness, personal and corporate, that Pusey, Newman and others sought, and nothing less. In this respect the early Catholics had much in common with the Evangelicals of their day. John Henry (later Cardinal) Newman's own religious journey began with an intense experience of conversion under Evangelical influence.

More than Evangelical influence, however, the early Catholics (usually called "Tractarians" after their great series of writings, *Tracts for the Times*) felt the weight of the Anglican writers of the all-important seventeenth century. Those "Caroline

Divines" reinforced the Tractarian interest in patristic writings, and we thus find the Tractarians taking a different tack than the Evangelicals, starting with emphasis on the Church, its life and work, rather than on individual conversion. The spiritual discipline which they urged on individuals was no less intense than that of Evangelicalism, and by bringing that discipline into the arena of the church and its sacramental life, Anglo-Catholicism may be said to be the completion of Evangelicalism and not its competitor.

The Oxford Movement is usually said to have begun with John Keble's sermon at the university on "National Apostasy," preached on July 14, 1833, at the opening of the summer term of the lawcourts. The issue which provoked the sermon was the government's plan to suppress ten Irish bishoprics. Taking as his text 1 Samuel 12:23, Keble attempted to correct the imbalance in the relationship between church and state in England, for that verse reads "God forbid that I should sin against the Lord in ceasing to pray for you; but I will teach you the good and right way." Recounting the struggle of the prophets in Israel to bring the nation's political life back to ideals of the Covenant, Keble told the assembled lawyers that the church which continued to pray for them also had plenty to teach at that moment:

> The point really to be considered is, whether, according to the coolest estimate, the fashionable liberality of this generation be not ascribable, in a great measure, to the same temper which led the Jews voluntarily to set about degrading themselves with idolatrous Gentiles. And if it be true anywhere, that such enactments are forced on the legislature by public opinion, is apostasy too hard a word to describe the temper of that nation?

Keble went on to call the whole English church to intercession for and remonstrance toward the national government. His call to the church to perceive itself and to act in a prophetic way in its relations with the state was revolution indeed.

The great religious crisis of 1833 passed, but the thought of Keble and his associates continued to grow. If the church was to be prophetic, it had to have integrity of its own, beyond any connection with the sovereign or parliament. Hardly a radical thought to contemporary Americans, used to religious pluralism as they are, but this inquiry into the nature of the church as an independent entity was an issue capable of arousing deep feeling in the England of the 1830's.

The Tractarians presented the Church as a divine institution, its ministry as having apostolic authority, and its prayerbook as standard of doctrine and life. For them participation in the sacramental life of the Church was to participate in the world beyond this one. Another of the movement's architects, Edward Bouverie Pusey, put it this way: "The less we live for things outward, the stronger burns our inward life. The more we live to things unseen, the less hold will this world of sense have over us."[22] Looking for the unseen, the greater reality, was the piety Tractarians urged. From this concern came the renewal of ascetical theology in Anglicanism, and the rebirth of spiritual direction on the parish level. Anglicans were once again taking auricular confession quite seriously, not as an obligation but as a help in building a holy life.

The search for the unseen world also resulted in the revival of religious life in Anglicanism. For the first time in three hundred years monastic communities appeared within its ranks. Nicholas Ferrar, a contemporary of Herbert's, had established a kind of religious house at Little Gidding, but now quite a few Anglicans began to appear with the initials of their orders behind their names. Marian Rebecca Hughes took her vows in 1841, becoming the first modern Anglican religious. Among the most familiar of these pioneer orders in Anglicanism are the Community of St. Mary the Virgin at Wantage, the Society of St. John the Evangelist (the "Cowley Fathers"), and the Community of the Resurrection at Mirfield. In the American church many of the English orders have been transplanted, and quite a few new ones have been founded. In 1983 the Episcopal Church recognized within its ranks fifteen orders for men, seventeen for women, and two for men and women. In teaching, writing, and most usually in the giving of retreats and spiritual direction, the revival of monasticism has been of the utmost assistance in carrying out the Anglo-Catholic program of personal and corporate renewal.

As the interior search for the unseen world continued, and as the Church's role as the prophet who both prays for and instructs the state became clearer to the Catholic party, its responsibility for social action became doctrine. Newman put it quite bluntly: "The church was formed for the express purpose of interfering or (as irreligious men would say) meddling with the world." Anglo-Catholic missions in the slums multiplied as care for the bodily needs of the urban poor received emphasis equal to that placed on their spiritual necessities.

The second half of the nineteenth century saw another aspect of the Catholic movement arise, that of Ritualism. Modern students of liturgy have enough anthropological knowledge to know that there is ritual in a Quaker meeting as surely as there is at a pontifical mass, but the very word "ritual" raised the hackles of those Anglicans who thought that because theirs was not a Roman church, talk of ritual was very seriously wrong. The originators of the Oxford Movement were not eager to see the ritual of Anglican liturgy become more elaborate, but their doctrine almost demanded it. The emphasis which they placed upon the Church and its sacraments and upon the apostolic nature of its ministry suggested dignity, awe, and more than a little touch of mystery in the outward circumstances of liturgical celebration.

The dramatic revision of the Church's ceremonial life was not the expression of fussy taste or a slight bent toward decadence. Rather it was an expression of the newly recovered realization that the Church is to be about the business of the divine things. It is not a contradiction that the churches most actively involved in serving the poor were the most "extreme" ceremonially. Both the increased attention to worship and the intensified devotion to service in the world were expressions of a church rediscovering itself as the body of Christ rather than an arm of the state.

In this country a similar pattern can be observed. The "missionary dioceses" were often the most extreme both in worship practices and in outreach. It was with no sensitivity to the judgment he was speaking on himself that an east coast critic of one midwestern Anglo-Catholic diocese attempted to discredit its worship by pointing out that besides its elaborate liturgy it ministered to Indians and poor immigrants from such *déclassé* places as eastern Europe![23] The Church of the Transfiguration in New York City ("The Little Church Around the Corner") is remembered for its willingness to serve people in the theater before theirs was a socially acceptable profession—but it was also a station on the Underground Railroad, smuggling escaped slaves to Canada.

By reappropriating the Church's awareness of its own call to holiness, the Catholic movement spurred Anglicanism on to new understandings of the meaning of worship and new commitment to the service of humanity, by urging men and women to see their lives as involved with the greater world of the things of God.

Sacrifice, Incarnation, and Social Action

Like the other churches of the reformation, early Anglicanism abolished the saying of masses for a stipend, and dropped completely any liturgical or catechetical suggestion that the eucharist was a propitiatory sacrifice offered to God. Eliminated also was the idea that each celebration released a quantum of merit or grace applicable to an equally quantifiable goal, getting grandmother out of purgatory, for instance.[24]

Knowing what to oppose does not necessarily help a reformer know what to support, and liturgy is a case in point. The New Testament presupposes an already worshiping community. Consequently, the biblicism of the reformers, especially as it was then entirely innocent of any knowledge of Jewish worship, was of really no practical use in their efforts to order worship on a primitive pattern. Today it is beyond argument that there is insufficient data from *any* source to permit us to reconstruct with any precision the worship of the first Christan communities. In those rough and ready reformation days, when people felt that they had just discovered the power of scripture, the solution seemed obvious: either reform the mass according to biblical teaching or write a new liturgy so as to do what the first Christians did. It did not occur to them that the New Testament could not be used as a liturgical textbook, or that they might need to turn to Jewish sources to discover what St. Paul meant by "the cup of blessing which we bless," for instance.

All of the reformers agreed on what they thought the first

Christians did, in its broad outlines. They were sure that they shared bread and wine in remembrance of Christ. Beyond that there is little unanimity. That sharing, that communion, was for Luther a sharing and eating of Christ's real body and blood, locally present in and with bread and wine. At the other extreme, the left wing of the reformation saw in bread and wine a bare sign, a psychological reminder of Christ's death. The views in between are many. All had some following in Anglicanism, and their evolution is traced ably in C. W. Dugmore's *Eucharistic Doctrine in England from Hooker to Waterland* (London, 1942).

From the Anglican point of view, the problem with the typical protestant approach to the question of eucharistic liturgy and the theology of eucharistic presence is that while they had discarded medieval western answers, the reformers and their generations of followers did not discard medieval questions. In the early days of the reformation the reasons for this attitude are clear: very little, if any, evidence was available to them of liturgies and theologies other than those of the late medieval west. However, protestants continued—and have not entirely ceased—to react to the question of sacrifice as though that word necessarily involves a commercial transaction, and to the question of eucharistic presence as though it were a problem in physics. The mother church of Anglicanism has not escaped this syndrome, as the liturgies of its new *Alternative Service Book* make clear, but other Anglicans have arrived at a different resolution of the eucharistic problems which so vexed protestantism.

There are a number of histories of the science of liturgiology available to the interested reader.[25] What is important for us as we investigate the spirituality of Anglicanism is to see how the scientific study of liturgy has determined how Anglicans worship and how they think about the eucharist.

The late sixteenth and the seventeenth centuries saw the collection and publication of many ancient liturgies, particularly those of the eastern churches. The liturgy of the eighth book of the *Apostolic Constitutions* and the *Liturgy of Saint James* had a great influence on post-reformation Anglican thinking. The realization came to many in Anglicanism that eucharistic sacrifice had by no means always and everywhere meant propitiation, and that the stuff of the sacrifice was not everywhere understood as the body and blood of Christ made present by priestly power in order that it be offered to the Father. Inspired by the ancient prayers Anglicans began to speak forthrightly of sacrifice in the eucharist, but in terms of what they read the ancients to be offering: thankful memory, praise, bread, and wine. Increasingly, "consecration" came less to be seen as a method of preparing a victim to offer than as a result of the sacrifice itself.

Thus since the first book of 1789, the prayerbooks of the Episcopal Church in the U.S.A. have gone far beyond Cranmer and followed the form of the ancient eastern prayers of the West Syrian type. Praise of the creator is followed by a thanksgiving for salvation and then by a supplicatory section which includes a petition for descent of the Holy Spirit upon the gifts. The thanksgiving for salvation concludes with the institution narrative and an act of remembrance and oblation. In the first American prayerbook the text was that of the Scottish book:

> . . . remembrance of me. Wherefore, O Lord and heavenly Father, according to the institution of thy dearly beloved Son our Savior Jesus Christ, we thy humble servants, do celebrate and make here before thy divine Majesty, with these thy holy gifts, which we now offer unto thee, the memorial thy Son hath commanded us to make; having in remembrance his blessed passion and precious death, his mighty resurrection and glorious ascension; rendering unto thee most hearty thanks for the innumerable benefits procured unto us by the same. (Rite I, Prayer I)

In the current American book, we find the same thought in more contemporary prose, although the original text is that of Basil of Caesarea:

> . . . remembrance of me. Father, we now celebrate this memorial of our redemption. Recalling Christ's death and his descent among the dead, proclaiming his resurrection and ascension to your right hand, awaiting his coming in glory; and offering to you, from the gifts you have given us, this bread and this cup, we praise you and we bless you. (Rite II, Prayer D)

The grammatical connection, present in the Greek original, sums up the eucharistic action: recalling, proclaiming, offering, we praise and bless God. The structure and content of this ancient prayer supports Alexander Schmemann's oft-quoted dictum that the essence of sacrifice is surrender, not value given.

In the late nineteenth and in the twentieth centuries, as studies of Jewish worship grew, and the Israelite concepts of communion sacrifice, memorial sacrifice and the sacrifice of thanksgiving became better known, the naturalness of the sacrificial language of the ancient liturgies became more and more apparent to Anglicans. Like the ancient Israelites, we thankfully recall our history in a meal shared in God's presence. Bread and wine used for such a purpose are holy food and drink indeed. Thus Anglicans have moved away from discussing a "moment of consecration," be it institution narrative or invocation of the Spirit upon the gifts, and now generally understand the entire eucharistic prayer to be consecratory.

Sacrifice and consecration are concepts which well illustrate how liturgical spirituality becomes active. F.D. Maurice (1805–1872) wrote of a universal law of sacrifice and its importance if human society were ever to become truly alive. He was convinced, as was St. Paul, that we are one in Christ, and that only as we reach out as he did can we live. "Kindness and Gentleness cease where there is no sense of a Kind or Gens. They grow with the growth of that sense. . . . A Creature sinking into itself dies; so long as it is associated with a kind, it lives."[26] Our sacrificial posture toward the rest of humanity cannot be an undisciplined goodwill, but must be shaped by "the confession and presentation of the perfect Sacrifice once made." This same thought must control the formulation of our personal prayers, for "if they are not petitions that the will which is expressed in that sacrifice may be done on earth as it is in Heaven, if they are not presented through the High Priest and Mediator within the veil, they are, in my judgment, not Christian prayers."[27]

Maurice was unremitting in his insistence that the Christian can have no other social or political policy than that of community and sacrifice. To pray for daily bread was not a prayer for personal wealth: "Bread for subsistence will not under any circumstances, be bread for mere display, for waste, for rivalry." Maurice's summary of the gospel proclaimed in the eucharistic action is distinguished by the words "family" and "share":

We shall tell them that a living and perpetual communion has been established between God and man; between earth and heaven; between all spiritual creatures; that the condition of this communion is that body and blood which the son of God and Son of Man offered up to His Father, in fulfillment of His Will, in manifestation of His love; that God is as careful to nourish their spirits as their bodies; that as He provides bread and wine for the strength and life of the one, so in this body and blood of His son is the Strength of the other; the Sacrament of His continual presence with His universal family; the witness to each man of his own place in that family, and of his share in all its blessing; the pledge and spring of a renewed life; the assurance that his life is his own eternal life.[28]

William Temple (1881–1944), who was to become Archbishop of Canterbury in 1942, also saw the social implications of the gospel as a plan for uniting and healing humanity. The intensely christocentric content of Temple's teaching makes it impossible to reduce his to a "social gospel." The theme of sacrifice pervades, as the aim of life is fellowship with man and God, "fellowship with Love—utter self-forgetful and self-giving love." Thus salvation itself "consists in the substitution of the Spirit of the Whole for the spirit of the particular self in the control of all life." Sacrifice means seeing in the eucharist a word of Christ, "As I treat this Bread, so I treat my Body, and you must do the same." Following Christ in this way is to reunite society through the Church, and this too is enacted in the eucharist:

[The eucharist is that] which is pre-eminently the Christian's means of access to the Eternal, and wherein he worships not as an individual but as a member of the Church of all times and places, [and where] the relevant conception of Christ is not that of the historic figure but that of the Universal Man. The sacrifice of Christ is potentially, but most really, the sacrifice of humanity. Our task is, by his spirit, to take our place in that sacrifice. In the strict sense there is only one sacrifice—the obedience of the Son to the Father, and of Humanity to the Father in the Son. This was manifest in actual achievement on Calvary; it is represented in the breaking of the Bread; it is reproduced in our self-dedication and resultant service; it is consummated in the final coming of the Kingdom.[29]

Temple urged Christians to think of the eucharist in terms of creation as well as redemption, and here again sacrifice is important, for the bread and wine we offer are nothing less than tokens of our economic life, a life dependent on God's goodness, a model for all human society:

> [In the eucharist] we take the bread and wine—man's industrial and commercial life in symbol—and offer it to God; because we have offered it to Him, He gives it back to us as a means of nurturing us, not in our animal nature alone, but as agents of His purpose, limbs of a body responsive to His will; and as we receive it back from Him, we share it with one another in true fellowship. If we think of the service in this way, it is a perfect picture of what secular society ought to be; and a Christian civilization is one where the citizens seek to make their ordered life something of which that service is the symbol.[30]

If the eucharist offers Anglicans a lens through which to look at God's purposes for the world and thus focus its spirituality, so does the doctrine of the Incarnation. The Incarnation is seen by Anglicans as not just a singular fact—or even as *the* singular fact—about the life of Jesus and restricted in its importance to him. Rather, taking a cue from eastern Christians, Anglicans have seen in the Incarnation an expression of God's total will. In the great Anglo-Catholic *Lux Mundi* of 1889, we find this paradigm of what Michael Marshall was to call in our day "the slow consecration of the universe":

> The Incarnation opened heaven, for it was the revelation of the Word; but it also reconsecrated earth, for the Word was made Flesh and dwelt among us. And is it impossible to read history without feeling how profoundly the religion of the Incarnation has been a religion of humanity. The human body itself, which heathendom had so degraded that noble minds could only view it as the enemy and prison of the soul, acquired a new meaning, exhibited new graces, shone with a

new lustre in the light of the Word made Flesh; and thence, in widening circles, the family, society, and state itself felt in their turn the impulse of the Christian spirit with its "touches of things common, 'till they rose to touch the spheres."[31]

This doctrine of the Incarnation was a mighty spur toward social action, particularly in the Anglo-Catholic circles in which it was articulated. We find it pervading that movement to such an extent that in an early edition of *The Parson's Handbook* Percy Dearmer warned against the use of Roman-style cassocks, which were fastened with many buttons. His reason was that he could not support the button trade, notorious in the England of his day for sweatshop conditions.[32]

Underhill, Spiritual Direction, and the Quest for Wholeness

For Evelyn Underhill (1875–1941), the main task of the writer about spirituality was to demonstrate that Christian commitment provided a unifying factor in life, not a cause for dividing life into departments sacred and profane. Her own experience of religious conversion as an adult, combined with her subsequent studies of the mystical tradition, had convinced her of this. Underhill's investigations into the spiritual life were catalytic in moving Anglican spirituality in new directions.

New directions were needed. The great strengths of the Catholic movement were also its weaknesses. In reclaiming the great tradition of the western church, it often worked uncritically. This was certainly the case in the cure of souls, where the Anglo-Catholics reclaimed the great traditions of the spiritual director, and the confessor. With that baby they also took some rather murky bath water, the priest's manuals of a somewhat ghettoized Irish and French Roman Catholicism a century before Vatican II.[33] Thus we find nineteenth century Anglicans writing in perfectly cold blood about "the tribunal of the confessional" and developing a system of casuistry based entirely on nineteenth century Roman models. One manual long in print in England goes on at length to warn against attendance at motion pictures (pre-talkies) as sin. Later editions warn against women receiving communion while wearing lipstick, as this might be a violation of the principle of fasting before communion (a practice not canon-ically required of Anglicans). Such a cultural transposition could not and did not work; the ethos of Anglicanism for good or ill resists the narrow approach. What came rather naturally to and fit fairly comfortably within a larger cultural pattern in Roman Catholicism appeared to be romantic posturing in Anglican cir-cles. Yet even those who were not extreme Anglo-Catholics rec-ognized that spiritual direction and the healing of confession and absolution were good things. After her conversion under Baron von Hügel, Underhill led the effort to get at the larger and deeper issues, the relation of the spiritual quest to the living of life.

Rather than arguing defensively for a greater place for reli-gion in a "normal person's" life, Underhill took the offensive: "Most of our conflicts and difficulties come from trying to deal with the spiritual and practical aspects of our life separately instead of realizing them as parts of a whole." Thus she spoke of three kinds of spiritual awareness that bind the person together:

> The cosmic, ontological, or transcendent; finding God as the
> infinite Reality outside and beyond us. The personal, finding
> Him as the living and responsive object of our love, in imme-
> diate touch with us. The dynamic, finding Him as the power
> that dwells within or energizes us. These are not exclusive but
> complementary apprehensions, giving objectives to intellect,
> feeling and will. They must all be taken into account in any
> attempt to estimate the full character of the spiritual life, and
> thus life can hardly achieve perfection unless all three be
> present in some measure.[34]

That Underhill's program immediately puts one in mind of the Trinity and classical approaches to spirituality was not acci-dent on her part. Like many before her she saw a path from the perception of God to an appropriation of God's love, to response in the painful process of inner transformation and loving acts toward others. That connectedness of belief, piety, and action was absolutely essential to her: "Man does not truly love the Per-fect until he is *driven* to seek its incarnation in the world of time."

Thus the "interior life" and Christian discipleship need each other. Meditation is not a luxury reserved for suburban matrons:

Without the inner life of prayer and meditation, lived for its
own sake and for no utilitarian motive, neither our judgments
upon the social order nor our active social service will be perfectly performed; because they will not be the channel of Creative Spirit expressing itself through us in the world today.[35]

In this way the active life becomes the fulfillment of the life of
prayer:

The final purification of love of the human spirit, and the full
achievement of its peculiar destiny as a collaborator in the
Spirit's work, must go together: obverse and reverse of the
unitive life. The soul's total prayer enters and is absorbed
into, that ceaseless Divine action by which the created order
is maintained and transformed. For by the prayer of self-
abandonment, she enters another region; and by adherence
is established in it. There the strange energy of will that is in
us and so often wasted on unworthy ends, can be applied for
the world's need—sometimes in particular actions, sometimes
by absorption into the pure act of God.[36]

For Underhill, immersed in the liturgy, it all fits into the pattern of the Cross where "life is offered, and being offered is
transformed in God: and by and through this life given and transformed" does the reality of life with God exist. Worship and life
revolve around sacrifice:

[Worship's] full meaning is disclosed in the absolute oblation
of the Cross. Cost is always essential to it. Thus wild animals
and fruits are never used by agricultural people for the purposes of sacrifice. They must give something into which they
have put their own life and work; for within that total, visible
offering which is ritual sacrifice, is always implied the total
invisible offering of the self, and everything the self best
loves.[37]

In the work of Underhill and her school was a call for intense
discipline to which Anglicans could respond, a link between faith
and life, and one which prompted one to invite direction, counsel
and absolution. And something of a spirituality industry has been
born, or reborn, in Anglicanism. No one spiritual method has

gained or can gain dominance, but Anglican writers after Underhill generally speak of interiority, personal and corporate dimensions in prayer, and works of love as stages in the process of Christian development.

Two writers in our own time follow Underhill's general pattern are Kenneth Leech in England and Alan Jones in the United States. Leech's *Soul Friend* (New York, 1977) and Jones' *Exploring Spiritual Direction* (New York, 1982) have a good deal in common, despite the difference in their intended audiences. Both are thoroughly Anglican in the best eclectic and synthesizing sense of the word. Personal history, the history of the cure of souls, classics of ascetical writing, and the insights of depth psychology are brought to bear on the question of how Christians help each other mature in Christ. Both prefer the model of friendship to that of guru or authority figure in the relationship of spiritual direction. Jones' own Center for Christian Spirituality at the General Theological Seminary educates seminarians and lay people in the broad tradition of Christian spiritual writing and also prepares spiritual directors in a graduate program that provides intensive practical experience. Confession is less and less the time or place of spiritual direction, and, following monastic and eastern tradition, Anglicans more and more separate the functions of confessor and spiritual director. This is not an accidental result of the fact that many fine directors are lay people who cannot pronounce priestly absolution, but a recognition that the gifts of discernment, patience, and love required in the direction relationship are conferred quite apart from ordination.

In this section we have met a seventeenth century poet priest whose personal journey is symbolic of the Anglican pilgrimage to acceptance of self and toleration of ambiguity all around. We have looked into the Evangelical and Catholic movements, which have had so much influence on the formation of the present day church. In Temple and Maurice we have seen "liberal" or Broad views connect the catholic tradition to the sacrificial worship and social action of Christians. In Evelyn Underhill we have seen the restructuring of classic ascetical theology for the ordinary Christian. There are few precise doctrinal formulations on which these people and movements would agree, outside of those given expression in the liturgy, but all were convinced that the Christian life involves personal discipline, corporate worship, sacrificial love. To one of the Broad Church views of church and history from which this essay is written they are complementary pieces of the ever-developing mosaic of Anglican identity and spirituality.

IV. ANGLICANISM'S ECUMENICAL VOCATION

Anglicanism is liberal, especially in its Broad Church (reason-oriented) wing. But for Anglicans "liberal" means not un-conservative, but un-bigoted and non-intransigent. "Liberality" rather than "liberalism" has been suggested as the identifying trait of Anglican spirituality. We have had recourse earlier in this chapter to the term "comprehension" as the Anglican ideal. It may be that Anglicanism's on-going commitment to being a church in which advocates of Bible, tradition, and reason remain in more-or-less friendly dialogue is the justification for our continued existense as a distinct Christian group. There really are special denominations in this age of pluralism for those who identify entirely with one of the strands in the Anglican tapestry and reject the others.

William Wolf has pointed out that in his view "the note of unreality that runs through many of the documents of Vatican II" is their "absence of any expectation of conflict, as though the bishops in verbally achieving agreement had supposedly eliminated conflict." Anglicans have learned, sometimes the hard way, that conflict is inevitable in a church which truly permits participation of all groups in decision making. They have also learned that out of conflict, unpleasant as it may be, often comes greater good than any side anticipated.

At its best the Anglican Communion seems to at least one Roman Catholic scholar to have a great deal to contribute to the life of world Christianity. And perhaps it is tempting to let him have the last word:

> All Anglican Churches . . . are one in the conscious endeavor
> to preserve the apostolic faith and character of the Church's
> worship of the first centuries, though trying to incorporate in

it the contributions of the Reformation and those of their own time so far as they have positive and permanent value. This typical Anglican attitude in respect to tradition and enrichment is at the basis of the moderation and comprehensiveness of Anglicanism. *It marks world Anglicanism as being, as it were, a provisional prototype of the reunited* Ecumene, *the world-Christianity of the future.* That Anglicanism comprises only a small number of Christians does not detract from that fact.[38]

Tempting as it is to end on that note, the last word must be given to Michael Ramsey, the one hundredth Archbishop of Canterbury, now retired:

While the Anglican Church is vindicated by its place in history, with a strikingly balanced witness to Gospel and church and sound learning, its greater vindication lies in its pointing through its own history to something of which it is a fragment. Its credentials are its incompleteness, with the tension and travail in its soul. For it is sent not to commend itself as 'the best type of Christianity,' but by its very brokeness to point to the universal church wherein all have died.[39]

NOTES

1. An essay presented in honor of thirty-five years of service by James L. Peck to the Episcopal Church in Long Island.

2. See, for example, the definitions in Alan Jones and Rachel Hosmer, *Living in the Spirit* (New York, 1980) and William J. Wolf, editor, *Anglican Spirituality* (Wilton, Ct., 1982).

3. The quadrilateral, originally the work of the American William Huntington Reed, states that all who are baptized with water in the name of the Trinity are members of the Holy Catholic Church of which the creeds speak. It commits this church to a ministry of unity: "co-operating with them on the basis of a common Faith and order, to discountenance schism, to heal the wounds of the Body of Christ, and to promote the charity which is the chief of Christian graces and the visible manifestation of

Christ to the world." They held that "Christian unity . . . can be restored only by return of all Christian communions to the principles of unity exemplified by the undivided Catholic Church during the first ages of its existence. . . . As inherent parts of this sacred deposit, and therefore as essential to the restoration of unity among the divided branches of Christendom, we account the following, to wit:

"1. the Holy Scriptures of the Old and New Testament as the revealed Word of God.

"2. The Nicene Creed as the sufficient statement of the Christian Faith. [The Lambeth version of 1888 added the Apostles' Creed here.]

"3. The two Sacraments,—Baptism and the Supper of the Lord,—ministered with unfailing use of Christ's words of institution and of the elements ordained by Him.

"4. The Historic Episcopate, locally adapted in the methods of its administration to the varying needs of the nations and people called of God into the unity of His Church."

The Lambeth Conference, the world congress of Anglican bishops, reminded the Anglican Communion in 1968 that the sixteenth century Thirty-Nine Articles of Religion are not imposed on any member church, and where they are retained, they are to be interpreted with reference to their historical setting.

4. Stephen Sykes, *The Integrity of Anglicanism* (New York, 1978) is a recent attempt to urge Anglicanism to adopt a denominational theology.

5. The Church of England is the only member of the Anglican Communion with state ties. Progressively, legislation in this century has freed the English Church to govern itself, although much remains to be done to complete its emancipation.

6. The real "settlement" of the English church did not occur until after the restoration of Charles II, by which time there was a working Anglican tradition of worship and theological inquiry. In the meantime the English Church had experienced the effects of the English Civil Wars, as well as the suppression of the Church and its liturgy under the Commonwealth, so the Anglican spirit could be said to have matured. See P.E. Moore and F.L. Cross, *Anglicanism* (London, 1962).

7. The *Soundings* movement is remembered fondly in Harry

Williams, *Someday I'll Find You* (London, 1982) and mercilessly lampooned as *Rumblings* in A.N. Wilson, *Unguarded Hours* (London, 1978), undoubtedly the cleverest satire upon Anglicanism written in this century.

8. The name, The Protestant Episcopal Church, arose in Maryland, "Episcopal" to distinguish Anglicans, who did retain the theology of episcopacy, from other protestants, and "Protestant" to distinguish them from the Roman Catholics. "Protestant Episcopalians" stuck, and at the first General Convention of the Church there was no real alternative in the choice of a name.

9. Without the latitude of belief and practice found in Anglicanism, the Anglo-Catholic and Ritualist movements *(q.v., infra)* could not have gotten off the ground, much less survived, despite significant canonical and, in England, legal steps taken against those movements.

10. In 1689 an attempt was made to revise the liturgy in a more protestant direction, to accommodate the puritan movement. Its failure resulted from the fact that the puritans had lost their desire for unity with and in the Church of England. The Methodists left the Church of England despite Wesley's pleas. In this country, the Reformed Episcopal Church was organized to promote particular doctrines, especially concerning baptism. In our own time, some have left because they could not countenance the ordination of women or certain aspects of liturgical revision. In every case known to the writer, groups have left Anglicanism because it was too comprehensive for them, not because it sought to exclude them.

11. W. Grisbrooke, in *Anglican Liturgies of the 17th and 18th Centuries* (London, 1958), has collected and commented on the attempts at liturgy writing which took place in England during the Commonwealth and after. A number of these attempts were adaptations of ancient texts, particularly those of The Liturgy of St. James.

12. See the description of the conflict in Horton Davies, *Worship and Theology in England,* vol. II (Princeton, 1975). Davies has reduced the troubles of the seventeenth century to a problem in etiquette: "Was it fitting, Anglicans asked, to approach the most high God . . . with casual and unpremeditated prayers, without appropriate etiquette, and elegant diction? *For these reasons* divine worship was appropriately expressed in a liturgy in which

dignity, formality, and order were the leading characteristics." (p. 187, emphasis added) This is to miss the point entirely, a point over which some men were deprived of their lives.

13. Stephen Neill, *Anglicanism* (New York, 1978), p. 149.

14. Daniel B. Stevick, "The Spirituality of the Book of Common Prayer," in Wolf, p. 117.

15. *Ibid.*, p. 115.

16. F.D. Maurice, *The Kingdom of Christ*, Part II, Chapter IV, sec. 3.

17. *The Book of Common Prayer* (1979), p. 372.

18. Quoted in *The Anglican Digest*, Pentecost 1983, p. 40.

19. *News of the Liturgy* and an invaluable series of *Liturgical Studies* come from Grove Books in Bramcotte, under the editorship of Colin Buchanan.

20. William Romaine, *The Life, Walk, and Triumph of Faith* (London, 1856), pp. 20f.

21. Hannah More, *Estimate of the Religion of the Fashionable World* (London, 1809), pp. 263f.

22. E.B. Pusey, *Sermons during the Season from Advent to Whitsuntide* (London, 1848), pp. 299f.

23. See John M. Kinney, "'The Fond du Lac Circus': The consecration of Reginald Heber Weller," *The Historical Magazine of the Protestant Episcopal Church*, Vol. 39 (1969) pp. 3–24.

24. Which is not meant to suggest that Anglicans do not have an evangelical doctrine of purgatory. Many do. See C.S. Lewis, *The Great Divorce* (many editions).

25. Generally, see L.R. Cabrol, *Introduction aux Etudes Liturgiques* (Paris, 1907), L. Eisenhofer, *Handbuch der katholischen Liturgik* (Frieburg, 1932), and P. Oppenheim, *Institutiones Systematico-Historicae In Sacram Liturgiam* (Rome, 1945). For the development of Anglican liturgiology, see Geoffrey Cuming, *A History of Anglican Liturgy* (London, 1982) and Paul Marshall, *Hamon L'Estrange and the Rise of Historical Liturgiology in 17th Century England* (Ann Arbor, 1982).

26. F.D. Maurice, *Moral and Metaphysical Philosophy* (London, 1872), 1:xxvi.

27. Maurice, *The Doctrine of Sacrifice* (London, 1893), p. 220f.

28. Maurice, *The Prayer Book . . . and the Lord's Supper* (London, 1880), pp. 230f.

29. William Temple, *Christus Veritas* (London, 1949), pp. 238f.

30. Temple, *The Hope of the World* (London, 1943), p. 70.

31. Charles Gore, ed., *Lux Mundi* (New York, 5th ed., n.d.), p. 176.

32. Percy Dearmer, *The Parson's Handbook*, 12th ed. (Oxford, 1932), p. 122. Dearmer took the same line on the late nineteenth century's shortened, ungathered surplice: " Now the worship of Mammon has so far intrenched on the honour due to God that the sweater has his own way with us . . . (*ibid*, p. 128).

33. For the comments of a Roman Catholic on the roles of subgroups, particularly the Irish, in English-speaking Roman Catholicism, see Mary Douglas, *Natural Symbols* (New York, 1963).

34. Evelyn Underhill, *The Life of the Spirit and the Life Today* (New York, 1922), pp. 13f.

35. *Ibid.*, p. 268.

36. Underhill, *The Golden Sequence*, pp. 182f., quoted in C.J.R. Armstrong, *Evelyn Underhill (1875–1941): An Introduction to her Life and Writings* (London, 1975), p. 269.

37. *Worship* (New York, 1937), p. 55.

38. Professor Van de Pol is quoted in William J. Wolf's "Anglicanism and Its Spirit" in his *The Spirit of Anglicanism* (Wilton, Ct., 1979). Wolf's essay is of great importance in understanding contemporary Anglicanism, and this writer remains in his debt.

39. *The Gospel and the Catholic Church*, quoted in Wolf, p. 183.

E. Glenn Hinson
PURITAN SPIRITUALITY

Puritanism was spirituality. Puritans were to Protestantism what contemplatives and ascetics were to the medieval church. They parted company with their medieval forbears chiefly in the locus of their efforts. Where monks sought sainthood in monasteries, Puritans sought it everywhere—in homes, schools, town halls, shops as well as churches. Sometimes knowingly, at other times unknowingly, they employed virtually the same methods monks used to obtain the same goal—"the saints' rest," heaven, or "full and glorious enjoyment of God." Like the monks, they were zealous of heart religion manifested in transformation of life and manners. Impatient with halfway commitments, they kindled fires for unreserved, enthusiastic embracing of the covenant. Everything they did, they did with solemnity and determination. The essence of piety, declared Lewis Bayly, Bishop of Bangor, in *The Practise of Pietie,* a work first published about 1610 which shaped the mold of Puritan spirituality, is

> to joyne together, in *watching, fasting, praying, reading* the *Scriptures,* keeping his *Sabboths,* hearing *Sermons,* receiving the holy *Communion,* relieving the *Poore,* exercising in all humilitie the workes of *Pietie to God,* and walking *conscionably* in the duties of our calling towards *men.*[1]

In those words he summed up the whole Puritan platform.

THE GOAL OF PURITAN SPIRITUALITY

The Puritan vision included both this world and the next. Ultimately they played out their own version of *contemptus mundi.*

Avid students of Hebrews, they "looked forward to the city which has foundations, whose builder and maker is God" (Heb 11:10); they journeyed to a "better country, that is, a heavenly one" (11:16). They were pilgrims on the way to "Mount Zion, the heavenly Jerusalem, the innumerable company of angels, and the spirits of just men made perfect" (12:22, 24), the Paradise of God in which dwelled the patriarchs, the prophets, the saints, the angels, and Christ himself. Or Revelation-like, they dreamed of a city which "shone like the sun" with gold-paved streets where the inhabitants continually praised God and where neither night nor suffering nor sorrow ever entered.[2]

It is not surprising that Puritans had a near-obsession about death and dying. Emerging in an age when infant mortality was high and the average life span less than thirty, they integrated this preoccupation realistically into their whole Calvinist scheme of divine omnipotence, human wretchedness, and predestination. They feared death, and they wanted none to forget that death brought punishment as well as reward. Those who did not fear had much to worry about. The saint should live as a dying person among dying persons. At the same time the Puritans, like saints of other ages, viewed death as a release and a relief. For the elect death opened the way to a life of unending bliss. Times of sickness and death could open one to the working of divine grace. In doubt and struggle lay assurance one knew the saying grace of God, the all important element in the whole pilgrimage.[3] In the Puritan scheme death was the fearsome river which separated Beulah Land from Mount Zion, the heavenly City itself. It was the most important stage on life's pilgrimage—infancy, youth, middle age, death, and after death. All life should prepare one for it.

Keen as was the Puritan longing for heaven, however, their chief focus of attention was not on the other world but on this one. Following their mentor John Calvin, they rejected medieval monastic otherworldliness. So long as they lived in the "wilderness" which this world is, they would practice "the life of heaven" on earth. As Christopher Hill has pointed out in his insightful study of *Society and Puritanism in Pre-Revolutionary England* Puritanism had to do with much more than religious matters. Puritans belonged to "the industrious sort of people," who stressed labor as a duty to one's neighbor, society, commonwealth, and human-kind, and viewed idleness with horror. They denounced popish religion as the mother of ineptitude in trade, hard work, and accumulation of wealth. Monks, nuns, and mendicants, they charged, lived in idleness and thus did not contribute to production. Unmarried clergy led to a declining population. Superstition permitted extravagance in adornment of churches. Too many holidays were detrimental to production. Friars lived on alms of the poor and thus inhibited their rise above poverty.[4]

In their quest for "a new Reformation" surpassing the "half-Reformation" of 1517,[5] Puritans emphasized the family as the basic unit of society. By reducing the authority of the clergy, the Reformation of the sixteenth century had simultaneously elevated the role of heads of households. Henry VIII, Edward VI, and Elizabeth all directed family heads " to have especial regard to the good government and ordering of the same."[6] Not surprisingly, therefore, Puritans emphasized still more vigorously the piety of the family. Arthur Dent printed family prayers in *The Plaine Mans Pathway to Heaven,* Lewis Bayly in *The Practise of Pietie.* "The family farm or workshop played in the world of early capitalism the part that the great noble household or monastery had played in mediaeval society," Christopher Hill observed.[7] Heads of families took charge of both the physical and the spiritual welfare of those under them. "Parents and masters of families are in God's stead to their children and servants," J. Mayne said in his explanation of the English catechism.[8]

THE WAY TO THE GOAL

Passing through "this world of sin" on the way to the heavenly Jerusalem, Puritans revived and adopted a regimen of self-examination and prayer which monks had employed for centuries. Thoroughly Augustinian, like their mentor John Calvin, they emphasized human sinfulness and divine grace. Christians, Richard Baxter declared, should "make it the great labor of their lives to grow in grace, to strengthen and advance the interest of Christ in their souls, and to weaken and subdue the interest of the flesh."[9] Grace alone could bring one to faith and repentance for sin and guide one in the way of salvation. It alone could soften the heart and energize the mind. Accordingly, the perpetual Puritan prayer went something like Cotton Mather's: "Lord, help mee now unto the Redeeming of time, and the Spending of as much as I can, of it, in a perpetual Exercise of Grace!"[10]

Prerequisite to the pilgrimage, the favorite Puritan metaphor for the Christian life, were election by God in the Son, being "born again," discovery of "a deep sense of divine things," awareness of a change of will, entrance into covenant with Christ, and perseverance in this covenant to the end.[11] Puritans unquestioningly accepted Calvin's predestinarian views. God is absolutely sovereign. Not a sparrow falls to the ground save by his design and decree. By his inscrutable will he has decreed that some would be saved, some lost. It behooves all, but especially the "elect," to inquire continually into the security of their "election." The important thing, Baxter, and most Puritans, would say, is "whether such or such a saving grace be in thee in sincerity or not."[12] Self-examination of this sort could and did lead to serious problems, since the Puritans made no special provision for spiritual direction which could mitigate the harsh and capricious aspects of self-criticism. John Bunyan, for instance, plunged into manic depression using the Puritan method. Relying on scriptures darting into his mind at random to tell him whether he belonged to the elect, he would sometimes hear a word of assurance, at other times one of judgment, especially from the passage in Hebrews about Esau selling his birthright. His moods went up. They went down. He feared he had committed the unpardonable sin. He reached the point of suicide. Little by little, a word of grace, which a spiritual guide might have spoken to him long before, broke through: in reading the preface to Luther's commentary on Galatians, in overhearing the conversation of some women at Bedford about a "new birth," in counsels of John Gifford, pastor at Bedford, and in "My grace is sufficient for thee" of 2 Corinthians 12:9 as he sat meditating in the Bedford congregation of which he later became pastor. Still tormented, he prayed that the Esau passage and the sufficiency passage might meet and do battle in his mind at the same time. They did, and, fortunately, the sufficiency passage won.[13]

However much everything depended on election, the "one

great qualification" from a human standpoint, according to Baxter, was being "born again" (Jn 3:3), conversion of heart, mind, and will. Conversion was the Spirit's work, requiring little if any human assistance. Early in the Puritan era, which was riding a wave of revival both in England and in New England, not much coaxing was required. Multitudes were engaging in the most rigorous soul-searching. A generation or two later, however, religious fervor dampened, and as it did some perceived an appropriate role for "means" to effect conversions. In the "Great Awakening" (1730–1760) Puritans split over the place of "religious affections" in conversion, some favoring and some opposing the use of means.

In the Calvinist scheme conversion was only the beginning of the pilgrimage. After and not before it came conviction of sin and redirection of the will toward God. Then one could enter into the covenant with God through Christ in which one must persevere to the end. The covenant stood at the center of Puritan thought and life. "We Covenant with the Lord and with an other," the Salem Covenant of 1629 read, "and doe bynd our selves in the presence of God, to walke together in all his waies, according as he is pleased to reveale himself unto us in his Blessed word of truth."[14] Seven years later, the Puritans spelled out particulars. Salvation lay in keeping the covenant by grace, but to most it must have seemed like living under law again.

Though the long range goal was heaven, therefore, the immediate task of the Puritan was to live a heavenly life on earth. Yet Puritans were well aware of obstacles on the way. Lewis Bayly listed misunderstanding of scriptures, the evil example of noted persons, prosperity, presumption of God's mercy, evil company, fear lest piety make one too sad or pensive, and the hope of long life.[15] Efforts to steer around such hindrances did much to create the Puritan ethos so often caricatured in modern thought. Where Puritanism lapsed into externalism, however, it did so unintentionally. Puritans coveted anything but "mere preparatives for the heavenly life, without any acquaintance with the thing itself."[16] They wanted authentic, sincere, soulful commitment which would overflow into every dimension of thought and activity.

The Puritans relied on a host of traditional techniques taken mostly from the ascetic and contemplative tradition, their critique of monasticism notwithstanding. We cannot assume any uniformity among these non-conformists, of course, but devout Puritans would have employed many of the same devotional exercises.

A practice expected of everyone was reading or, perhaps one should say, praying and poring over the scriptures in search of the Word of God. Puritans were "people of the Book." Thus when Christian, in *Pilgrim's Progress,* left his "roll" behind inadvertently, he had to return for it, for it was "the assurance of his life, and acceptance at the desired haven."[17] Lewis Bayly directed the devout to read a chapter morning, noon, and night so as to read through the entire Bible in a year, then to meditate on its exhortations and counsels to good works and a holy life, threatenings of judgment for sins, blessings, God's promises for Christian virtues (patience, chastity, mercy, almsgiving, zeal in his service, charity, faith, and trust in God), and God's gracious deliverance and special blessings. These chapters, he insisted, should not be read as history but as letters sent directly from God, and therefore be read with reverence as if God stood by and spoke the words directly to the reader, thus inciting to virtue and repentance of sin.[18] Cotton Mather developed what he called "porismatic" reading, which entailed reading "with such a devout Attention, as to fetch at least one *Observation,* and one *Supplication,* a *Note* and a *Wish,* out of every *Verse* in all the Bible" (*Diary,* I:103; II:578).

Puritans were a highly literate people, turning out vast amounts of devotional material. The devout kept daily logs of both their inner perceptions and their outward activities in diaries and journals. They wrote biographies, autobiographies, and pious fiction modeling the pilgrimage. They did searching critiques of contemporary society.[19]

The heart of Puritan, as of monastic, devotion was prayer and meditation. To be true prayer, it had to come from the heart. Prayer, John Bunyan insisted,

> is a sincere, sensible, affectionate pouring out of the heart or
> soul to God through Christ, in the strength and assistance of
> the holy Spirit, for such things as God hath promised, or,

according to the Word, for the good of the Church, with submission, in Faith, to the Will of God.[20]

Not all Puritans would have gone to the extreme Bunyan did in
rejecting all forms, even the Lord's Prayer, as a hindrance to the
Spirit. Some wrote commentaries on the latter. But they would
have agreed with Bunyan in emphasizing the heart. A test frequently applied to commitment was the disposition of the heart
in prayer for mercy. And Puritans could report experiences worthy of a Bernard of Clairvaux or a Teresa of Avila. Cotton
Mather, for instance, spoke of his heart being "rapt into those
heavenly Frames, which would have turned a Dungeon into a Paradise" or "raised unto Raptures almost Insupportable, when I
was Expressing my *Love* to God, and Beleeving His *Love* to
me. . ."[21]
    Puritans knew too the power of tears, "compunction" the
monks called it, as a conditioner of the heart for prayer. A youth-
ful Cotton Mather had the habit of prostrating himself on the
floor and pouring out tears concerning his "wickedness" as "the
most filthy Sinner out of Hell."[22] On another occasion emptying
his heart in confession, he "melted into a Flood of Tears."[23]
    Puritans emphasized both public and private confession as a
remedy for sin. Calvin, of course, included confession and absolution in the liturgy in Geneva. His heirs followed in his footsteps.
A substantial part of the Puritan formation process, however,
revolved around examination of one's conscience as a sinner in a
manner very like Ignatius Loyola's. If sickness struck, one should
inquire into sin, for in the Puritan view illness almost certainly
indicated divine disfavor and need of repentance. And "where sin
abounded, grace superabounded" (Rom 5:15), especially to those
who confessed. "A Stream of Tears gushed out of my Eyes, upon
my Floor," Cotton Mather testified, "while I had my Soul inexpressibly irradiated with Assurances, of especially two or three
Things, bore in upon me."[24]
    Another conditioner which figured prominently in the Puri-
tan regimen, both publicly and privately, was fasting or "humiliation." In both Old and New England officials called for fasts
during times of crisis, convinced that the public welfare
depended on the piety of the faithful. The General Court of Mas-

sachusetts, for instance, set July 7, 1681 as "a day of public Humiliation" on the grounds that the time required "greater fervency and frequency in the most solemn seekings of God in the face of Jesus Christ, then wee have ordinarily had experience of . . ." The decree ticked off concern about Puritan woes in Great Britain and anti-Christian sentiment, a drought, and other awful circumstances in New England.[25] Fasts, whether public or private, aimed at the abasing of the sinner so as to soften the heart and get it in condition for divine direction and assurance. "Inexpressible *Self-Abhorrence,* for my abominable Sinfulness before the Holy Lord," wrote Cotton Mather of one "secret" fast, "was the Design, and the very Spirit of my Devotions this Day." By humbling himself, however, he "received a new, a strong, a wonderful Assurance from Heaven (melting mee into Tears of Joy!) that my Sins are all pardoned thro' the Blood of Christ, and that notwithstanding all my horrid Sinfulness, I shall be employ'd in great Services for His Name."[26]

Puritans knew they could take nothing for granted in their march toward Beulah Land. For persons adamant in their opposition to Roman Catholic works-righteousness or salvation by works, they spoke surprisingly often and emphatically of *duties* the Covenant imposed upon them. For those who would maintain a heavenly walk, Richard Baxter prescribed conviction that heaven is one's only treasure, labor to know it as one's own and how near it is, frequent and serious talk about it, effort to raise one's affections nearer to it in every activity, "improvement of every object and event," much "evangelical work and praise," careful observing and cherishing of motions of the Spirit, and care for bodily health.[27] Their verbal gymnastics notwithstanding, these prescriptions differed not at all in any essential way from the program of medieval monks and nuns![28]

Early on, Puritans perfected methods of meditation and contemplation supportive of heart religion. According to the master guide of Puritan contemplation, Richard Baxter, contemplation should occur at stated times to avoid omission, frequently to prevent shyness between God and the soul and prevent unskillfulness and "loss of heat and life," and seasonably. Prayer should be engaged in several times daily, more frequently on the sabbath, on special occasions when God warms the heart, when sick, and when dying.[29] Devout Puritans often spent entire days in prayer. They frequently threw up "ejaculatory" prayers as occasion demanded. Obviously the goal was to "pray without ceasing" (1 Thes 5:17).

Puritans emphasized privacy in prayer and literally arranged "closets" for that purpose. One's covenant is an intimate matter requiring highly personal conversation. At the same time they made prayer a visible public concern in the family, church gatherings, especially on the sabbath, and other settings. In public prayer Puritans made much use of the Psalms. They peppered their prayers with scripture quotations, which was natural in view of their constant searching through the Bible.

Although Puritans would not have distinguished as precisely as the monks did between levels of prayer (*cogitatio, meditatio,* and *contemplatio* of Hugo of St. Victor), they did differentiate meditation or contemplation from ordinary prayer, which is perhaps best characterized as "mental" prayer. Given their strong accentuation of individual piety, we should not be surprised to find much improvisation in prayer and meditation, but the best specimens reveal remarkable likeness to medieval forms.

Contemplation, instructed Baxter, requires preparation of the heart by freeing it of the world—business, troubles, joys— and by attaining the greatest solemnity of heart and mind through apprehension of the presence of God and his incomprehensible greatness. Detachment, Meister Eckhart would say. "The most powerful prayer . . . is that which proceeds from an empty spirit."[30]

"Consideration," rational control of the whole process, is "the great instrument by which this heavenly work is carried on." The Puritans knew that the heart is "where it's at," but they feared the emotions and the imagination. Both could go wild. Consideration, a concept used also by Loyola in the *Spiritual Exercises,* would establish a proper direction in meditation. As Baxter described its effects, it "opens the door between the head and the heart," "presents to the affections those things which are most important," "reasons the case with a man's own heart," "exalts reason to its just authority," "makes reason strong and active," and "can continue and persevere in this rational employment."[31]

Capricious as they may be, nevertheless, in the Puritan view the affections count most in heart religion. Meditation has to do with affective rather than cognitive capacities. And here is where imagination enters in. To incite love, desire, hope, courage or boldness, and joy or their opposites (hatred of sin, godly fear, godly shame and grief, unfeigned repentance, self-indignation, jealousy regarding one's heart, and pity for those in danger of losing immortal salvation), Baxter urged use of biblical images, soliloquies, and "sensible objects," warning, however, "Don't, like the papists, draw them (Moses, Jesus or other biblical characters) in pictures but get the liveliest picture of them in thy mind that thou possibly canst by contemplating the scripture account of them . . ."[32] (A tall order, surely, for the "papist" Loyola, whose spirituality exerted much influence on Catholic spirituality, insisted on exact mental images, too.) Biblical images would supposedly arouse the right emotions and thus increase love or desire for God, hope, courage, etc. Again like medieval contemplatives such as Bernard of Clairvaux, the Puritans relied on the Song of Songs as well as New Testament passages such as the passion narratives to do a job on them, but they spent most of their time on heaven or hell. The soliloquy, a meditative style handed down from Augustine, entailed "a pleading the case with thyself."

Puritans complained of the straying heart just as contemplatives did in other ages. Baxter attributed such excursions to excuse-making, trifling, diversion to other concerns, and abruptly ending the work of meditation before it was well begun. His suggested remedy: "Use violence on your heart!"[33]

ON THE WAY TOGETHER

What has been said up to now might leave the mistaken impression that Puritan spirituality was almost wholly individual and private. Radicals, such as Quakers and Baptists, it is true, did go to an extreme there, just as extremists among monks did. For most Puritans, however, it is only partially true, for their spirituality also embraced a powerful sacramental and liturgical element which we cannot gloss over, and it spilled over into all of public life, from the family to the government of a commonwealth.

For one thing, the sabbath played a powerful role in Puritan piety. Their commitment to it was motivated by much more than social necessity, changes in the character of labor, as Christopher Hill has argued.[24] Not even the interaction of Calvinism with social and economic forces would be adequate to explain the fervor with which Puritans fought to preserve it. They saw it, as Solberg has contended, as an integral part of their "program for revitalizing personal religion and building a holy commonwealth."[35] God commanded it as a part of the covenant. "The *conscionable* keeping of the Sabbath," Bishop Lewis Bayly judged, "is the *Mother* of all Religion, and good discipline in the Church. Take away the Sabbath . . . and what will shortly become of Religion. . . .?"[36] Cotton Mather agreed:

> "The Lord expresses the whole of *Religion,* under that Phrase, *keep my Sabbaths.*
>
> "Tis true concerning both Persons and Peoples,
>
> "That if *Religion* desirably flourish, *Sabbaths* will bee duely kept.
>
> "But *Religion* will decay and wither, if Strictness about the Sabbaths do go.
>
> "Indeed, not to keep *Sabbaths* exactly, is both the Guise of, and the *Way* to, in the greatest Irreligion.
>
> As has been said of Prayer, either *Sin will make Men leave off praying, or Prayer will make Men leave off sinning:* so may wee say of the *Sabbath.*"[37]

A devout Puritan such as John Winthrop, later governor of Massachusetts Bay Colony, could feel his "herte was very much unsettled" because he waited until after three o'clock Saturday afternoon (when devout Puritans began the Sabbath) to begin reading and prayer.[38]

Despite a high regard for preaching as *the* means for communication of grace, Puritans, like their mentor Calvin, also made much of the Lord's Supper. They took pains to prepare for reception, meditating on the worthiness of the sacrament, their personal worthiness for receiving it, and the means whereby one might become a worthy recipient. Puritan expectations of the sacrament were not far from those a Roman Catholic might have had. According to Lewis Bayly, one should look for forgiveness of sins, the Spirit and breath of grace, all saving graces, communion with Christ, a pledge of resurrection, assurance of everlasting life, and union with other Christians.[39] During the observance, he admonished, one should carry on "a sweet soliloquy" with oneself. Even after returning home, one should reflect on whether he or she received diligently, were reconciled to God, and desired to receive again.

Puritans gained considerable notoriety for the discipline with which they sought to maintain the covenant. It is quite clear that they intended to create a visible society of saints which, without discipline, would have been quite impossible. Most would have subscribed to Milton's conviction in the matter.

> There is not that thing in the world of more grace and urgent importance throughout the whole life of man, than discipline. The flourishing and decaying of all civil societies, all the movements and turnings of human occasions are moved to and fro upon the axle of discipline. . . . Nor is there any sociable perfection in this life, civil or sacred, that can be above discipline; but she is that which with her musical cords preserves and holds all the parts thereof together. . . . Discipline is not only the removal of disorder, but if any visible shape can be given to divine things, the very visible shape and image of virtue.[40]

Such an outlook was rooted, as the last sentence suggests,[41] in Puritan concern for order. God has created an orderly world, down to the least item in creation. Human beings, therefore, should regulate their society, else the latter might end up in chaos. Certainly the aim of a restored human community could be achieved only if Christians assumed their obligation to exercise discipline, and the brotherhood of preachers which stood at the core of Puritanism did not want to fail in this task.[42]

Puritan spirituality did not limit itself to the individual nor even to the religious community. Heart religion had to manifest itself in transformed lifestyle and social concern. The work of grace in one's life is discovered, Faithful informed Talkative in *Pilgrim's Progress,*

1. By an experimental confession of his faith in Christ.
2. By a life answerable to that confession; to wit, a life of holi-

> ness, heart-holiness: family-holiness, (if he hath a family,)
> and by conversation-holiness in the world; which in the
> general teacheth him inwardly to abhor his sin, and him-
> self for that in secret; to suppress it in his family, and to
> promote holiness in the world: not by talk only, as an hyp-
> ocrite or talkative person may do, but by a practical sub-
> jection in faith and love to the power of the word.[43]

Citing James 1:22, 27, Christian observed, "The soul of religion is the practical part. . . ." At the day of judgment one will not be asked, "Did you believe?" but "Were you *doers*, or *talkers* only?"[44]

As part of a social revolution cresting during the seventeenth century, themselves oppressed, Puritans identified with the suffering and oppressed. In *The Plaine Mans Pathway to Heaven* Arthur Dent listed "honest, just, and conscionable dealing in all our actions among men" among infallible signs of election. Sounding like a Latin American liberationist, he proceeded to catalogue areas in which oppression might occur: usury, bribery, racking of rents, taking of excessive fines, bargaining, letting of leases, letting of houses, letting of grounds, binding the poor to unreasonable covenants, thrusting the poor out of their houses, hiring the houses of the poor over their heads, and taking of fees.[45] After heaping up a pile of scripture texts against such injustices, he enumerated the causes—cruelty, covetousness, hardheartedness, evil conscience, and the Devil—and cures—pity, contentment, tender affections, a good conscience, and much prayer.[46]

Being a part of the "industrious sort" gave a peculiar twist to the Puritan view of wealth. They did not regard wealth as a blessing and poverty as a curse, as often accused. From Calvin, rather, they inherited a concept of calling which encouraged ceaseless effort. One's calling belonged to the divine order of things. Its primary goal was to serve God and humankind, not to amass wealth. Thus one had to pursue a vocation with diligence, zeal, and persistence to the glory of God and out of gratitude to God. Should one prosper, one must be a good steward. A good steward would live frugally—the Puritan version of monastic asceticism. Good stewardship would not mean careless liberality toward the poor. Puritans were severe toward vagabonds and freeloaders, and Cotton Mather was more the exception than the rule in his preoccupation with the poor in his parish.[47]

PURITAN SPIRITUALITY IN RETROSPECT AND PROSPECT

Puritanism has often been caricatured from its negative side. "Don't dance. Don't drink. Don't smoke. Don't chew. Don't go with those who do." Admittedly some of the caricature fits when one evaluates Puritanism in terms of convention rather than in terms of tradition. The Puritan tradition, by which I mean its essence, was commendable and laudable, entailing a spirited search for heart religion manifested in transformation of both individuals and society. Like the prophets of old, the Puritans too wanted holiness and justice to "roll down like waters." Like Jesus, they too denounced play acting at religion by legalistic and trivialistic observances which diverted people from sincere and authentic commitment; saying "Lord! Lord!" mattered little, if one did not do what he said.

Where did Puritan spirituality fail? Not in its intention surely. If so, you would have to fault biblical spirituality which Puritans sought so assiduously to emulate and to realize in their own lives. Or medieval spirituality which they borrowed from in so many ways. No, if they fell short of their aims, it would have been because they were so ambitious as to be unrealistic. They wanted and they expected by grace to be a society of redeemed and saintly human beings, restoring the order disrupted by the Fall; being faithful to the Covenant. This is why discipline was so crucial. In their zeal, however, they forgot some of their own basic tenets.

The Puritans were voluntarists. The sovereign God alone has a claim on the conscience. Only if people *freely* enter into covenant, therefore, with God and with one another, can discipline be exercised. What happens when they no longer "own the covenant"? This is the crucial question which the Puritans confronted within a generation, and they had to admit the failure of their noble experiment with the "halfway covenant." Those who had remonstrated with the Church of England for being only "halfly reformed" were no more than that themselves. If they had remembered their premise about human nature, far more realistic than their goal for society, they might have seen greater wisdom in the monastic vision. The monks did not try to reform everybody, a whole society. They, being voluntarists too, were content to work with those who were willing to withdraw from society into disciplined communities. Or the Puritans might also have settled for the Anabaptist model of the "gathered church" composed only of the regenerate. By expanding their vision to the outer margins of society, they became coercive. Magistrates imposed covenant obligations, religious as well as civil, on all and sundry. They levied fines, imprisoned, whipped, and even hanged persons who stepped outside the lines. By 1700 the Puritan vision, so luminous at one time, was scarcely a flicker.

What can we learn from the Puritan experience which might help us today? Some well-meaning Christians seem to suggest that we might return to the Puritan era and again recapture their vision and program for the United States. Godliness and holiness should again pervade the White House, the Capitol, the schools, the businesses, the homes, as well as the churches. The American will stand as the bulwark of a Christian commonwealth against the tide of godless Communism and secularism. Appealing as these words may sound to some ears, they ignore the failure of the Puritan plan. The Puritans' own realism—"We have no enduring City here"—should have tempered their effort to realize the Kingdom of God in Old or New England, at least putting some controls on misguided zeal to mold all and sundry in one mold. Unfortunately it took the deterioration of religion to remind them again of the validity of their voluntarist principle, that to be authentic, faith must be free.

If we can keep this principle in the forefront, then Puritan spirituality can help us. By way of the Puritan tradition we can find our way back to the Catholic mainstream, for that is where Puritanism headed in its drive to obtain a fuller reformation. The essence of Puritan spirituality is also the essence of Christian spirituality. Indeed a student of the history of Christian spirituality will find little that is new in Puritan spirituality. For the Puritans the newness lay in rediscovery, in the joy of coming once more upon a discarded item long forgotten, and in the zeal with which they pursued the old. Many persons are having a similar experience today in this era of the "New Pentecost" introduced by Pope John XXIII.

NOTES

1. Lewis Bayly, *The Practise of Pietie* (3rd ed.; London: J. Hodges, 1613), p. 163.

2. John Bunyan, *The Pilgrim's Progress*, ch. xx. Hebrews fascinated the Puritans. See William Perkins' *A Cloud of Faithful Witnesses, a Commentary on Hebrews* xi (London: H. Lownes, 1608).

3. See David E. Stannard, *The Puritan Way of Death: A Study in Religion, Culture, and Social Change* (New York: Oxford University Press, 1977), pp. 72–95.

4. Christopher Hill, *Society and Puritanism in Pre-Revolutionary England* (2nd ed.; New York: Schocken Books, 1965, 1967), pp. 20, 129, 132.

5. Cotton Mather, *Diary of Cotton Mather* (New York: Frederick Ungar Publishing Co., n.d.), I: 262f.

6. 35 Eliz. cap. I; cited by Hill, p. 447.

7. Hill, p. 449.

8. J. Mayne, *The English Catechism Explained* (3rd ed.; 1623), p. 278.

9. Richard Baxter, *The Saints' Everlasting Rest* in *Doubleday Devotional Classics*, ed. E. Glenn Hinson (Garden City, NY: Doubleday & Co., Inc., 1978), p. 90.

10. Mather, *Diary* I: 87f.

11. See Baxter, *Saints*, pp. 55–70.

12. Ibid., p. 86.

13. See my fuller reconstruction in *Doubleday Devotional Classics*, I: 211–212.

14. In Williston Walker, *The Creeds and Platforms of Congregationalism* (Boston: Pilgrim Press, 1960), p. 116.

15. Bayly, *The Practise of Pietie*, pp. 234–290.

16. Baxter, *Saints*, p. 112

17. John Bunyan, *Pilgrim's Progress*, in *Doubleday Devotional Classics*, I: 355.

18. Bayly, *The Practise of Pietie*, pp. 156–7. Cotton Mather,

Paterna: The Autobiography of Cotton Mather, ed. Ronald A. Bosco (Delmar, NY: Scholars' Facsimiles and Reprints, 1976), p. 6, read *fifteen* chapters a day as a child of seven or eight!

19. On the literature of Puritan spirituality see Owen C. Watkins, *The Puritan Experience* (London: Routledge & Kegan Paul, 1972.

20. John Bunyan, *I Will Pray with the Spirit,* ed. Richard L. Greaves (Oxford: Clarendon Press, 1976), p. 235.

21. *Diary,* I: 110; *Paterna,* p. 16.

22. *Diary,* I: 187, 233, 227.

23. Ibid., p. 199.

24. Ibid., p. 187.

25. *Mass. Archives,* XI.8; cited in Cotton Mather, *Diary,* I: 22, n. 2.

26. Mather, *Diary,* I: 237.

27. Baxter, *Saints,* pp. 120–9.

28. For a more detailed comparison of Puritan with earlier disciplines see Charles E. Hambrick-Stowe, *The Practice of Piety: Puritan Devotional Disciplines in Seventeenth-Century New England* (Chapel Hill: University of North Carolina Press, 1982), pp. 25–39.

29. Baxter, *Saints,* pp. 130–8.

30. Meister Eckhart, *Counsels of Discernment,* 2; in *Meister Eckhart,* trans. Edmund Colledge, O.S.A. and Bernard McGinn, "Classics of Western Spirituality" (New York: Paulist Press, 1981), p. 248.

31. Baxter, *Saints,* p. 143.

32. Ibid., p. 159.

33. Baxter, *Saints,* pp. 169–73.

34. Hill, pp. 145–218.

35. Winton U. Solberg, *Redeeming the Time* (Cambridge, MA: Harvard University Press, 1977), p. 31.

36. Bayly, *The Practise of Piety,* p. 513.

37. Mather, *Diary,* I: 30.

38. *Winthrop Papers,* 162; cited by Solberg, p. 69.

39. Bayly, *The Practise of Piety,* pp. 664–791. On Calvin's high view of eucharist see Kilian McDonnell, OSB, *John Calvin, the Church, and the Eucharist* (Princeton, NJ: Princeton University Press, 1967), pp. 223ff.

40. John Milton, *Prose Works* (Bohn Edition), II: 441–2; cited by Hill, p. 225.

41. Cf. Stephen Foster, *Their Solitary Way* (New Haven & London: Yale University Press, 1971), pp. 11–40.

42. Patrick Collison, *The Elizabethan Puritan Movement* (London & New York: Metheun, 1967), p. 59, has traced the origins of the Puritan party in England to preachers who regarded the Church of England as only "halfly reformed." Composed mostly of persons who had spend some time of exile either in Zürich or Geneva, this fellowship complained about the Elizabethan Settlement as regards the role of preaching, the importance of Bible study, discipline, and ecclesiastical preferments. By 1566, under royal pressure toward uniformity, they began to emerge as an underground movement. These "privy" congregations attached to their preachers rather than to parish churches emphasized disciplined observance of the Covenant.

43. John Bunyan, *Pilgrim's Progress*, p. 387.

44. Ibid., p. 384.

45. Arthur Dent, *The Plaine Mans Pathway to Heaven*, pp. 182–3.

46. Ibid., p. 197.

47. See Foster, pp. 148–52.

John Weborg

PIETISM: "THE FIRE OF GOD WHICH ...
FLAMES IN THE HEART OF GERMANY"[1]

Classical Lutheran Pietism, born out of a dimension of depth, rooted in the devotional writings of the church, including especially Luther, took its rise in and for the sake of the church in order to restore a dimension of depth to personal religious life.[2] The experience of the dimension of depth in life, whether evoked by pain or prosperity, guilt or grace, occasioned the awareness of the mystery of life, of the "coming and going of God," thus raising the need for due regard for the *experiential* part of life. Pietism provided a congenial receptivity for experience and for a living encounter with a living Lord who could speak a word that makes faith, hope and love come alive.

At the same time that Pietism was preoccupied with the regeneration of persons it occupied itself with the renewal of the church. It sought to revive a certain apostolic simplicity that centered in the love each member had for the other rather than on a highly polemicized form of relation that set Lutheran against Lutheran as well as Lutheran against Reformed, Anabaptist, etc. By means of group Bible study, free prayer and testimony, Pietism sought to raise the consciousness of Christians that they were priests of God and to exercise their spiritual priesthood in prayer and service to neighbor. Pietism longed for the day when it could be said of the church in Germany as was said of the church in Jerusalem: "And with great power the apostles gave their testimony to the resurrection of the Lord Jesus, and great grace was upon them all. There was not a needy person among them, for as many as were possessors of lands or houses sold them, and brought the proceeds of what was sold and laid it at the apostles' feet; and distribution was made to each as any had need" (Acts

4:33–35). What was not lost to the Pietists was the close connection between the power of apostolic preaching and the quality of congregational life. The freedom to share and the spontaneous character of love were to them immediate fruits of the gospel. And more: in some intrinsic fashion, Pietism saw a connection between the credibility of the gospel and the consistency of congregational life. To be sure, they did *not* mean that inconsistent congregational life undid the kerygma and robbed the gospel of its truthfulness. Its objective character and content stood fast. But they did see that congregational life was a part of the proclamation of the gospel since among and through the People of God the fruit of the Spirit was made visible and the power of God made public in its capacity to transform wicked persons into graceful and caring persons.

Various proposals for reform were made such as would contribute to the renewal of the spiritual life of persons and congregations investing as it were "soul" into the music and manner of life. These reforms, to be looked at later in this paper, contributed the *experimental* aspect to the pietistic movement. I have chosen this word because Pietists did not necessarily see a cause-effect relation between these proposals for reform and their results. Rather, they sought to create occasions within the context of which God's Holy Spirit in, with and under Word and Sacrament, could do the work of renewal and regeneration in persons and in the church. God had made certain promises to the church regarding the future as such and regarding the power of the Word of God itself. It was a human responsibility, motivated by the obedience of faith, to provide tangible instances whereby this Word could embody itself in creative and regenerative activity.

What concerned the movement called Pietism was the passion for a congruence of profession and practice. To be sure, doctrine *denoted* certain fixed elements of the Gospel such as the distinctive content of the Christian religion but at the same time doctrine *described* the mind and manner of the Christian life. If in doctrine as *denotation* one sought purity of teaching and consistency in systematic development, in doctrine as *description* one sought purity of motive and consistency in manner of life consonant with the life of Christ recorded in Scripture. Piety denoted the *congruence* of profession and practice, confession and character. This congruence was to be *seen* in the lives of persons and congregations. Granting some allowance for hyperbole, to the Pietists, theology should not terminate in propositions but the propositions of the faith should find their outcome in lives formed by the faith, the hope, and the love of Jesus Christ. Spener said, "The reformation begun by Luther is far from completed as far as it regards life and morality."[3]

SETTING IN LIFE

War

The period immediately preceding the beginning of Pietism was a period of pervasive dissolution. The Thirty Years War ended in 1648 and left in its wake a most pitiable situation. According to one historian, by either death or immigration, the population had been reduced by one third. Since supply lines were not as yet used to furnish needed material at the front, the soldiers had to get this material by pillaging land, forest and livestock and by harassing, torturing and raping the citizenry. So dehumanized had conditions become that the dead were found with grass in their mouths and cannibalism was not unknown. It has been argued further that perhaps even the wars of the twentieth century were in part compensaiton for the losses of this period.[4]

In Wurttemberg in south Germany for example, W.H. Bruford reports that by 1654 eight towns, forty-five villages and thirty thousand buildings were in ashes. It is estimated that between 1634–1654 the population was reduced from three hundred thirteen thousand to sixty thousand.[5] As if this were not enough, later in the century the area suffered three invasions by France, once again opening land and people to rape. At the same time as this was going on, there was a noticeable admiration of things French—clothing for example, and even French scissors for trimming German beards!—but especially the opulence at the court of Versailles. What the latter admiration led to was increased taxes for the support of their "coveteousness" on the part of rulers.[6] In addition to the losses of the Thirty Years War, the losses of the French invasions amounted to six cities and thirty-seven smaller villages.[7] What it all added up to was a depopulation of the land, dehumanization of people due to the sheer need to survive, and a dissolution of morals and manners.

The recovery of the person was high on the agenda of needs. Pietism sought to address that need by means of an emphasis on the experiential side of Christianity, thereby opening up a dimension of depth, and on the experimental side, by showing how Christians could employ their gifts for service in fulfillment of their calling in the priesthood of all believers, which doctrine had lapsed into obscurity as the next section will show.

Cultural/Intellectual

There had been a gradual transfer of power to the states at the expense of the feudal lords, a process begun in the Middle Ages but greatly exacerbated by the Thirty Years War. The concentration of power led to abuses, and, as already mentioned, to a striving for opulence on the part of rulers at the expense of the citizenry. Rulers seemed to be a law unto themselves, including a growing power over the church, a major concern of the Pietists.

A rigid class distinction emerged with disastrous consequences for a church that had preached the priesthood of all believers. For example, people from the upper classes insisted on receiving Holy Communion separate from the lower classes, or, if there must be communion together, at least from a separate cup.[8] The same happened with baptism. Stoeffler reports that upper class families would not have their children baptized in the church because that would involve the use of water already used by the lower classes.[9] This is likewise the era in which the address "Herr Pastor" became part of proper etiquette.[10] Since the "lordly" bearing was transferred to the clergy, it may not be surprising but it is offensive to learn that since duties were clearly differentiated according to class, there was a case of a woman in Wittenberg who had to get the bishop's permission to give consolation to a sick friend since consolation was the proper function of a pastor.[11] The recovery of the priesthood of all believers, and the service of God and neighbor, rooted in the spontaneous character of love, was a cardinal matter to the Pietists. The credibility of the Gospel was at stake as well as that of the church.

There had also been stirrings in the intellectual community that gave pause to the Pietists. Copernicus (1473–1543) had upset things cosmologically by assigning the central place in the universe to the sun. Further scientific elaboration and confirmation took shape in the mathematical work of Kepler (1571–1630) and explorations by telescope in the work of Galileo (1564–1642). Along with scientific discovery comes reflection on the activity of science such as is found in Francis Bacon's *Advancement of Learning* and *Novum Organum* wherein he urges the acquisition of knowledge by observation and experimentation, a concern that found a more complete exposition in the work of Isaac Newton, who did much to secure a firm place for what is called the scientific method, i.e. all hypotheses are to be tested by experimentation, and wherever possible, all natural laws and relations are to be expressed mathematically. Inevitably these ideas led to a more mechanical view of nature and left less room for a view of God's providential activity.[12]

Philosophical thought was not unaffected by these developments. Spinoza (1632–1677), for example, employed geometric language and form as a way of constructing his philosophy. Essentially his view of God was pantheistic, hence immanent and not transcendent, impersonal not personal. And Leibnitz (1646–1716) too was of a mathematical orientation having discovered, along with Newton, the infinitesimal calculus. But he too was not free of a somewhat mechanical understanding of nature and life. Sin, for example, received its due because of the way the natural order meted out its judgment.[13] In these more impersonal views concerning the operation of reality, he shared similarities with Descartes, Locke, and earlier, Bacon and the general scientific and mathematical way of conceiving reality. When this got worked into the philosophical notion that every possibility had a claim to existence and that the best possible world would exist on its own right, almost forcing itself into existence, the whole enterprise shows some affinity to Spinoza's idea of identifying the totality of things with God.[14] This wide ranging vision of the totality of things did not exclude religion, for Leibnitz had hoped to find a way of uniting the religions of humankind, a matter that did not fail to arouse the opposition of August Hermann Francke of Halle, who had corresponded with Leibnitz and opposed him on this issue, thinking that such an eventuality would force revelation to be subservient to reason and that the uniqueness of Christianity would get lost in an improper universalism.[15]

The influence of Liebnitz found its way into Pietism via the work of philosopher Christian Wolff (1679–1754) who had imbibed the rationalist spirit and was banished from Halle in 1723 where he was teaching, only to be returned to the faculty by Frederick the Great. Wolff sought to show that reason could attain to certain knowledge in every aspect of life, including the knowledge of one's moral duty. In support of this he adduced the philosophy of Confucius as an example of exemplary moral knowledge. As might be expected, the Pietists reacted vigorously to this point as to another teaching to Wolff. He had compared the universe to a vast interconnected machine, each part working in concert. Furthermore, in his anthropology, Wolff taught that human being always tended toward the best and that once the right conduct was known, it would be followed. What offended the Pietists in this notion was a compromise of human freedom and an overestimation of human capacity.[16]

This material was not strange to the Pietists. Spener had written a thesis on Thomas Hobbes, and Bengel, who had a degree in philosophy, had given special attention to Spinoza. If Bengel may be taken as representative, his views will enable one to get a glimpse of how Pietists viewed the philosophical enterprise. "All the real advantages which *divines* can derive from philosophical training may be comprised in a very small compass; its chief use to them is for teaching good arrangement and methodological inferences."[17] And as for speculative questions, in this case Leibnitz's theodicy, Bengel says,

> . . . the more we talk upon such things, the less we know about them. Is it to promote piety? Knowledge of this sort will not at all promote our recovery from sin; and when we are recovered enough, we shall know enough; wisdom will then be spontaneously manifested to us. This is all I have now to say upon speculative philosophy; for though I meant to have said a great deal more, the desire has left me, because I know that God cannot be pleased with our too curiously inquiring into the secret things which belong to him.[18]

To a degree, the major concerns of Pietism emerge: practicality and the promotion of piety. While it may sound both naive and anti-intellectual, the Pietists sincerely believed that the acquisition and practice of wisdom was aligned with a pure heart, for we both know more and know more of what is right than what we *want* to do. Therefore there is a connection between "recovery from sin" and "wisdom . . . spontaneously manifested to us and the power to do what is right." The corrective they sought in the case of intellectual activities was the same as in the case of orthodoxy: intellectual activity should not become intellectualism and orthodoxy should not become orthodoxism. In an increasingly impersonal world in the realm of nature and an increasingly institutionalized world in the realm of the church, Pietism sought to restore the dimension of depth, the personal, and the experiential which to be sure were at home in an increasingly experimental world.

Orthodoxy

For Luther, the doctrine of justification by grace through faith was the doctrine by which the church stood or fell. Justification is a two-sided doctrine. On the one hand, it is a doctrine of incomparable comfort. Freely God acquits anyone who has faith in Christ Jesus as the one sufficient and total sacrifice for sin. The old words serve well to denote the exclusively Christological basis of this salvation: Christ alone; grace alone; faith alone; promised on the authority of Scripture alone.

On the other hand, justification by grace through faith is a polemical doctrine. As the reformers saw it, the doctrine was a body-blow against works righteousness, a staple charge against Roman Catholicism. Viewed from the standpoint of the Reformers, the free grace of God was compromised by the notion that love formed faith rather than that faith formed love. Based on Galatians 5:6, they invariably asserted that faith must act in love, faith being both primal and primary. No merit whatsoever could attach to works and good intentions, be they church works such as masses, indulgences, or obedience to bishops and priors or works of ordinary Christians in service of their neighbors. None of these works could be added up so that the total would compensate for a previous lack of righteousness. Works by themselves were but one half of the problem; there was also required a quality of love that made them meritorious. And as if this were not enough, how does one know that what one has done is sufficient to merit God's approval? The whole scheme lacked certainty and was not medicine for a sin-sick soul.

This doctrine became established into an order of salvation, the so-called *ordo salutis*. In the period of Orthodoxy, great intellectual effort was expended, especially with the help of Aristotelian philosophy, to make this doctrine impregnable and to develop in detail the exclusively divine activity in grace. In short, it was to show precisely how salvation was God's work both *for* us and external *to* us in contrast to what will emerge in Pietism, namely, a concern to delineate God's work *in* us as a work of regeneration and the creation of a new nature. This of course elevates the doctrine of sanctification to a level that the Orthodox party thought would threaten the doctrine of justification by grace through faith by stressing good works and would eventually lead to a doctrine of perfectionism, a doctrine emerging in Pietism and which reached its culmination in Wesley. The *ordo salutis* in classical Lutheranism looked like this: election, calling, illumination, conversion, regeneration, justification, mystical union, renovation, conservation and glorification.[19]

The intervening years between 1580, the acceptance of *The Book of Concord* by the various Lutheran bodies, and the onset of Pietism, usually dated 1675, the publication of the *Pia Desideria*, were filled with a sustained effort to secure the objective and external character of the saving work of Christ. Since this period was a period of definition of Lutheran over against Lutherans, Reformed, Anabaptists, Spiritualists, Catholics, etc. it was filled with polemical preaching and writing. With some allowance for exaggeration, it might be called the polemical captivity of theology and preaching. Alan Deeter's research has given particular force to this phenomenon. Some pastors devoted an entire year to preaching sermons against other Christians—Calvinists, Zwinglians, Anabaptists, Catholics. The upshot of this as the Pietists saw it was that the sermons were not thereby aimed at the congregation which looked for a living word. It all seemed contradictory: a congregation listening to a sermon it could not understand, laced as it was with Latin and Greek quotes left untranslated, and, to top it off, aimed elsewhere! Apparently such was often true in the schools also. One report of a student speaks of compiling a notebook, subdivided in detail and systematic fashion, made replete with passages from Scripture to refute the heathen, the Turks, the Greeks, the Calvinists and the Papists. Those students particularly being trained to be schoolmasters were to distribute themselves in the various churches, take notes on the sermons and submit them to the inspectors.[20] According to Tappert it was not uncommon to hear such epithets as "stupid dog," "blasphemous bitch," "ass," "grasshopper," "Turk," etc. hurled back and forth. And in America, the tension continued even to the extent that in the case of death, Lutherans in some cases were reluctant to have their children buried in graves dug by persons of Reformed background.[21] To us, this seems incredulous; to the Pietists it was incongruous. The Psalmist's vision remained unfulfilled: righteousness and peace had not kissed each other.

The rise in polemics is rooted in a change in theological method. Jaroslav Pelikan points out that there is a shift from exegesis to dogmatics, due in substantial part to the influence of Aristotle's philosophy. With that shift comes another. To be sure, Lutheranism had spoken of faith as *fiducia* or a trusting confidence in God's mercy revealed in Christ and as *assensus* or assent to doctrine as explicated in the Confessions. But to what does one assent? The creeds? The Confessions? One Daniel Hofman, a professor of theology at Helmstedt, became critical of the undue influence of Aristotle on Lutheran theological method and was first censured and then dismissed from the faculty in 1598. Was assent to Aristotelian philosophy also implied in being a Lutheran? It appeared that *assensus* was winning out and that the fiduciary aspect was giving way to formal subscription to articles of the faith. This development also entailed a shift in the use of the Bible. Increasingly the formal authority of the Bible came into view with the elaboration of the doctrine of verbal inspiration, bringing it into close relation to the theological system. The more exclusively the Bible was linked to a system and made part of the larger polemical enterprise, the less the Bible was used pastorally in feeding the souls of the people who comprised congregations.[22] Ironically, the same thing was happening to Lutheranism as Luther asserted had happened to the Roman Catholic Church: it existed apart from a congregation of people. If the Roman

Church seemed to find its existence in the hierarchy, the sacramental system and canonical books, Lutheranism also seemed to exist apart from the people in a confessional system, an increasing *ex opere operato* (by the work, worked) view of the sacraments, politicization of the Church and clergy dominance. The Pietists wanted to restore a balance, to bring doctrine and life into congruity and pastor and people together around the Scripture as the source of promise and power. Then, to use Bonhoeffer's striking phrase, both can dare to be sinners under the cross.

THE EMERGENCE OF PIETISM

Pre-Pietism: Johann Arndt (1555–1621)

Ernst Benz has argued that at least part of Pietism's reaction to Lutheran Orthodoxy was a reaction to the indolence which the conventional teaching of justification by grace through faith had engendered.[23] Just how such indolence could arise is indicated in the Majoristic controversy. George Major (1502–1574), following Melancthon, had spoken of good works as necessary to salvation. The statement, as can be imagined, sparked a conflagration. On its face, such a proposition contradicted salvation by grace *alone* on the basis of Christ's work *alone*. What Major meant was that good works did not merit or effect salvation but were related to the preservation of salvation. The opposite extreme was represented by Luther's friend, Nicholas Amsdorf (1483–1565), who asserted that good works were injurious to salvation. What he wanted to communicate was that good works belong to the Christian life but not in the article of faith that pertains to salvation.[24] The effort in the direction in which Amsdorf pointed was the direction of developing a secure doctrine of objective justification. But when a doctrine is construed with such a radical objectivity it runs the risk of subsuming other doctrines such as sanctification or the growth of the Christian in holiness. Baldly stated, the doctrine of justification, foundational as it is, can be perverted into meaning "justification no matter what." At that point the freedom that the gospel offers has a way of becoming a caricature of itself, issuing in an illegitimate libertinism.

For that reason, Benz spoke of a certain "indolence" resulting from a misuse of the doctrine of justification. Swedish
Lutheran theologian Einar Billing gets even stronger in his warning: " . . . the forgiveness of sins degenerates into an opiate . . ."
and a certain "slackness."[25] And W.H. Auden's poem "Luther"
will reinforce the concerns of Benz and Billing:

> 'The Just shall live by faith . . .' he cried in dread. And men
> and women of the world were glad, Who'd never cared or
> trembled in their lives.[26]

Johann Arndt was the son of a Lutheran pastor and was
raised in a home where the writings of Luther, Tauler and à Kempis found a congenial receptivity. Educated at Helmstedt, Wittenberg, Strasbourg and Basel, he had the good fortune of being a
student at Wittenberg in 1577 shortly after the principles of the
Formula of Concord (published in 1580) had brought order and
unity to Lutheranism and had given Wittenberg a strictly
Lutheran character. Arndt had also studied medicine, but after
recovering from a serious illness he gave himself entirely to the
service of the church as a pastor during the first period of
Lutheran Orthodoxy which began with Martin Chemnitz (1522–
1586) and lasted until 1618. As an author/editor, he edited the
1518 Luther printing of *The German Theology,* a major devotional
work, Staupitz's *The Love of God,* and between 1605–1610 saw the
publication of his major work, *True Christianity.* Later he published a work on how to study the Bible and a popular prayer
book, *A Paradise Garden Full of Christian Virtues.* The latter book
contains reworked prayers from the Bible and from Catholic and
Protestant sources. And in *True Christianity,* recent scholarship
has demonstrated Arndt's dependence on Angela of Foligno's (d.
1309) writings, especially in the second book, and Tauler in the
third.[27] A brief look at *True Christianity,* the staple devotional
book of later Pietism, will show how the later themes of Pietism
are present in Arndt.

The work begins with a lament: "Christian reader! That the
holy Gospel is subjected, in our age, to a great and shameful
abuse, is fully proved by the ungodly and impenitent life of those
who loudly boast of Christ and his word, while their unchristian

life resembles that of persons who dwell in a land of heathens and not of Christians." Then Arndt makes an assertion: " . . . true Christianity consists namely, in the exhibition of a true, living, and active faith, which manifests itself in genuine godliness and the fruits of righteousness."[28] In contrast Arndt says of his own time, " . . . the Christian life, true repentance, love and godliness, are, as it were, forgotten; as if the sum and substance of the Christian religion consisted in arguing and writing books of controversy rather than in the unfeigned holiness of life, and purity of manners, which the gospel requires,"[29] for "without a holy life, purity of doctrine cannot be preserved."[30] At the conclusion of Book II he maintains that purity of doctrine is of no benefit if it is not adorned by a holy life and that holiness of life should be guarded with more earnestness than purity of doctrine. And when it comes to training, it is better to train up a devout person than a learned person.[31]

Compared with the polemical efforts described earlier in this paper, Arndt's efforts represent the beginning of a major shift. The move in emphasis is from doctrine to life. In doing so he precipitates a change in the way faith is conceptualized. Classical Reformation theology paid great attention to the origin of faith. In explaining the third article of the Creed (I believe in the Holy Spirit, the Holy Christian Church, etc.) Luther says, "I believe that by my own reason or strength I cannot believe in Jesus Christ my Lord or come to him. But the Holy Spirit has called me through the Gospel, enlightened me with his gifts, and sanctified and preserved me in true faith. . . ."[32] An implication of this is that faith is a gift, not a human work, " . . . by which in the Word of the Gospel we recognize Christ aright as our redeemer. . . ."[33] Reformation theology clearly establishes that faith is of divine origin. But Arndt, while denying none of the above, begins to stress the *fruits* of faith, a metaphor that will come to full term in Spener's writings. Now the main issue becomes not the *origin* of faith but its *outcome*.[34]

What comes to the fore is the experiential dimension of faith. Arndt writes:

> When, therefore, this true knowledge of God is attained, by which God offers himself, as it were, to be touched and tasted

by the soul, according to that Psalm, 'O taste and see that the
Lord is good' (Psalm 34:8); it is impossible that a sincere
repentance should not immediately ensue; that is, a real renovation of the mind, and reformation of life. For, from a
sense and knowledge of the divine Omnipotence, proceeds
humility; since he must necessarily submit himself unto the
mighty hand of God, who has perceived its irresistible power
and energy. From the experience of the divine mercy arises
charity to our neighbor; for no man can be uncharitable who
has ever been affected by a sense of divine compassion.

And what does the consideration of this divine wisdom and charity produce? The *"Fear of God,"*[35] which Arndt calls an "experimental" knowledge of God.[36]

A later Pietist, Johann Albrecht Bengel of Wurttemburg
(1687–1752) thought that this exposition of the experiential fear
of God was one of Arndt's primary contributions to the ecclesial
life of Germany. Bengel was a classicist and for the greater part
of his life was the headmaster of a preparatory school in Denken-
dorf near Tübingen. This school provided the pre-seminary training necessary for entry into the university. Later, Bengel served
congregations near Tübingen, and at the conclusion of his life
was an official in the Consistory at Tübingen, providing supervision for the Lutheran churches of the area.

Bengel was a prolific author in three specific areas: textual
criticism, apocalyptic studies and edification literature. His most
well known work is the *Gnomon* (1742), a commentary on the New
Testament prefaced by an extensive treatise of textual criticism
in particular and on Bible reading in general.

According to Bengel, prior to Luther's time, people were sat-
urated with fear, fear of hell, of judgment, of not doing enough
good works to please God. Luther preached a gospel of pure
grace producing a rich fear—fear of taking advantage of this free
grace. But then, under the pretext of justification by grace
through faith, people fell into a false security and become impu-
dent. Between the time of Luther and Arndt, a "wild generation
arose." "Fear God!" became the rubric for Arndt's testimony.[37]

How does Bengel understand fear? In Revelation 14:6 it says
" . . . fear God and give him glory." Bengel speaks of this as a
"voluntary fear" which consists in a proper respect before the

divine majesty since the creature recognizes an immeasurable difference between himself/herself and the creator, yet finds a certain pleasantness accompanying this fear. On the other hand, without fear, one is a vile outrage in that one does not recognize God's omnipresence, omniscience, righteousness, and one misuses God's mercy,[38] the very themes that are strewn throughout Arndt's *True Christianity*.

Bengel distinguishes two kinds of fear: one kind is distressing or scrupulous (peinlich, Ger.) and the other is a delicate respect (zarter, Respect). It is the latter variety that he seeks to inculcate.[39] Since grace is the source of all of God's work, the element of fear might conceivably seem out of place since grace implies self-giving, vulnerability and sacrifice. Certainly a scrupulous fear is out of place since it never really receives grace but fears that grace is insufficient. A scrupulous fear borders on a fear grounded more in the sense of one's unworthiness and in an uncertainty about God's gracious will. A delicate fear, on the other hand, takes God's will seriously, i.e. his desire to save persons and to count them worthy of his favor for Christ's sake out of his grace alone. This fear is delicate because it knows both the costliness of grace (Christ's suffering and death) and the uncleanness of the one seeking grace. When this delicate fear is missing, one makes the terrifying error of just assuming God's desire is to forgive and thus one presumes on God's mercy. A presumptive sin is an insult.

Bengel, following Arndt, perceived that the doctrine of justification by grace through faith, as then popularly understood, engendered neither a scrupulous nor a delicate fear of God. Persons just assumed their justification and lived both freely and carelessly. Bengel referred to this as the pretext (Vorwand, Ger.) of justification and asserted that it bred a false security.[40] The condition under consideration here is what we have previously noted in other scholars' description of this phenomenon of taking advantage of the divine mercy without a due repentance for one's sin in the face of the holy love that seeks to redeem the lost: Benz called it indolence; Billing called it an opiate and a slackness; Arndt called it the absence of fear and trembling; Bonhoeffer called it cheap grace. What was needed, in my view, was the restoration of the religious dimension to the doctrine of justification or the dimension of depth in which the sinner felt the incomparable generosity of God and the delicate character of his grace. Hence Bengel called God's glory of the chief cause of conversion.[41] If there ever is a term that exudes the religious dimension, it is glory. Glory fascinates and frightens, invites but also intimidates. Both Arndt and Bengel found this mystery lacking in the theology and practice of the church and most certainly saw virtually no experiential evidence of the "fear" of God. The experiential dimension of Pietism owes its source to a profound awareness of the glory and majesty of God.

For Arndt, there is to be a congruity of faith and the fruit of faith. This is piety. To Arndt as to Bengel, this piety is intrinsic to a faith that is grounded in the glory, majesty and mystery of God, for it fears offending God's grace and presuming upon his mercy. Faith without fruit is inconceivable and requires no separation— a distinction but not a separation. And as if he anticipated trouble by propounding the intrinsic connection between faith and its fruit, at the end of the Preface to Book I, Arndt specifically disavowed any notion that he was an heir of George Major: good works are necessary to salvation! Nevertheless it stands written: "By their fruits you shall know them."

THE EXPERIENTIAL ASPECT

Philipp Jakob Spener (1635–1705)

Spener was born in Roppoltsweiler (near Strasbourg), Upper Alsace on January 23, 1635. His educational experience was gained at Strasbourg, Basel, Geneva and Tübingen. While at Geneva he met the former Jesuit, Jean de Labadie, who had converted to the Reformed confession and who had begun to gather Christians in small groups, a possible influence for the later extensive use of such groups (conventicles) by Spener and others. Spener was profoundly influenced by Arndt's *True Christianity* and a host of devotional writings such as Bayly's *Practice of Piety,* Baxter's *Self-Denial* and others. After serving as a pastor in Strasbourg in 1666 he moved to Frankfurt am Main where he published the most crucial document in Pietism, the *Pia Desideria* or

Pious Desires. This work was published as a "long introduction"to a new edition of Arndt's sermons. In 1675 the *Pia Desideria* was published separately.

The work is divided into three parts. In part one Spener discusses the defects among the civil authorities, the clergy, and the common people. Part two describes the possibility for better church conditions and part three offers proposals to correct the defects in the church. As the exposition of this work unfolds it is well to keep the thesis of this paper in mind: piety is the congruence in life of what is professed and what is practiced; it is the congruence of faith and the fruits of holiness and righteousness. Furthermore, piety is rooted in the experiential reality known here as the fear of God in which the believer seeks in no way to presume on God's grace but to do everything possible to be an embodiment of truth and godliness. Mere morality is insufficient. Spener writes:

> . . . Our whole Christian religion consists of the inner man or the new man, whose soul is faith and whose expressions are the fruits of life, and all sermons should be aimed at this. On the one hand, the precious benefactions of God, which are directed toward this inner man, should be presented in such a way that faith, and hence the inner man may ever be strengthened more and more. On the other hand, works should be so set in motion that we may by no means be content merely to have the people refrain from outward vices and practice outward virtues and thus be concerned only with the outward man, which the ethics of the heathen can also accomplish, but that we lay the right foundation in the heart, show that what does not proceed from this foundation is mere hypocrisy, and hence accustom the people first to work on what is inward (awaken love of God and neighbor through suitable means) and only then act accordingly.[42]

Here is Pietism! The perennial themes are all present: the new man; faith and its fruits; sermons aimed at edification and the creation of this "new man"; all external works are rooted in an inner soil and are sourced from a heart invested in the works. The congruity of the inner and outer is the assumed nature of piety.

Theologically, the key concept at this point is the *Wiedergeburt* or the second or new birth upon which theme Spener preached over sixty sermons.[43] The congruence of faith and its fruits is rooted in the work of God in the re-creation of the human heart or the creation of the new person. This act of God takes place in three stages: the kindling of faith, since, for Spener, the new birth brings forth faith, faith does not bring forth the new birth; second, justification and the adoption as children of God occurs; finally there is the completion of the new person. In all of this, the human person is passive just as, in natural life, conception and birth are passive and the person "comes into being." What this stress on the new birth allowed Spener to do was to establish a theological foundation for a stress on sanctification or a growth in holiness. For Spener, a complete doctrine of redemption required that one speak not only of Christ's work in justification but also of his role in sanctification. It would be an anomaly to him if a person were justified but unchanged. For Spener, therefore, a person was changed from the inside out and as a tree brings forth its fruit so a regenerated person ought to yield its fruit.[44] And with this, the experiential element receives a primal place although experience as such does not produce the new birth and experience as such is not a criterion for the new birth. What Spener sought to establish was that God's work for us in Christ does not exclude one's participation in this work of God but draws the human person into the sphere of God's creative activity. As Spener said in the quotation cited at the beginning of this section: "Our whole Christian religion consists of the inner man or the new man, whose soul is faith and whose expressions are the fruits of life. . . ."

August Hermann Francke (1663–1727)

Francke was a close friend of Spener and might be called Spener's Melancthon. He was the organizational genius of Pietism. Francke's father, trained in law, spent his life serving in the upper echelons of society and in civil service, one responsibility of which was to be the supervisor for the reconstruction of an area devastated by the Thirty Years War. Here young Hermann got insight which later served him well as he created the social programs at Halle. As might be expected, Arndt was staple spiritual food in the Francke household.

Francke was trained as a classicist and as a Hebrew scholar, receiving a master's degree in 1685. In 1686 he and his friend Paul Anton began to gather students together to read the Bible in Hebrew and Greek and called it the *Collegium Philo-biblicum*. What was new was that the scriptures were discussed, not merely for ascertaining a theology but for nurture of the spirit. There Leipzig students met for spiritual edification. Francke was ordained in June 1690 and served in Erfurt where he distinguished himself in catechetical work. His ministry in Halle commenced in 1691 when he became a professor of Greek at the newly formed university, where the express object of education was an education toward living an exemplary and intentional Christian life. At about the same time, he became pastor of St. George's Church in Glaucha, a suburb of Halle.

Francke had a dramatic conversion experience in 1686.[45] Spener did not. Despite his own experience, Francke never delineated a method of conversion or an order of conversion. But he, like Spener, spoke of the foundational character of the new birth. The following summary of Francke's sermon on the new birth will illustrate his views, a sermon preached in 1697 on Trinity Sunday, based on John 3:1–6.

Luther spoke of the doctrine of justification by grace through faith as the doctrine by which the church stood or fell. Francke virtually assigns the same place to the doctrine of rebirth—it is the ground upon which Christianity stands and is in its own way a doctrine of recreation. When one is born of God, one receives a divine nature, manner, mind and character.

This rebirth comes about through the word of God as Law and Gospel. The Law shows one how he or she lives in sin, stripping one of any self-righteousness and, finally, striking the person down in defenselessness. In Francke's metaphor, the law is a plow opening the soil to the seed of the Word of God as Gospel. The Gospel is the good seed of grace, which, when received in faith, has the power to come to life in a person regenerating the person from within.

Likewise baptism is what Francke calls a "means of rebirth."

However, Francke does not treat baptism as working merely by the virtue of its administration, but baptism is to be kept in a living relation to faith so that in effect faith is the continuation of the baptismal act. Persons can fall from baptismal grace by ceasing to trust in Christ, by just assuming their acceptability on the basis of a past act totally divorced from present circumstances. For persons who have not remained in a living baptismal faith, Francke teaches that they must undergo rebirth.

Spener taught an identical position. He spoke of the power of baptism to regenerate and, citing Luther, to effect the forgiveness of sins and grant eternal salvation.[46] But then, like Francke, he warns his people not to pervert their baptism into a false sense of justification.

> Thereby these blind people turn the holy intention of God upside down. Your God has indeed given you Baptism and you may be baptized only once. But he has made a covenant with you—from his side a covenant of grace and from your side a covenant of faith and good conscience. This covenant must last through your whole life. It will be in vain that you comfort yourself in your Baptism and in its promise of grace and salvation if for your part you do not also remain in the covenant of faith and a good conscience, or having departed therefrom, return to it with sincere repentance. Accordingly, if your Baptism is to benefit you, it must remain in constant use throughout your life.[47]

Thus repentance takes place in the context of the betrayal of baptism, when, by the preaching of the law, one comes to an experiential awareness of one's shame, of one's hypocrisy and of how one has not loved God's will from the heart.

Francke calls upon such persons to acknowledge the rightness of the Law's judgment and to let the Gospel not only forgive sin but recreate the person from the inside out. While Spener and Francke both stressed the new birth, Francke showed a more specific interest in conversion and the struggle of repentance and particularly the role of law and discipline as a way of forming life. In fact all of his educational theory had in mind the formation of the Christian persons, designed to lead one to repentance and

then to preserve one in that new life. Manfred Kohl has summarized the *élan vital* of this process from Francke's writings.

1. *Realization of one's invalidity and sinfulness.* One is to reach
one's vanishing point before the new can arise. Is this similar
to AA's having to hit bottom before a true recovery from alco-
holism can be made?

2. *Recognition of divine illumination.* Resulting from point 1,
this illumination, engendered by divine activity, helps one to
see oneself truly and admit what one is. Here Pietism understands illumination, not as a light to the mind in order to
understand truth but as an illumination of the will in order to
do the truth, including the performance of the very primal
move, namely the grace to repent.

3. *Experience of God's act of conversion.* As one experiences the
battle of repentance and the struggle against the old nature,
God's grace works its change in persons so that by the power
of the Holy Spirit one can both love and do what God
commands.

4. *Assurance of salvation.* Along with the grace and power of
new life, one now is aware of God's working in one's life and
thus enjoys assurance.

5. *The walk of the re-created one.* The new person enjoys not
only a new relation with God but a new style of life. Francke
distinguished between a risk-taking-faith (Glaubens-Wagnisse)
and the faith present in rational Christianity (Vernunfts-
Christenthum). The person who is newly born undertakes
new ministries theretofore untried or attempts to renew relationships that have virtually dissolved. Faith acts in love and
lives in hope that God's promises will come to pass in one's
obedience of faith.[48]

This demonstrates very clearly both the dimension of depth
and the experiential character of Pietism's concern for a new life
and a new walk. But point 5 also adds a crucial dimension to the
spirituality of Pietism, namely its active character. Francke's category of risk-taking-faith entails what I have called the *experimental* character of Pietism.

EXPERIMENTAL ASPECTS OF PIETISM

The Pietists fostered new ideas and proposals by which to engender congruence of the faith preached and the faith practiced. Classical Lutheran Pietism was not quietistic. Energized by the promises of God, the Pietists sought to find ways or occasions by which a growing congruence between the church's profession and practice might be effected. It is important to note that they did not view themselves as engineering these changes, as for example might be inferred from Charles Finney's assertion that there is a cause-effect relation between the use of certain means and the production of a certain end, namely revivals. To be sure, Francke did see a close relation between his educational methods and the onset of conversion, but he, like Spener, had another source of confidence that renewal would come to the church and regeneration to persons. I refer to their confidence in the promise of God for better times for the church. Implied in this notion of promise is that only God knows the times and reasons for the fulfillment of these promises and hence no human being can speak of a cause-effect relation between certain proposals for renewal and their immediate fruition. But the obedience of faith seeks ways of ministry that offer both to God and the church the occasions by which renewal might come. By its very nature, Christianity thrives on a risk-taking-faith.

Spener, convinced of Scripture's promise for better times, writes:

> Since this has been promised to us by God, the fulfillment of the promise must necessarily follow in time, inasmuch as not a word of the Lord will fall to the ground and remain without fruit. While hoping for such fruit, however, it is not enough idly to wait for it and be killed by desire . . . but it is incumbent on all of us to see to it that as much as possible is done, on the one hand, to convert the Jews and weaken the spiritual power of the papacy, and on the other hand to reform our church. Even if it may be evident that we cannot achieve the whole and complete purpose, we can at least do as much as possible.[49]

Lying behind this passage is, of course, Scripture. Spener understood Hosea 3:4–5 and Romans 11:25–26 to teach the conversion of the Jews after the full number of the Gentiles had been converted. Furthermore, he understood Revelation 18 and 19 to teach the triumph of the evangelical church over the papacy. But in order for these two events to come to pass, the entire church needed to be reborn because, as Spener avers, given the debilitated conditions of the church, no outsider would want to come in. Stated another way, the church lacked a social apologetic. The lives of persons and the lives of congregations did not commend the gospel. The orthodox concern for purity of doctrine needed to be matched with an equal concern for purity of life. As Spener instinctively knew, the gospel is commended both by logic and by life. Hence to some extent the credibility of the gospel is connected with consistency of life, both of persons and of congregations. To be sure, this is from the point of view of those *perceiving* the church and persons. For this reason, Arndt and Spener both struggle with some kind of "necessary" connection between faith and works, although the latter never contributes anything to the substance of salvation. The fruits of faith do attract people to Christ and do become the signs of the work of Christ in the lives of people. But how does one establish an occasion for such a social apologetic to take shape?

Spener had preached a sermon in which he assailed hypocrisy among Christians, especially among those who lean on the doctrine of justification by grace through faith as though it justifies whatever course of life they take. A lay member of the congregation at Frankfurt asked Spener for guidance in how to live a more consistent life and how to use the Bible to that end. Spener proposed that members of the congregation be invited to come to a small group meeting, usually referred to as a conventicle. The Monday conventicle heard the Sunday sermon summarized and then discussed it. Then a large portion of time was given over to prayer. Sometimes English devotional writings were read in German translation.[50]

How did the Pietists understand the practice of Bible reading since Scripture discussion dominated the conventicle? Both Spener[51] and Francke[52] wrote guides for reading Scripture, a summary comparison of which follows. Both agree that it is preferable to learn the languages in which Scripture is written and that it is most advantageous to read entire books. Francke counsels the reader to pay close attention to what the text commands, teaches, and promises, or to what one is to believe, to do and to hope. Both Spener and Francke stress in particular how one is to enact and to embody Scripture. Spener: "All knowledge of God and his will . . . does not exist in mere knowing but must come forth in praxis and action." In the process of obeying the word, the word becomes clearer and its truthfulness reinforced. Francke: "Remember that you may know no truth in Scripture for which you will not have to give an account (I Timothy 6:14), of whether you have transformed it into life as one transforms food and drink into flesh and blood." In this emphasis on "doing the word" they follow Arndt who tried to show that Jesus placed doing before teaching.[53] This activistic reading of Scripture fits well with Francke's view of risk-taking-faith wherein as one obeys Scripture, Scripture vindicates itself and him or her who has faith in its promise.

In addition, Scripture stands in close relation to the doctrine of the priesthood of all believers. The Reformers spoke of the "perspicuity" or clarity of the Scriptures, thereby meaning that Scripture was open and plain to any reader and that its meaning was not contingent on the teaching authority of the church. The reading and interpretation is a priestly work, pertinent to any Christian. This also means that Christians are to speak the Scriptures to each other in rebuke or encouragement. For that reason, Christians are to know Scripture. But the Christian is not just to speak words. Francke admonishes believers to know more than the literal meaning of words and sentences. By the aid of the Holy Spirit, the reader of Scripture is to know the "mind" and the "emotions" of the Apostles so that such may also become a part of the reader.[54] When the Pietists sought to know the "mind" and "emotions," they were cognizant that communication is more than the use of words. Communication includes the investment of persons in their communication. Thus, the Apostles were not just mouthpieces. What they said, they said with conviction. So when the Christian communicates in the exercise of his/her priesthood, he/she does more than recite words. Persons communicate themselves. The communication of the gospel is to be done faithfully to the gospel and with the feeling of the gospel. To read Scripture is to read the mind of the Apostle. Communication, on this score, is also communion, both in relation to Scripture and its authors and in relation to those who speak and here Scripture.

The conventicle provided an ideal place for communication and communion. It was ideal for discipline and discernment. But for Spener, the conventicle was a parallel idea to the notion of the new person. Just as the individual is renewed from the inside out, so is the church. The conventicle, as a group of awakened and committed people, is the ideal means by which to renew the church. It earned the name, *ecclesiolae in ecclesia,* the little churches in the church. It is the place where Scripture is read, interpreted and implemented—an experiment in obedient faith.

Spener then made six concrete proposals—an experiment in faith based on God's promised better times for the church.

1. *A more extensive use of the word of God.* In this proposition he seeks to use more of the Bible in teaching and preaching than what was prescribed in the pericopes for each Sunday and a more sustained encounter with Scripture by use of the conventicle.

2. *More exercise of the Spiritual priesthood.* In this proposal Spener seeks to lay the groundwork for developing a lay ministry. That there was a need for such is illustrated by the 1688 report of Johan Winckler in Hamburg who wondered how in the world he could care for thirty thousand souls? If the conventicles could develop properly and lay persons assume their rightful priesthood, then renewal had a chance and pastoral care could truly be pastoral.[55]

3. *It is not enough to have knowledge of Christianity, for Christianity consists of practice.* In this thesis, Spener seeks to show how Christianity comes to life in one's circumstances and how in particular each Christian needs a confessor.

4. *Great care must be exercised in the conduct of religious controversies.* The erring must be enlightened but in such a way that conduct enhances the teaching, i.e. the *practice* of Christianity is part of the apologetic in any defense of the gospel or reproof of error. When this new spirit is present, it even

enhances the chance for an ecumenism that does not rest on dogma alone.

5. *Seminaries are to be places of spiritual formation, not just places of intellectual exercises.* As Spener says, " . . . study without piety is worthless." Theology is a practical discipline which thrives in a school which is a "workshop of the Holy Spirit."

6. *Seminaries are to provide practical experience in ministry.* Professors are to take students with them on pastoral calls. In particular, homiletical instruction is to aim at edification of believers and not at polemical warfare.[56]

The proposals are modest and, in a way, non-programmatic. But they are an experimental venture.

Count Ludwig von Zinzendorf (1700–1760)

Other Pietists were programmatic. Count Ludwig von Zinzendorf was from an aristocratic family, was a godson of Spener and had been a student at Halle where he was an active member of conventicles. He left the study of law at Wittenberg, purchased an estate at Berthelsdorf at Dresden which he opened to refugees from Moravia in 1722, and named in Herrnhut—the Lord's watch. The community was made up of Lutherans, Brethren, Reformed, Separatists, and Roman Catholics which eventuated in tensions. In August of 1727, a visitation of the Holy Spirit created the occasion for reconciliation and renewal of relationships.

The idea of an *ecclesiola in ecclesia* was given a highly specialized role at Herrnhut, so much so that Stoeffler argues that Spener's *ecclesiola* became a distinct religious society under Zinzendorf where life was governed by a religious ideal.[57] He organized the entire community into ten choirs, not of the musical variety but groups organized according to sex, age and marital status for purposes of discipline, direction, discernment, confession of faults and prayer. Choirs in turn had bands, groups of two or three, for purposes of more personal care and individual attention.

The *ecclesiola* idea was extended to the idea of a *tropus* which was used in Greek to describe ways of training. Zinzendorf considered each denomination as a *tropus* in the one great body of Christ. Thus each church group was a school by means of which God taught his truth. Each denominational group is a temporary station on the way to a greater unity, the upshot of which is to relativize the claims of all churches. Zinzendorf viewed the Moravians as a *tropus* whose function it was to engender renewal and a sense of mission to the world in each tradition hastening the day when the church of Christ might become one. Thus the Moravians were servants of all of the churches.

Zinzendorf's understanding of the vocation of the Moravians as *tropoi* in and among the churches led to another major concept, namely that of the *Diaspora*. The Moravian *Diaspora*, based on I Peter 1:1, was the scattering of teams of Moravians throughout the Christian world as missioners of renewal and unity. Thus, an innovation begun experimentally in faith by Spener became an expert instrument in the hands of Zinzendorf.[58]

The piety at Herrnhut was more cheerful than at Halle. The stress at Herrnhut was not on the struggle of repentance but on the joy of the gift of salvation. The context for this lyrical piety was in part rooted in a familial understanding of the Trinity where the Holy Spirit was thought of as the "mother" or the "nurse." Communities filled with the Spirit are gifted at nurturing and inclusiveness.[59]

The intentionality of Zinzendorf is matched by that of Francke, to say nothing of his ingenuity. German Lutheran Pietism is inexplicable apart from two fundamental Lutheran themes: faith and the doctrine of creation. Attention has already been given to faith, what Francke called risk-taking-faith, in contrast to the inert and passive stance of the church, what he called "rational Christianity." Francke, like Luther, thought of faith as "a busy, active, mighty thing" and a "daring confidence in God's grace so sure that the believer would stake his life on it."[60]

Francke did. Horrified at the plight of orphans and challenged by the need for a comprehensive educational system, Francke went to work with virtually no resources but an incredible supply of risk-taking-faith ready to experiment with God. Between 1695 and 1702 four kinds of schools suited to levels of

German society were constructed. By 1698, five hundred had enrolled and the enrollment figure proposed at the time of his death was twenty-three hundred. He began his orphanage by renting rooms in 1695, and in 1698 the number had reached one hundred, and by Easter 1700 the complex was dedicated. In addition, he constructed a hospital, printing press, bookstore and bindery, tailor shop, smithy, carpenter shop and cooper shops.[61]

In the midst of this poverty seeking redress and adversity caused by opponents, Francke launched out. What is striking is that as Francke reports his progress, the work is treated under the rubric of the first article of the Creed, i.e. creation. The omnipotent creator who created the world out of nothing will create out of nothing in our day as well.[62] Hence the risk of faith for Francke is grounded in the doctrine of creation while for Spener the risk of faith is grounded in God's promise. The "piety of Pietism" has a profoundly experimental character, rooted in the conviction that Scripture is not only to be interpreted but also implemented. This piety, like the faith that infused it, is a "living, busy, active, mighty thing."

But piety was not identical with being busy. It was not activity as such but what the activity activated in the recipient that concerned the Pietists. Spener wrote an explanation of Luther's catechism[63] and treated the doctrine of the priesthood of all believers, not in the section on the church but under the commandment prohibiting murder and under the doctrine of Christ. The latter reaction is understandable since Christ was the chief servant. But why the former? Because personal presence is an enormous power. It either evokes intimacy or intimidation. It establishes the environment for communication and communion. That is why the Pietists spoke of the affections as being present in language. The demeanor of the servant has to be caring but not condescending lest the recipient be demeaned. If the service is condescending it "kills" the recipient. The piety of service in the pietistic tradition implies the congruence of word, acts, and affection so that the recipient feels neither put upon nor put down. Piety gives life. Those who serve only with professional acumen but without personal care are called hirelings by Francke because they cannot create "new tempers" or, we might say, new dispositions.[64] The Pietists understood piety to be a creative force, capable of engendering faith, hope and love in people, a derivative no doubt of their strong doctrine of creation. True piety, the congruence of words, acts, and love, activates the person's will to meaning and prepares the person for the hearing of the gospel, which is the aim of Pietism's social apologetic.

CONCLUSION

Cotton Mather referred to Pietism as "the fire of God which . . . flames in the heart of Germany." Fire is an appropriate metaphor in two ways. First it picks up the emotional warmth generated by the experience of God's free grace. Second, fire spreads. So did Pietism. Both the Halle and Herrnhut varieties spread to the Baltic states and Scandinavia, to England by the enormous influence of Bengel on Wesley, to America by Halle's influence on Muhlenberg (the patriarch of American Lutheranism) and by Cotton Mather's correspondence with Francke and by the rise of the missionary movement. Finally, in the great immigrations of the 1800's Pietism came to America both as part of established traditions such as the Hauge Movement among Norwegian Lutherans and in the churches spawned by the movement such as the Covenant Church in Sweden or the United Brethren from German background before its merger with Methodism.

Pietists need to be careful. In being serious about a true congruity between the inner will and outer action, an unhealthy scrupulosity often develops resulting in moralism, not piety. Likewise, the experiential and subjective components of Pietism are vulnerable to the quest for new experiences to outdo the previous one. That is an unhealthy compulsiveness and a debilitating narcissism. Finally, Pietists need to learn the distinction between withdrawing from worldliness and withdrawing from the world. The latter has been all too characteristic. All Pietists would be helped if they viewed piety as for the greater glory of God and the good of the neighbor rather than as a source of personal gratification. That would go a long way toward equalizing the experiential and the experimental.

NOTES

1. From Cotton Mather, *Nuncia bona e Terra Longinqua* (1715) quoted in John T. McNeill, *Modern Christian Movements* (Philadelphia: The Westminster Press, 1954), p. 74.

2. This definition is the author's. It can be found originally in the author's dissertation "The Eschatological Ethics of Johann Albrecht Bengel: Personal and Ecclesial Piety and the Literature of Edification in the Letters to the Seven Churches in Revelation 2 and 3" (Ph.D. dissertation, Northwestern University, 1983), p. 2. Hereafter references to this work will be abbreviated as "JAB: Ethics and Piety."

3. Quoted in Amand Saintes, *A Critical History of Rationalism in Germany* (London: Simpkin, Marshall, and Co., 1849), p. 51.

4. Louis Gottschalk and Donald Lach, *Europe and the Modern World*, Vol. I: *The Rise of Modern Europe* (Chicago, et al.: Scott Foresman and Co., 1951), p. 306.

5. W.H. Bruford, *Germany in the Eighteenth Century: The Social Background of the Literary Revival* (Cambridge: At The University Press, 1965), pp. 152–53.

6. Ibid., pp. 154–155.

7. See Gottlieb Geiss, *Johann Albrecht Bengel Gottesgelehrter und Ewigkeitsmensch* (Giessen und Basel: Brunnen-Verlag, 1933), p. 69 and Heinrich Hermelink, *Geschichte der Evangelische Kirche in Württemberg von der Reformation bis zus Gegenwart* (Stuttgart und Tübingen: Ranier Wunderlich Verlag Herman Leins, 1949), pp. 208–209.

8. Theodore E. Tappert, "Orthodoxism, Pietism, and Rationalism," in Harold C. Letts, ed., *Christian Social Responsibility*, Vol 1: *The Lutheran Heritage* (Philadephia: Muhlenburg Press, 1957), p. 42.

9. F. Ernest Stoeffler, *The Rise of Evangelical Pietism* (Leiden: E. J. Brill, 1971), p. 181.

10. Tappert, "Orthodoxism, Pietism, and Rationalism," p. 43.

11. Ibid.

12. Robert G. Clouse, *The Church in the Age of Orthodoxy and the Enlightenment*, Church in History Series (St. Louis: Concordia Publishing House, 1980), pp. 45–48.

13. Colin Brown, *Philosophy and the Christian Faith* (Downers Grove: Inter Varsity Press, 1968), pp. 53–57.

14. *Encyclopedia Britannica,* 1971 ed., s.v. "Gottfried Wilhelm Leibnitz," by Marcel Karman, pp. 913–916.

15. F. Ernest Stoeffler, *German Pietism During the Eighteenth Century* (Leiden: E. J. Brill, 1973), p. 36.

16. *Encyclopedia Britannica,* 1971 ed., s.v. "Christian Wolff," by Ruth Lydia Saw, pp. 617–618.

17. *A Memoir of the Life and Writings of John Albert Bengel* compiled by John Christian Frederic Burk and translated by Robert Francis Walker (London: William Ball, 1837), p. 57.

18. Ibid., p. 55.

19. For an extended discussion of this, see the collection of theological comments in Heinrich Schmid, *The Doctrinal Theology of the Evangelical Lutheran Church,* trans. Charles A. Hay and Henry E. Jacobs (Philadelphia: 1876; reprinted by the Augsburg Publishing House, 1961), pp. 407–499.

20. Allan C. Deeter, "An Historical and Theological Introduction to Philipp Jakob Spener's *Pia Desideria:* A Study in Early German Pietism" (Ph.D. dissertation, Princeton University, 1963), pp. 10–12. The citation of the reference to education is found in Carl Philipp Mortiz, *Anton Reiser,* tr. P. E. Matheson, "World's Classics" (Oxford: Oxford University Press, 1926), pp. 98ff.

21. Tappert, "Orthodoxism, Pietism, and Rationalism," pp. 39–40.

22. Jaroslav Pelikan, *From Luther to Kierkegaard* (St. Louis: Concordia Publishing House, 1950), pp. 57–66.

23. Ernst Benz, *Die Protestantische Thebias* (Wiesbaden: Franz Steiner Verlag, 1963), pp. 16–19, 129–131.

24. For a technical discussion of this problem cf. F. Bente, *Historical Introductions to the Book of Concord* (St. Louis: Concordia Publishing House, 1965), pp. 112–124. For a more "popular"

discussion cf. Eugene F. Klug and Otto F. Stahlke, *Getting Into the Formula of Concord* (St. Louis: Concordia Publishing House, 1977), pp. 38–41.

25. Einar Billing, *Our Calling*, trans. Conrad Bergendoff, Facet Books (Philadelphia: Fortress Press, 1947), pp. 15 and 35.

26. In W.H. Auden, *Collected Shorter Poems 1927–1937* (New York: Random House, 1937), p. 193.

27. This data is summarized from the material found in *Johann Arndt*, trans. and Introduction by Peter Erb and Preface by Hieko Obermann, Classics of Western Spirituality (New York, et al.: Paulist Press, 1979), pp. 1–12 and Johann Arndt, *True Christianity: A Treatise on Sincere Repentance, True Faith, The Holy Walk of the True Christian, etc.*, trans. A.W. Boehm, new Am. ed. with Introduction by Charles F. Schaeffer (Philadelphia: General Council Publication House, 1906), Intro., pp. xi ff. Quotations used in this essay are quoted from this text and will be cited as *TC*, book no., chap. no., paragraph and page.

28. *TC*, Preface to the First Book, par. 1. XXXXIX. Book I. x. 1. 27.

29. Ibid., I. XXXIX. 3. 133.

30. Ibid., I. XXXIX. 6. 134.

31. Ibid., II. Concl. 1. 374.

32. *The Book of Concord*, ed. and trans. Theodore G. Tappert (Philadelphia: Fortress Press, 1959), Small Catechism, p. 343. 5–6.

33. Ibid., Formula of Concord, Epitome, Article III, p. 473. #4.

34. Martin Schmidt, "Philipp Jakob Spener und die Bibel," *Pietismus und Bibel*, hsgb. von Kurt Aland, Arbeiten Zur Geschichte der Pietismus, 9 (Witten: Luther-Verlag, 1970), pp. 14, 15, and 27.

35. *TC*, I. XXI. 10. 68. This footnote covers both the quote and the expression, "Fear of God."

36. Ibid., I. XI. 18. 34.

37. Johan Albrecht Bengel, *Sechzig Erbauliche Reden über die Offenbarung Johannes oder vielmehr Jesu Christi samt einer Nachlese gleichen Inhalts*, 2 aufl. (Stuttgart: Johann Christian Erhard, 1758), pp. 747–749. Hereafter cited as *SeR* and the page. See also his *Gnomon*, Übersetzt von C.F. Werner und Vorwort von

Egon Gerdes und von Johann Albrecht Bengel, 2 Bände (Stutt-gart: J.F. Steinkopf Verlag, 1970), II. 841. And *Erklärte Offenba-rung Johannis oder vielmehr, Jesu Christi*, 3. aufl. (Stuttgart: Johann Christoph Erhard, 1758) pp. 756–764. Hereafter abbreviated as *EO*.

38. *SeR*, pp. 750–752, 1033.

39. Ibid., p. 845.

40. Ibid., p. 749 and *EO*, pp. 756–764.

41. *EO*, p. 544. The entire section on Bengel draws heavily on the author's dissertation *JAB: Ethics and Piety*, pp. 101–106.

42. *Pia Desideria*, trans., ed. and Introduction by Theodore G. Tappert, Seminar Editions (Philadelphia: Fortress Press, 1964), pp. 116–117. Hereafter this work will be abbreviated as *PD*.

43. In abridged form, some of these sermons are now avail-able in Philipp Jakob Spener, *Von der Wiedergeburt*, hsgb. Hans-Georg Feller (Stuttgart: J.F. Steinkopf Verlag, 1963). A corollary work of Spener's should also be mentioned: *Der neue Mensch*, hsgb. Hans-Georg Feller (Stuttgart: J.F. Steinkopf Verlag, 1966). The unabridged edition of the sermons on the new birth is *Der Hochwichtige Articul von der Wiedergeburt* (Frankfurt: 1696).

44. This summary paragraph depends on the work of Manfred Kohl, "*Wiedergeburt* as the Central Theme in Pietism," *Covenant Quarterly* 32 (November, 1974), pp. 15–20. Cf. Stoef-fler, *The Rise of Evangelical Pietism*, pp. 240–241.

45. Francke's narrative of this experience can be found in translation in Gary Sattler's work, *God's Glory, Neighbor's Good* (Chicago: Covenant Press, 1982), pp. 29–33. The summary of Francke's sermon on the new birth comes from pages 133–153.

46. *PD*, p. 63.

47. Ibid., p. 66.

48. Kohl, "*Wiedergeburt* as the Central Theme in Pietism," pp. 22–23. I have added some personal commentary to each point.

49. *PD*, p. 78.

50. Deeter, "An Historical and Theological Introduction to Philipp Jakob Spener's *Pia Desideria*," pp. 146–149.

51. "The Necessary and Useful Reading of the Holy Scrip-tures" (1694), in *Pietists: Selected Writings*, ed. and with Introduc-

tion by Peter C. Erb and Preface by F. Ernest Stoeffler, The Classics of Western Spirituality (New York, et al.: Paulist Press, 1983), pp. 71–75.

52. "Scriptural Rules of Life" (1695), in Sattler, *God's Glory, Neighbor's Good*, Part II, nos. 26–31, pp. 222–226.

53. *TC*, I. XI. 1. 29.

54. Francke also wrote *A Guide to the Reading and Study of the Holy Scripture*, trans. and augmented with notes by William Jacques, First American ed. from the last London ed. (Philadelphia: David Hogan, 1823). This is a complete guide to how to study the Bible according to the spirit and letter with an extensive discussion of the affections of the apostles and the important relation between the affections and language.

55. John T. McNeill, *A History of the Cure of Souls* (New York, et al.: Harper Torchbooks, 1951), p. 183.

56. These six proposals are summarized from *PD*, pp. 87–118. Spener wrote an entire catechism dealing with the priesthood of all believers called *The Spiritual Priesthood*, trans. A.G. Voight, Lutheran Monograph Series (Philadelphia: The Lutheran Publication Society, 1917).

57. Stoeffler, *German Pietism in the Eighteenth Century*, p. 196.

58. This summary of Zinzendorf's contributions is heavily indebted to Howard Snyder, "Pietism, Moravianism, and Methodism as Renewal Movements: A Comparative and Thematic Study" (Ph.D. dissertation, University of Notre Dame, 1983), pp. 84–101 and 196–202. An important primary source at this point is Zinzendorf, *Maxims, Theological Ideas and Sentences, Out of the Present Ordinary of the Brethren's Churches*, extracted by J. Gambold (London: J. Beecroft, 1751). Another important primary source is Zinzendorf, *Nine Public Lectures on Important Subjects in Religion*, trans. and ed. by George W. Forell (Iowa City: University of Iowa Press, 1973).

59. Kohl, "Wiedergeburt as the Central Theme in Pietism," p. 26 and Synder, "Pietism, Moravianism . . .," pp. 207–208.

60. *Luther's Works*, ed. Jaroslav Pelikan (St. Louis: Concordia Publishing House and Philadelphia: Fortress Press, 1955–1976), 35: 370–371.

61. This summary is dependent upon Sattler, *God's Glory, Neighbor's Good*, pp. 57–59 and 60ff; Stoeffler, *German Pietism*

During the Eighteenth Century, pp. 25–26 and James O. Duke, "Pietism Versus the Establishment: The Halle Phase," *Covenant Quarterly* 36 (November, 1978):8.

62. August Hermann Francke, *Segens-Volle Fussstapfen des noch lebenden und waltenden leibreichen und getreuen Gottes/Zur Beschämung der Unglaubens und Stärckung des Glaubens entdecket durch eine wahrhafte und umständliche Nachricht von dem Wäysen-Hause und Übrigen Anstalten zu Glaucha vor Halle* (Halle: im Verlegung des Wäysen-Hauses, 1709). This contains reports year by year of Francke's work together with letters from his supporters.

63. Philipp Jakob Spener, *Einfältige Erklärung der Christlichen Lehr Nach der Ordnung dess Kleinen Catechismi dess Theuren Manns Gottes Lutheri* (Frankfurt: Johann Dietrich Friedgen, 1677), Q. 232, p. 135.

64. August Hermann Francke, *Pietas Hallensis Or a Publick Demonstration of the Foot-Steps of a Divine Being Yet in the World In a Historical Narration of the Orphan House and Other Charitable Institutions at Glaucha near Halle in Saxony*, n.t. (London: J. Downing, 1705), pp. 192–193.

David Lowes Watson
METHODIST SPIRITUALITY

I. WESLEYAN FOUNDATIONS

Methodist spirituality begins of course with John Wesley. This is not to say that the spirituality which emerged with a distinctively Methodist imprint did not have roots in the writings by which Wesley was guided and formed in his spiritual pilgrimage; nor yet is it to imply that Methodist spirituality was uniquely Wesleyan.[1] Even so, it was Wesley who gave shape to the Methodist movement, and his spiritual insights provided its bedrock. His genius was to create a theological synthesis between the two major strands of English Protestant spirituality—Anglican holiness of intent and Puritan inward assurance—and apply it in the practical outworking of an accountable discipleship.

1. Anglican Holiness of Intent

By John Wesley's own account, it was while he was a student at Oxford that he began to seek a more disciplined spiritual life by following the advice given by Bishop Jeremy Taylor in *Rules for Holy Living and Dying*. "I began to take a more exact Account than I had done before, of the manner wherein I spent my Time, writing down how I had employed every Hour."[2] He notes that he was "exceedingly affected" by "that part in particular which relates to *purity of intention*. Instantly I resolved to dedicate *all my life* to God, *all* my thoughts, and words, and actions, being thoroughly convinced, there was no medium; but that *every part* of my life (not *some* only) must either be a sacrifice to God or myself, that is, in effect, to the devil."[3]

Taylor is perhaps *the* exemplar of Anglican spirituality. He

217

described the purpose of life as a constant walk with God, so that personal holiness was the necessary concern of the Christian. And since the goal in life was perfection, even the perfection which was in Christ, sin had to be strictly analyzed and overcome. For faith, "if it be true, living and justifying, cannot be separated from a good life. It works miracles . . . and makes us diligently to do, and cheerfully to suffer, whatsoever God hath placed in our way to heaven."[4]

A concern for right intent, however, was not to be pursued in a spiritual vacuum. Taylor saw the continuing life of the visible church, with its sacraments and observances, as at once the setting and the means of implementation for the growth of a personal spiritual life. From the very beginning of the Reformation, liturgy had played an important part in the English church. Drawing on the doctrines and liturgies of the Eastern church, the English reformers had provided corporate spiritual disciplines—as, for example, in the *Book of Common Prayer*. And the touchstone of this spirituality was a concern to avoid any disjuncture between what was holy and what was experienced in the world. The focus of spiritual discernment was to see God at work in the spectrum of daily life.

Nor yet was holiness of intent to be pursued for its own sake, but rather as a means of opening the whole of one's life to the will of God. It was to infuse one's works with divine grace, which alone could ensure that they were good. As Wesley was to note in the opening paragraphs of *A Plain Account of Christian Perfection*, "the giving even *all my life* to God (supposing it possible to do this and go no farther) would profit me nothing, unless I *gave my heart*, yea, *all my heart*, to him. I saw that 'simplicity of intention, and purity of affection,' *one design* in all we speak or do, and *one desire* ruling all our tempers, are indeed 'the wings of the soul,' without which she can never ascend to the mount of God."[5]

Wesley's conviction of the need for inward holiness of intent was further confirmed by his reading of Thomas à Kempis' *Christian Pattern*[6] and William Law's *Christian Perfection* and *Serious Call*.[7] Like Taylor, Law regarded the end of salvation as the regeneration of the *imago Dei*, perfection in the very likeness of God, but with a focus on the will:

This doctrine does not suppose, that we have no need of divine grace, or that it is in our own power to make ourselves perfect. It only supposes, that through the want of a *sincere* intention of pleasing God in *all our actions,* we fall into such irregularities of life, as by the *ordinary* means of grace, we should have power to avoid.

And that we have not that perfection, which our present state of grace makes us capable of, because we do not so much as *intend* to have it.[8]

A right intention, marking a transformation of the will, would change Christians, and through them, the world:

And when you have this *intention to please God in all your actions, as the happiest and best thing in the world,* you will find in you as great an aversion to everything that is *vain* and *impertinent* in common life. . . . You will be as fearful of living in any foolish way, as you are now fearful of neglecting the publick Worship.

Now who that wants this general sincere *intention,* can be reckon'd a Christian? And yet if it was amongst Christians, it would change the whole face of the world; true piety, and exemplary holiness, would be as common and visible, as *buying* and *selling,* or any trade in life.[9]

Wesley's relationship with Law continued for some years, exposing him to a High Churchmanship rooted in the patristic writings and traditions. Yet the context of these years of spiritual development was to prove just as important as the expansion of his reading. In 1729, he had returned to Oxford to assume the duties of his fellowship at Lincoln College, and had found himself acting as spiritual mentor to a group of students, known as the "Holy Club," which included his brother Charles. The group had made a commitment to engage in the intentional disciplines of personal and corporate devotions, especially the study of the Scriptures and frequent holy communion, and to pursue an inquiry into the liturgical and devotional practices of the early church.[10] But they were also committed to works of practical charity in the city of Oxford, among the poor, the illiterate, and the imprisoned.

Wesley was thus engaged in a twofold spiritual formation. In his readings, he imbibed some of the greatest writings in the Roman Catholic mystical tradition—those of Pascal, Fenelon, de Renty, and the *Theologia Germanica,* for example—and, through "Macarius the Egyptian," the Byzantine tradition of spirituality, in which the Christian life is seen as a growth toward a goal rather than a static state. But he was also engaged in an active discipleship in the world, which was to have a profound effect on the spiritual leadership which he exercised through the Methodist societies.

2. Puritan Assurance

Yet the very mysticism of Wesley's spirituality was dialectical.[11] He perceived the path to perfection to be a constant tension between the irresistibility of the will of God and the resistance of the human will empowered by prevenient grace.[12] And it was at this point that he drew on the great riches of the Puritan tradition, most particularly on its doctrine of the "inner witness," the assurance that comes from the indwelling Spirit of God.

Wesley was indebted primarily to the Moravians for his introduction to this spiritual heritage. Beginning with a shared voyage to Georgia in 1735, when Wesley was sufficiently impressed by a group of them on board to learn German so that he might converse with them more freely, they brought him to see that a perfectionism of right intent and right endeavor lacked the Augustinian dimension of grace. While William Law's mysticism could instruct in the spiritual self-discipline through which a person could find God, it did little to foster an expectancy of the divine initiative. As opposed to the "stern, objective, moralistic piety of High Churchmanship,"[13] Moravian piety was a discerning of the pattern of God's initiative toward the believer.

During his stay in Georgia, Wesley remained in dialogue with the Moravians, though they would not permit him to join their community. When he pressed them for conditions of acceptance, he was told by one of their members, John Toltschig, that the first step in the spiritual formation which they practiced was to try to "lead people out of themselves," so that the "word of power" might break in on them and "pierce them through." When they

were thus "apprehended by grace," their souls were tended so
that they might grow in grace from one step to the next. But persons were not admitted into full fellowship until they had "genuine forgiveness of sins" and "peace with God" from which
would proceed a "glad and willing submission" to the Moravian
discipline.[14]

The wrestling which brought John and Charles Wesley alike
to an acceptance of this inward peace is poignantly expressed in
the hymn which, as John was to state in his obituary tribute to
Charles in 1788, no less a writer than Isaac Watts had described
as "worth all the verses he himself had written."[15]

> Come, O thou Traveler unknown,
> Whom still I hold, but cannot see!
> My company before is gone,
> And I am left alone with thee;
> With thee all night I mean to stay,
> And wrestle till the break of day.
>
> . . .
>
> Yield to me now—for I am weak,
> But confident in self-despair!
> Speak to my heart, in blessings speak,
> Be conquered by my instant prayer:
> Speak, or thou never hence shall move,
> And tell me if thy name is LOVE.
>
> . . .
>
> 'Tis Love! 'Tis Love! Thou diedst for me;
> I hear thy whisper in my heart.
> The morning breaks, the shadows flee,
> Pure Universal Love thou art:
> To me, to all, thy bowels move—
> Thy nature, and Thy name, is LOVE.[16]

Wesley came to know this assurance on May 24, 1738, at a
religious society meeting in Aldersgate Street, London, where he
records that his heart was "strangely warmed."[17] The account he
gives of his pilgrimage to that point is a clear indication that he
was appropriating what R. Newton Flew has described as the tra-

dition of "the evangelical succession of believers."[18] It was what
his father had described as the "inward witness," as had the Puritan scholar, John Preston, a hundred years earlier:

> "If any man love me, and keepe my Commandements, I will
> shew myself to him;" that is, hee shall have an extraordinary
> manifestation of my selfe, hee shall have such an expression
> of love and peace and joy, such a thing that no an knowes but
> himselfe. Beloved, this is the testimony of the Spirit. I con-
> fesse, it is a wondrous thing, and if there were not some Chris-
> tians that did feele it, and know it, you might beleeve there
> were no such thing, that it were but a fancie or enthusiasme;
> but, beloved, it is certaine, there are a generation of men, that
> know what this seale of the Lord is.[19]

The traditioning may have been Moravian, but Wesley's
experience at Aldersgate Street was unmistakably the spirit of
Puritanism.[20] When he came to publish the fifty volumes of *A
Christian Library*, consisting of "Extracts from, and Abridgements
of, the choicest Pieces of practical Divinity which have been published in the English Tongue," the list of Puritan authors was
impressive, including Samuel Clarke, Robert Bolton, John Preston, Richard Alleine, John Bunyan, Richard Baxter and Edmund
Calamy.[21]

And indeed, the power of this inward assurance led Wesley
to turn away from the mystical writers for a time—though not
for long. His acceptance of the divine initiative as the *dynamic* of
his spirituality did not negate the importance of spiritual disciplines as its *form*. Nor yet did it negate the impact of mystical writers such as Henry Scougal, who defined true religion as "an
Union of the Soul with God, a real participation of the Divine
Nature, the very image of God drawn upon the Soul, or, in the
Apostles' phrase, it is Christ formed within us."[22] The quest for
Christ-likeness continued to be integral to Wesley's spirituality.

3. Theological Synthesis

The key to Wesley's synthesis of Anglican and Puritan spirituality is discernible first of all in the Oxford Holy Club, where
the name "Methodist" seems first to have been used, initially as

a term of derision. Wesley himself disliked the name, and frequently preferred to use the phrase "The People Called Methodists." But the occasion of the word is significant. These were young men who took the working out of their faith seriously. They engaged in the study of the Scriptures, in private and public prayer, in frequent Holy Communion, and in works of practical piety among the poor and underprivileged people of Oxford. They may have brought to these outworkings an inner pursuit of holy intent, but the form of their spirituality was sufficiently self-evident for others to discern it to the point of ridicule.

Wesley's appropriation of the evangelical tradition, the inward witness of the Spirit, meant that he could now affirm the assurance of faith as a manifest gift of the Spirit, a divine *elenchos*,

> the demonstrative evidence of things unseen, the supernatural evidence of things invisible, not perceivable by eyes of flesh, or by any of our natural senses or faculties. Faith is that divine evidence whereby the spiritual man discerneth God and the things of God. It is with regard to the spiritual world what sense is with regard to the natural. It is the spiritual sensation of every soul that is born of God.[23]

But he did not equate this assurance with salvation, which was at once a more inclusive and a more extensive work of God. For Wesley, salvation in the fullest sense was enfolded in a catholicity of God's initiatives, "from the first dawning of grace in the soul till it is consummated in glory." It began with "what is frequently termed 'natural conscience,' but more properly 'preventing grace'; all the 'drawings of the Father'; the desires after God which, if we yield to them, increase more and more . . . although, it is true, the generality of men stifle them as soon as possible." It proceeded to justifying grace, "another word for pardon," "the forgiveness of all our sins and, what is necessarily implied therein, our acceptance with God," the immediate effect of which was "a peace that passeth all understanding" and "a rejoicing in hope of the glory of God." And then, even at the very moment of justification, there was a real as well as a relative change in the believer, the beginning of sanctification—an inward renewal by the power of God, "expelling the love of the world [and] changing the 'earthly, sensual, devilish mind' into 'the mind that was in Christ Jesus.'"[24]

The significance of this *ordo salutis* is that Wesley's spirituality was accountable to a disciplined theological reflection, in which he was faithful to the tenets of the English Reformation. From the beginnings of Protestantism in the English Church, its theologians had been concerned to retain the necessary place of good works in the doctrine of salvation. And it is no accident that Wesley, after his return from a visit to the Moravian community at Herrnhut in the fall of 1738, should have begun "more narrowly to inquire what the doctrine of the Church of England is concerning the much-controverted point of justification by faith."[25] The following year, he published editions not only of the Anglican Homilies on salvation, faith and good works, but also a treatise on justification by Robert Barnes, who had been one of the first English scholars to study with Luther at Wittenberg.

Under the scrutiny of Wesley's theological reflection, the spiritualities of right intent and divine illumination were brought together in an outworking of grace which was not optional, nor merely fruitful, but necessary. The dynamic of this was a divine initiative which the human will was always able, with the freedom of prevenient grace, to resist. The path to perfection, therefore, was a growth in obedience to the divine initiative—a learning how not to resist the grace of God. And the way to this obedience was through the disciplines of right intent.

The scheme is at once awesome and straightforward. By grace, God permits a freedom of choice to the human creature. Yet because of sin, it is not a freedom to choose between good and evil, but rather between resistance or submission to the divine initiative. When the human will ceases to resist, then grace affords a new relationship with God which, moment by moment, is sustained by grace in obedience. Thus the believer grows in grace, and the mind of Christ is formed within.

Wesley's synthesis was especially distinctive, however, in the further step he took to identify a maturity of obedience which renders the believer so in tune with the will of God that love controls every thought, word and deed—truly a Christian perfection. This does not imply a state which can be attained so much as a stage in the process of sanctification. The work of sanctifying grace is of course limitless. But there is a point at which the new relationship with God in Christ is so sealed that we can, by grace, come to love God "with all our heart, mind, soul and strength," in which "all thoughts, words and deeds are governed by pure love." Such a perfection does not exclude "infirmities, ignorance, and mistake." On this, Wesley was quite clear. The definition of sin which he used in expounding the doctrine was that of a "voluntary transgression of a known law"—which is why he resisted the term "sinless perfection," even though the doctrine connoted a cleansing from sin.[26] There is always the possibility of mistake, of "falling away," or "backsliding," because the faith of the believer, however seasoned and mature, is dependent at all times on an openness to grace, for which the believer is responsible.

Of prior importance, therefore, is the relationship of justifying faith. It is this which is the occasion of spiritual growth, which sustains the believer in an obedient discipleship. In short, grace is the occasion of the whole of Christian discipleship: the discreet invitations of God; the immediacy of a new relationship with God; and the necessary outworking of this relationship in works of obedience which engendered a transformation in the believer. Rather than a state to be *attained,* spiritual communion with God is a relationship to be *sustained* in the midst of a constant twofold struggle of the human will: with residual resistance in the individual sinner, and with the resistance of a world which does not yet acknowledge its sovereign God.

The extent to which Wesley worked through these issues and forged the essence of his theological and spiritual synthesis is evident in a short treatise which he published in 1740, entitled *The Principles of a Methodist.*[27] The next step was how to implement it in the rough and tumble of the eighteenth-century England, where the vanguard of spirituality was a religious revival among common people.

4. Accountable Discipleship

The genius of Methodist spirituality lay in the guidance of ordinary people into a discipleship which, empowered by grace and shaped by the doctrines and ordinances of the church, was accountable for good works. Wesley accomplished this with a connectional polity that remains a paradigm of spiritual formation.

Not that Methodist polity was forged *de novo.* Wesley built first of all on the religious societies of the Church of England which had evolved during the latter years of the seventeenth century. Founded in London and thence throughout the country, they were an expression of the religious hunger which had its parallel in German pietism; and in fact, it was an immigrant Lutheran minister, Anthony Horneck, who initially provided guidance for these groups of young men who wanted a more disciplined spiritual life.[28] They met according to a set of rules, by which they prayed together, sang hymns, conversed on matters of practical religion, and took regular collections of money for distribution to the poor. Before the end of the century, the societies had an extensive organization for the relief of debt, visiting the sick, caring for orphans, and providing up to a hundred schools in London and its suburbs alone.[29]

Though they had ceased to be the movement they once were, there were still many of these societies in existence when Wesley began his evangelistic ministry in 1738. They provided him with a structural base, and, more important, a supportive context. The Anglican emphasis was clear: inward holiness of intent applied to practical works in the world, on the assumption that the world is also God's sphere of salvation.

The importance of the Moravians' influence on the form of Wesley's spirituality lay in their intentional analysis of the divine initiative in the life of a believer.[30] Under the religious freedom afforded by Count Ludwig von Zinzendorf on his estates at Berthelsdorf, they had developed in their Herrnhut community a discipline of internal direction within a residential structure, segregated by age, sex and marital status. The members were assessed by the elders of the community as being "dead," "awaked," "ignorant," "willing disciples," and "disciples that have made a progress."[31]

In smaller groupings, known as *bands,* there was intensive confessional inquiry, an exercise regarded as highly important for the spiritual life of the community. Not only did it foster the spiritual growth of each person; it also engendered a spirituality of *koinonia.* Zinzendorf himself was quite specific:

> This day, twenty years ago, whilst the gospel was being preached at Berthelsdorf, Herrnhut and elsewhere to an

incredible number of people, a gracious wind from the Lord was felt, which was the commencement of an uninterrupted work of the Holy Spirit in Herrnhut during the remainder of the year. The visit of Mary to Elizabeth, which is that day commemorated in the Christian Church, gave rise to the idea of bands, or societies; these were established throughout the whole community the following week, and have been productive of such blessed effects that I believe, without such an institution, the church would never have become what it is now. The Societies called bands consist of a few individuals met together in the name of Jesus, amongst whom Jesus is; who converse together in a particularly cordial and childlike manner, on the whole state of their hearts, and conceal nothing from each other, but who have wholly committed themselves to each other's care in the Lord.[32]

That Wesley was influenced by the bands as a means of spiritual oversight and nurture is apparent from his account of his ministry in Georgia:

Not finding, as yet, any door open for the pursuing our main design, we considered in what manner we might be most useful to the little flock at Savannah. And we agreed (1) to advise the more serious among them to form themselves into a sort of little society, and to meet once or twice a week, in order to reprove, instruct, and exhort one another. (2) To select out of these a smaller number for a more intimate union with each other, which might be forwarded, partly by our conversing singly with each, and partly by inviting them all together to our house; and this, accordingly, we determined to do every Sunday in the afternoon.[33]

Wesley did not use the word "band" to describe these small groups in Savannah, nor yet was there an appreciation of the immediacy evinced by the Moravian fellowship. But clearly he had accepted the importance of intimate fellowship as a form of spiritual oversight. On his return to England early in 1738, and largely as a result of his fellowship with a Moravian, Peter Bohler, he helped to form a society at Fetter Lane in London, which was divided into bands according to the Moravian pattern.

In the months which followed, however, we can discern some

reservations in Wesley's attitude toward the Moravian disciplines. There was, of course, the important experience at Aldersgate Street, where in effect he ceased to become their pupil, and joined them in their assurance of the inner witness. But even more significant was his visit to their community at Herrnhut in the summer of 1738, during which he observed what he felt to be a degree of immaturity in the strict monitoring of their spiritual oversight.[34] He expressed disapproval of this practice in the Fetter Lane Society,[35] and in his own *Rules of the Band Societies,* drawn up in the December of 1738, he stressed the principle of mutual confession and accountability.

In these Band Rules, it was stipulated that the leader, "some person among us," was to "speak his own state first, and then ask the rest, in order, as many and as searching questions as may be," such as:

Have you the forgiveness of your sins? . . .

Have you the witness of God's Spirit with your spirit? . . .

Has no sin, inward or outward, dominion over you? . . .

Do you desire to be told of all your faults? . . .

Do you desire that, in doing this, we should come as close as possible, that we should cut to the quick, and search your heart to the bottom?[36]

And at every meeting, there were five questions to be asked of everyone:

1. What known Sin have you committed since our last meeting?

2. What Temptations have you met with?

3. How was [sic] you delivered?

4. What have you thought, said or done, of which you doubt whether it be a Sin or not?

5. Have you nothing you desire to keep secret?

The bands did not, however, become the basic pattern of Methodist spiritual practice, even though they remained as an important dimension of the movement's connectional polity. To understand why this was so, we must be aware of how Wesley was inexorably drawn into the mainstream of the eighteenth century evangelical revival.[37] The turning point was his venture into "field preaching"—proclaiming the gospel in the open air. He agreed to do this with some reluctance, and did so primarily at the urging of George Whitefield, who was making plans to come to North America. But it proved to be a pivotal move, not only in establishing Methodism as a distinctive component of the Revival, but also in determining the shape of Methodist spirituality.

Field preaching ensured that God's gracious initiative reached people with power and effect—ordinary people, who were "utterly inaccessible every other way,"[38] and who were largely neglected by the Church of England. They heard the gospel message in a manner which moved them deeply, and in some instances converted them soundly. The question then became how to nurture these converts in the faith. A sampling of membership lists of the early societies indicates that by and large they were from the artisan stratum of society. This meant that they had little time, even if they were ready, to engage in the intensive spiritual disciplines to which Wesley, with the leisure afforded by years at Oxford, had applied himself.

In a word, Methodist spirituality was honed by the context of its practice—the necessary, though often neglected, Christian discipline of taking the gospel message into the world. To do so was to find that the illumination of faith was indeed available to all—a witness of the Spirit which was not forensic, but dynamic and organic. People were born of the Spirit, but then had to grow in the Spirit; and the intensive mutual searching of the bands presumed too much of those whose spiritual birth was relatively new and sudden.

As Wesley himself described it, those who responded to the preaching of himself and his brother, and who made a commitment to Christian discipleship, found themselves immediately

surrounded with difficulties;—all the world rose up against them; neighbors, strangers, acquaintances, relations, friends, began to cry out amain, "Be not righteous overmuch; why shouldest thou destroy thyself?" Let not "much religion make thee mad." One, and another, and another came to us, asking what they should do, being distressed on every side; as every one strove to weaken, and none to strengthen, their hands in God. We advised them, "Strengthen you one another. Talk together, as often as you can. . . . "[39]

The implication was clear: the path to perfection did not lie through neutral territory. The disciplines of the spiritual life had to be forged in the immediate reality of a world resistant to its God, in which the Christian had been placed, not to be tested and matured for his or her own sake, but rather as a messenger with the announcement of God's salvation. *Methodist spirituality had a purpose which transcended the personal formation of its practitioners. It was the appropriation and application of those disciplines which equip and empower the believer to be a faithful disciple in the world. The goal of their spiritual pilgrimage was the mind that was in Christ. But their immediate task was to be the ambassadors of God to a sinful and resistant world—of which they were also a part.*[40]

II. THE FORMATION OF METHODIST SPIRITUALITY

1. The Class Meeting: Mutual Accountability

The key to this essentially pragmatic spirituality emerged during a discussion in February, 1742, on how to clear the building debt on the New Room at Bristol. Wesley had personally signed the note, but income had fallen far short of the amount needed; so it was suggested that every member of the society should give a penny a week toward the debt. This seemed to be a good solution, until it was pointed out that not everyone might be able to afford the weekly amount. A retired sea captain, named Foy, then offered to take twelve names, and collect the money personally, putting in himself whatever anyone could not afford. Others offered to do the same, and before long the whole membership had been divided into "little companies, or classes," of twelve according to where they lived, with one person, styled as the leader, to collect the weekly contributions.[41]

As Wesley was to comment in his *Thoughts upon Methodism,* this was the very thing the societies had needed. The class leaders were "the persons who may not only receive the contributions, but also watch over the souls of their brethren."[42] As they made the rounds to collect the weekly contributions, they found themselves involved in the work of spiritual guidance. In some instances, this meant giving advice or even reproof. But more important, the weekly visit was a time of spiritual support and encouragement, for the very reason already cited: that to be a Methodist was not an easy task. Society members were marked persons in the community or the household. They were to be watched, and if possible made to stumble. The society meeting did not always provide a time to give an account of these spiritual battles, but the class leader was there each week to listen and to guide. And in due course, instead of the leader going around to collect the weekly contributions, the members came together to meet with the leader. There had proved to be too many occasions when the leader could not talk with the members alone; besides which, there were misunderstandings which could only be resolved by seeing everyone together, "face to face."[43]

As we might expect from our vantage point of late twentieth-century group dynamics, a sense of Christian fellowship quickly developed. Wesley records that members began to "bear one another's burdens," and to "care for each other." As they now had "a more intimate acquaintance with, so they had a more endeared affection for each other." They felt free to be open with each other, and, "speaking the truth in love, they grew up into Him in all things, who is the head, even Christ."[44]

Many of the classes became as intimate as the bands, especially where the class leader had become skilled and perceptive. It is important to note, therefore, that the bands were by no means neglected. They continued as before, though with significant differences from the classes. The bands were organized according to age, sex and marital status; the classes were divided according to where the members lived. The bands were structured for intensive sharing and mutual confession; the classes were formed around the leaders, whose duties were specified even before the class meetings as such were functioning.

Perhaps the most significant difference was the role of the

leader. Indeed, if there is a pivotal figure in early Methodist spirituality, it is the class leader. Wesley acknowledged this by reserving to himself or his assistants the right to appoint or remove them. He was quick to answer their critics by pointing out that God had "blessed their labour,"[45] and there is little question that they developed into as skilled a group of spiritual mentors as the church has ever produced. They combined spiritual discernment with the practical disciplines necessary for accountable discipleship in the world, and it was largely through their office that ordered guidance and oversight in the societies provided a means of growth and maturity among the members.

Class meetings were much less intense than those of the bands, being a mixture of informality and firmness. They would begin with a hymn and a prayer, and would then proceed to a catechesis. The leader, starting with himself or herself,[46] would ask each member to give an account of the past week's spiritual journey; and in response to each account, the leader would clarify what had been said, and then give appropriate guidance.[47] In addition to the weekly catechesis, the members were examined once each quarter by Wesley or one of his assistant preachers, upon satisfactory completion of which, the member was issued a quarterly class ticket, coded in sequence with a letter of the alphabet. This examination was a quiet way of dropping negligent members, and the ticket was an important symbol of identity.

Class leaders were encouraged from an early date to evaluate the spiritual state of their members. For example, one of the leaders at the Foundery society, Abraham Jones, reported to Wesley on December 12, 1742 that his members "do all walk orderly, & keep close to the Word, and the means of grace." One member complained of being "under strong temptations, as to doubt the being of a God, or of ability to hold out, that if the Lord did not destroy the man of sin in her that it would destroy her."[48] Another Foundery leader, John Hague, reported variously on his members in 1747 that there were those who "retain their confidence in the Lord," are "shut up in a fog," are "very dead, and yet very sore," are "earnestly seeking the Lord," and "appear to have a desire, and to be widely seeking something."[49] When class papers were later introduced to record the weekly attendance and contribution of each member, there was a column in which the leader was to insert the letter "a" for one who was "awakened," a period for one who "professed justification," and a colon for one who professed the "perfect love of God."[50] The language may be dated, but the principle was profound: *No dimension of human existence is devoid of the grace of God.*

2. A Catholicity of Grace

It was this very principle which proved to be the occasion of Wesley's rift with the Moravians, causing him to leave the Fetter Lane society and base his London activities at the old Foundery in Moorfields. The issue surfaced initially as a dispute over the efficacy of the means of grace, and in particular whether a person should receive the sacrament without "full assurance of faith." There were those in the Moravian community who advocated a "stillness" in waiting for this gift from God, a "quietism" which might have been practicable in the refined seclusion of Herrnhut, but which for ordinary people in the city of London was leading to damaging self-doubt. Wesley's position was clear:

> (1) There are means of grace—that is, outward ordinances— whereby the faith that brings salvation is conveyed to them who before had it not; (2) that one of these means is the Lord's Supper; and (3) that he who has not this faith ought to wait for it in the use both of this and of the other means which God hath ordained.[51]

The implications were to prove significant for the course of Methodist spirituality. Having come to acknowledge, and to receive, the gift of inward assurance, Wesley did not thereby deny the efficacy of grace in the lives of those who had not. The following month, after a long conversation with Philip Molther, the Moravian who was responsible for most of this "quietism" at Fetter Lane, Wesley recorded what he perceived to be their differences:

> As to faith, you believe:
> 1. There are no degrees of faith, and that no man has any degree of it before all things in him are become new, before he has the full assurance of faith, the abiding witness of the Spirit, or the clear perception that Christ dwelleth in him. . . .

Whereas I believe:
1. There are degrees in faith, and that a man may have some degree of it before all things in him are become new—before he has the full assurance of faith, the abiding witness of the Spirit, or the clear perception that Christ dwelleth in him.
2. Accordingly, I believe there is a degree of justifying faith (and consequently a state of justification) short of, and commonly antecedent to, this. . . .

As to the way to faith, you believe:
That the way to attain it is to wait for Christ, and be still— that is, Not to use (what we term) the means of grace; . . (Because you believe these are not means of grace; that is, do not ordinarily convey God's grace to unbelievers; . . .); Not to do temporal good; Nor to attempt doing spiritual good. (Because, you believe, no fruit of the Spirit is given by those who have it not themselves; . . .)

Whereas I believe:
The way to attain it is to wait for Christ and be still;
In using all the means of grace.
Therefore I believe it right for him who knows he has not faith (that is, that conquering faith),
To go to church;
To communicate;
To fast;
To use as much private prayer as he can, and
To read the Scripture.
(Because I believe these are 'means of grace'; that is, do ordinarily convey God's grace to unbelievers; and
That it is possible for a man to use them, without trusting in them.)
To do all the temporal good he can; And to endeavour after doing spiritual good.
(Because I know many fruits of the Spirit are given by those who have them not themselves;
And that those who have not faith, or but in the lowest degree, may have more light from God, more wisdom for the guiding of other souls, than many that are strong in faith.)[52]

This statement might well have been a blueprint for *The Nature, Design, and General Rules of the United Societies,* published in 1743. Only one pre-condition was required of those who wished to join—"a desire to flee from the wrath to come, to be saved from their sins." But it was expected that all who wished to *continue* in a society should give evidence of this desire in three ways: First, "by doing no harm, by avoiding evil in every kind." Second, by "doing good of every possible sort, and as far as possible, to all men." Third, by "attending upon all the ordinances of God. Such are, the public worship of God; the ministry of the word, either read or expounded; the supper of the Lord; family and private prayer; searching the scriptures; and fasting, or abstinence."[53]

In one stroke, Methodist discipleship and spirituality were fused in a catholicity of grace. God awakens, invites, draws a sinner into the way of salvation, the assurance of which is a justifying faith. But because this gift of new life is real, and not forensic, it cannot not be regarded as an isolated occurrence.[54] It is preceded by grace, and then nurtured by grace. Wesley could not regard those who were "doing the best they could" as beyond God's plan of salvation any more than he could regard those who were "striving for perfection" as falling short of it.[55]

The class meeting was where all of these variables found a place. Since the means of grace were ordinances of the visible church, and since grace was the dynamic of every level of spirituality, no person, whether beginning the quest for faith or advancing to its fullness, could afford to disregard these basic disciplines. Nor yet could they neglect the works of obedience—doing no harm, and doing every possible good—for these were the outworkings of grace in the world.

3. The Path to Perfection

The bands, on the other hand, continued to function in the Methodist societies as a means of grace for those who wanted and needed some "means of closer union." Band members were those who, "being justified by faith," had peace with God. They "felt a more tender affection than before"; they were "partakers of like precious faith." They

> poured out their souls into each other's bosom. Indeed they
> had great need so to do; for the war was not over, as they had

supposed; but they still had to wrestle both with flesh and blood, and with principalities and powers: So that temptations were on every side; and often temptations of such a kind, as they knew not how to speak in a class; in which persons of every sort, young and old, men and women, met together.[56]

Band members were accordingly held more strictly accountable than the classes. In the December of 1744, Wesley provided them a set of Directions which particularized the General Rules. Their class tickets were marked with the letter "b" in addition to the quarterly code letter, identifying them as those within a society who were firmly committed to the quest for Christian perfection. And there evolved in due course a meeting known as the *public bands,* or the *body band,* when all the band members of a society met together, with a preacher presiding, for a time of intimate mutual sharing.

A further means of grace which at first was the privilege of band members only was the *lovefeast.* Wesley had been introduced to this practice of the early church by the Moravians, and had incorporated it into the rules of the Fetter Lane society. A lovefeast was a common meal, usually consisting of bread distributed by the stewards of the society, and water, or sometimes tea, passed around in a "loving-cup." There would be testimonies from those present, spontaneous prayers, and the singing of hymns; and frequently, when the Spirit moved with power among the company, they would remain in prayer and testimony well into the night.[57]

The quest for Christian perfection was most clearly expressed, however, in the formation of an even more intimate grouping, the *select societies.* Wesley's purpose in forming these groups was to direct those members whom he regarded as "continually walking in the light of God, and having fellowship with the Father, and with his Son Jesus Christ," in the path to perfection. In these meetings, the members learned how to "improve every talent they had received," how to "love one another more, and to watch carefully over each other." And Wesley also notes, with a disarming disclosure of his own spiritual quest, that the select societies consisted of those "to whom I might unbosom myself on all occasions, without reserve; and whom I could propose to their brethren as a pattern of love, of holiness, and of good works."[58] There were no rules for these groups, since they had "the best rule of all in their hearts." They were free to share in their fellowship, speaking openly, with no leader appointed.

It is important to note that the progression to membership of a select society seems frequently to have included a period of "backsliding" and "recovering." Those who "fell from the faith, either all at once, by falling into known, wilful sin; or gradually, and almost insensibly, by giving way in what they called little things," and whose fall was not checked by "exhortations and prayers used among the believers," were classified by Wesley as *penitents,* and given special instruction and advice. Those who "recovered the ground they had lost" proved even stronger in the faith, "being more watchful than ever, and more meek and lowly."[59]

This was another instance where the synthesis of Wesley's spirituality was proved in practice. The striving for perfection was the conscious desire on the part of the band member for holiness of right intent; but the occasion of this striving was justifying grace, the inward assurance. Even though a believer might be advanced in the faith, the relationship could be broken at any time by disobedience, resulting not only in a lack of spiritual progress, but in a breach, however temporary, of the new relationship with God. Christian perfection, therefore, was a consistency of relationship with God in Christ, sustained by disciplined obedience; and those pressing on to perfection were to be accountable no less than those who were awakened. They were to seek the gift of perfect love,

> not in careless indifference, or indolent inactivity; but in vigorous, universal obedience, in a zealous keeping of all the commandments, in watchfulness and painfulness. . . . It is true, we receive it by simple faith; But God does not, will not, give that faith, unless we seek it with all diligence, in the way which he hath ordained.[60]

The center of this perfect love was Christ, and Christ alone; and the path to perfection lay in obedience to Christ, a constant trust in his forgiveness and reconciliation. In the closing months of his life, Wesley could still write: "I do not believe any single person in your Select Society scruples saying, 'Every moment, Lord, I need the merit of thy death.'"[61]

4. The Means of Grace

As we shall see, the doctrine of Christian perfection came to prominence and took on new forms in the spirituality of nineteenth-century Methodism. But in its eighteenth-century origins, the Wesleyan dialectic is clear: Whatever experience of the Holy Spirit might be granted to a person by grace, the means of grace were the necessary structure of that person's spiritual life.

Nowhere is this more clearly articulated than in the tract known as *The Large Minutes,* an abstract of various annual conference minutes, in which Wesley gave definitive shape to Methodist polity, including the spiritual disciplines he enjoined upon his preachers. These are worth excerpting in detail, for they represent as well as anything in his writings the taproot of Methodist spiritual formation.

> We might consider those that are with us as our pupils; into whose behaviour and studies we should enquire every day. Should we not frequently ask each, Do you walk closely with God? Have you now fellowship with the Father and the Son? At what hour do you rise? Do you punctually observe the morning and evening hour of retirement? Do you spend the day in the manner which we advise? Do you converse seriously, usefully, and closely? To be more particular: Do you use all the means of grace yourself, and enforce the use of them on all other persons?
>
> They are either Instituted or Prudential:
>
> I. *The Instituted* are,
>
> (1) Prayer; private, family, public; consisting of deprecation, petition, intercession, and thanksgiving. Do you use each of these? Do you use private prayer every morning and evening? if you can, at five in the evening; and the hour before or after morning preaching? Do you forecast daily, wherever you are, how to secure these hours? Do you avow it

everywhere? Do you ask everywhere, "Have you family prayer?" Do you retire at five o'clock?

(2) Searching the Scriptures by,

(i) Reading: Constantly, some part of every day; regularly, all the Bible in order; carefully, with the Notes; seriously, with prayer before and after; fruitfully, immediately practising what you learn there?

(ii) Meditating: At set times? by any rule?

(iii) Hearing: Every morning? carefully; with prayer before, at, after; immediately putting in practice? Have you a New Testament always about you?

(3) The Lord's supper: Do you use this at every opportunity? with solemn prayer before; with earnest and deliberate self-devotion?

(4) Fasting: How do you fast every Friday?

(5) Christian conference: Are you convinced how important and how difficult it is to "order your conversation right?" Is it "always in grace? seasoned with salt? meet to minister grace to the hearers?" Do not you converse too long at a time? Is not an hour commonly enough? Would it not be well always to have a determinate end in view; and to pray before and after it?

II. *Prudential Means* we may use either as common Christians, as Methodists, as Preachers, or as Assistants.

(1) As common Christians. What particular rules have you in order to grow in grace? What arts of holy living?

(2) As Methodists. Do you never miss your class, or Band?

(3) As Preachers. Do you meet every society; also the Leaders and Bands, if any?

(4) As Assistants. Have you thoroughly considered your office; and do you make a conscience of executing every part of it?

   These means may be used without fruit: But there are some means which cannot; namely, watching, denying ourselves, taking up our cross, exercise of the presence of God.

(1) Do you steadily watch against the world, the devil, yourselves, your besetting sin?

(2) Do you deny yourself every useless pleasure of sense, imagination, honour? Are you temperate in all things? instance in food: Do you use only that kind and that degree which is best for your body and soul? Do you see the necessity of this?

(3) Do you eat no flesh suppers? no late suppers?

(4) Do you eat no more at each meal than is necessary? Are you not heavy or drowsy after dinner?

(5) Do you use only that kind and that degree of drink which is best for your body and soul?

(6) Do you drink water? Why not? Did you ever? Why did you leave it off? If not for health, when will you begin again? today?

(7) How often do you drink wine or ale? every day? Do you want it?

(8) Wherein do you "take up your cross daily?" Do you cheerfully bear your cross (whatever is grievous to nature) as a gift of God, and labour to profit thereby?

(9) Do you endeavour to set God always before you; to see his eye continually fixed upon you? Never can you use these means but a blessing will ensue. And the more you use them, the more you will grow in grace.[62]

5. The Hymns of Methodism

To all of which, we must add the hymns of early Methodism, in which the means of grace came to matchless expression. Most of them were written by Charles Wesley, though John exercised considerable editorial responsibility, and added a number of important translations, notably of German hymns. Rightly does the preface to the 1933 British Methodist Hymn Book begin with the simple statement, "Methodism was born in song." The Wesleys took the tunes of the day, some by serious composers such as Handel, some popular, some rowdy, and set words to them which gave the society members a ready means of articulating their deepest beliefs.

The definitive edition published in Wesley's lifetime was the 1780 *Collection of Hymns for the Use of the People called Methodists.* This was for many years the standard referent for every dimension of Methodist spiritual life. It went through countless editions, and was issued in many formats, for use in pocket, pew and pulpit. As I write, I have in front of me the copy which was used by my great-great-grandfather, George Watson, of Shotley Bridge, Northumberland, England. It is one of the many popular editions of the mid-nineteenth century, solidly bound, and designed to be carried to and from Sunday worship as well as the weekly class meetings. There is no date of publication, though the inscription is dated January 1, 1856.

The list of contents gives an indication of the breadth and the depth of this distinctively Methodist means of grace:

PART FIRST

SECTION I. Exhorting Sinners to return to God

       II. Describing, 1. The Pleasantness of Religion
                         2. The goodness of God
                         3. Death
                         4. Judgment
                         5. Heaven
                         6. Hell

      III. Praying for a Blessing

PART SECOND

SECTION I. Describing Formal Religion
       II.   Inward Religion

PART THIRD

SECTION I. Praying for Repentance
       II. For Mourners convinced of Sin
     III. For Persons convinced of Backsliding
     IV. For Backsliders recovered

PART FOURTH

SECTION I. For Believers Rejoicing
       II.   Fighting
     III.   Praying
     IV.   Watching
      V.   Working
     VI.   Suffering
    VII.   Seeking for Full Redemption
   VIII.   Saved
     IX.   Interceding for the World

PART FIFTH

ADDITIONAL HYMNS

SUPPLEMENT

Since the Collection is once again available, and in a new and scholarly edition, this is not the place to cite the hymns in any detail. But one can at least be reproduced as an example of the worldly compassion of Methodist spirituality and the depth of its experience both:

Sinners, obey the gospel word!
Haste to the supper of my Lord,
Be wise to know your gracious day!
All things are ready; come away!

Ready the Father is to own
And kiss his late-returning son;

Ready your loving Saviour stands,
And spreads for you his bleeding hands.

Ready the Spirit of his Love
Just now the stony to remove;
To' apply and witness with the blood,
And wash and seal the sons of God.

Ready for you the angels wait,
To triumph in your blest estate:
Tuning their harps, they long to praise
The wonders of redeeming grace.

The Father, Son, and Holy Ghost,
Is ready, with their shining host:
All heaven is ready to resound,
"The dead's alive! the lost is found!"

Come, then, ye sinners, to your Lord,
In Christ to paradise restored;
His proffer'd benefits embrace,
The plenitude of gospel grace:

A pardon written with his blood,
The favour and the peace of God;
The seeing eye, the feeling sense,
The mystic joys of penitence:

The godly grief, the pleasing smart,
The meltings of a broken heart;
The tears that tell your sins forgiven,
The sighs that waft your souls to heaven:

The guiltless shame, the sweet distress;
The' unutterable tenderness;
The genuine, meek humility;
The wonder, "Why such love to me!"

The' o'erwhelming power of saving grace,
The sight that veils the seraph's face;
The speechless awe that dares not move,
And all the silent heaven of love.[63]

III. THE PRACTICE OF METHODIST SPIRITUALITY

Two Biographical Vignettes

In 1778, John Wesley founded the *Arminian Magazine*.[64] As the title suggests, it was intended in part to be a polemical publication, though this purpose was quickly subsumed by Wesley's broader vision of the Christian life. The early issues, and especially those which appeared in Wesley's lifetime, are a goldmine of Methodist spirituality, not least because Wesley asked a number of his early preachers to submit vignettes of their Christian pilgrimages. Many of these accounts were later compiled by Thomas Jackson in *The Lives of Early Methodist Preachers*, one of the classics of Methodist spirituality,[65] from which we shall make two brief selections: an excerpt from the account of John Nelson, one of Wesley's most faithful assistants; and from that of Thomas Rankin, who spent some years in North America as Wesley's superintendent before concluding his ministry in England.

1. John Nelson[66]

John Nelson was born in Yorkshire in 1707, and was trained to be a stone mason, like his father. He had a marked spiritual sensitivity from an early age:

> God had followed me with convictions ever since I was ten
> years old; and whenever I had committed any known sin,
> either against God or man, I used to be so terrified afterwards
> that I shed many tears in private; yet, when I came to my com-
> panions, I wiped my face, and went on again in sin and folly.

His father, who seems to have been a devout man, reading the Scriptures to the family, and ensuring that his children were instructed in the faith, died when John was aged sixteen. That he died at peace with God made a strong impression on the young boy.

At the age of nineteen, John found himself in "great danger of falling into scandalous sins," and prayed that God would give him a wife, "that I might live with her to His glory." He married shortly thereafter, but although they were happy together, he still "loved pleasure more than God." Looking for work, he traveled to London, where his "concern for salvation increased for some time"; but again,

> I looked at men for example, and fell from my seriousness. The workmen cursed and abused me, because I would not drink with them, and spend my money as they did. . . . But when they took my tools from me, and said if I did not drink with them I should not work while they were drinking, that provoked me, so I fought with several of them; then they let me alone. But that stifled my concern for salvation, and I left off prayer and reading in a great measure.

The ensuing years were unsettled, moving between his home in the North of England, and London, where something seemed to be drawing him. When his friends pressed him about this "wandering," he replied: "I have something to learn that I have not yet learned." Here was a man who was clearly being impelled by the gracious initiatives of the Holy Spirit. He had all that a person of his station in life could want or need, yet still he was unsettled:

> I said to myself, "What can I desire that I have not? I enjoy as good health as any man can do; I have as agreeable a wife as I can wish for; I am clothed as well as I can desire; I have, at present, more gold and silver than I have need of; yet still I keep wandering from one part of the kingdom to another, seeking rest, and I cannot find it." Then I cried out, "Oh that I had been a cow, or a sheep!" for I looked back to see how I had spent above thirty years; and thought, rather than live thirty years more so, I would choose strangling. . . . Yet I thought I would set out once more; for I said, "Surely God never made man to be such a riddle to himself, and to leave him so; there must be something in religion, that I am unacquainted with, o satisfy the empty mind of man; or he is in a worse state than the beasts that perish."

The spiritual quest became more intense. He went from church to church, but "found no ease." The preachers he heard seemed to talk about Christian duty: that God required a man "to do all he could, and Christ would make out the rest." But this was of little comfort, since he knew very well that he had not done all that he could. Indeed, if this was the road to salvation, then "none could be saved but little children."

Then he heard George Whitefield proclaim the gospel in Moorfields, preaching like "a man who could play well on an instrument. . . . I loved the man, so that if any one offered to disturb him, I was ready to fight for him. But I did not understand him. . . . " This brought Nelson closer to the moment of spiritual truth, but clearly there was another step still be taken. He was brought closer yet on Sunday, June 17, when he heard Wesley preach in the same place:

> His countenance struck such an awful dread upon me, before I heard him speak, that it made my heart beat like the pendulum of a clock; and, when he did speak, I thought his whole discourse was aimed at me. When he had done, I said, "This man can tell the secrets of my heart: he hath not left me there; for he hath showed the remedy, even the blood of Jesus." Then was my soul filled with consolation, through hope that God for Christ's sake would save me; neither did I doubt in such a manner any more, till within twenty-four hours of the time when the Lord wrote a pardon on my heart.

Nelson continued to hear Wesley preach, and he had "many flashes of love under the word," when he was at prayer and "at the table of the Lord." His friends tried to persuade him "not to go too far in religion," saying they "should be glad to knock Mr. Wesley's brains out," and avowing that "they would not hear him preach for fifty pounds." But Nelson stood his ground, saying that he intended to "seek to be born again, and experience a spiritual birth."

It was the testimony of an old soldier which brought his search to its crisis. The soldier too had been convicted by Wesley's preaching, and likewise had been discouraged by his friends. They had found him reading the Bible, and had dragged him to an ale-house, where he began to reason with them. But it was not long before they had him as drunk as they were—"how dangerous is it to encounter Satan on his ground!"—and this had brought him to the critical point of surrender. One Sunday morning, at Whitehall Chapel, he had gone to receive the sacrament. And no sooner had he received, than he had "found power to believe that Jesus Christ had shed His blood for me, and that God, for His sake, had forgiven my offences. Then was my heart filled with love to God and man; and since then sin hath not had dominion over me."

This testimony deeply affected Nelson. He found his soul "much refreshed" at the sacrament the Sunday after, and was "mightily encouraged" by Wesley's sermon in the afternoon. During the following week, he "felt an awful sense of God" resting upon him, as his own spiritual pilgrimage reached its critical point of surrender:

> When I went back to my lodging at noon, dinner was ready; and the gentlewoman said, "Come, sit down: you have need of your dinner, for you have eaten nothing today." But when I looked on the meat, I said, "Shall such a wretch as I devour the good creatures of God in the state I am now in? No; I deserve to be thrust into hell." I then went into my chamber, shut the door, and fell down on my knees, crying, "Lord, save, or I perish!" When I had prayed till I could pray no more, I got up and walked to and fro, being resolved I would neither eat nor drink til I had found the kingdom of God. I fell downto prayer again, but found no relief; got up and walked again: then tears began to flow from my eyes, like great drops of rain, and I fell on my knees a third time; but now I was as dumb as a beast, and could not put one petition, if it would have saved my soul. I kneeled before the Lord some time, and saw myself a criminal before the Judge; then I said, "Lord, Thy will be done; damn or save!" That moment Jesus Christ was as evidently set before the eye of my mind, as crucified for my sins, as if I had seen Him with my bodily eyes: and in that instant my heart was set at liberty from guilt and tormenting fear, and filled with a calm and serene peace. I could then say, without any dread of fear, "Thou art my Lord and my God." Now did I begin to sing that part of the 12th chapter of Isaiah, "O Lord, I will praise Thee; though Thou wast angry with me, Thine anger is turned away, and Thou comfortest me. Behold, God is my salvation; I will trust,

and not be afraid: for the Lord Jehovah is my strength and my song; He also is become my salvation." My heart was filled with love to God and every soul of man: next to my wife and children, my mother, brethren, and sisters, my greatest enemies had an interest in my prayers; and I cried, "O Lord, give me to see my desire on them: let them experience Thy redeeming love!"

We should note in the narrative the worldly context of Nelson's spiritual journey. As with the old soldier who so impressed him, the struggle was not just with himself, but with the people whom he knew and who knew him. The inner working of grace was rarely without its testing in the world. And indeed, shortly after Nelson's conversion (which, as with so many of these first-hand accounts in the *Arminian Magazine,* took place in private), he found himself faced with the possibility of being thrown out of his job because he would not work on the Sabbath. In spite of the foreman's threats, he stood firm, and found that on the Monday morning his job was still there. The foreman who had told him on Saturday that Wesley had made a fool of him, welcomed him back on Monday with "good words." The character of Methodist spirituality emerges with some cogency—a quest for obedience to God in the midst of worldly living.

We should also note the importance of the sacrament of the Lord's Supper in Nelson's spiritual journey as an efficacious means of grace. It is prominent in Rankin's account also, and it occurs frequently throughout Jackson's *Lives.* Wesley established its priority in Methodist spirituality when he refuted Moravian quietism,[67] and it remained a central focus of his evangelistic ministry. Moreover, as we shall presently observe, it figured prominently in the spirituality of the Second Great Awakening in North America.

Nelson became one of Wesley's most trusted preachers, and the remainder of his account is noteworthy among other things for his arrest and impressment into the army in 1744. This was a hazard for all Methodist preachers, since magistrates could order a man into the military if he did not appear to be gainfully employed—which many clergy were quick to declare that the Methodist preachers were not. Nelson was released after several months, during which time, of course, he continued to preach to his fellow soldiers and to whoever would hear him in the open air. Quite apart from the spiritual testimony, the episode is a fascinating glimpse of life in eighteenth-century England.

2. *Thomas Rankin*[68]

Thomas Rankin was born in Scotland, and, like John Nelson, was "early taught the principles of religion." His father catechized the family (and the servants), and he was likewise catechized at school. At the age of eleven or twelve, he was

> deeply affected at a sacramental occasion, being permitted to stay at the administration of the ordinance. When I saw the ministers and people receive the bread and wine, and heard the address from the former to the communicants, I frequently burst into tears.

The occasion of Rankin's first real exposure to the spirit of the Revival was the visit of a company of dragoons to his home town. Among their number were some who had formed religious societies in Germany under the leadership of John Haime.[69]

> The news of soldiers meeting for prayer and praise, and reading the Word of God, soon spread through the town: curiosity led many to attend their meetings, and I was one of that number. . . . It was not long before several were enabled to testify that they had redemption in the blood of Christ, the forgiveness of all their sins. This soon spread abroad, and made a great noise in the town; . . . but I could not understand them when they spoke of God's Spirit bearing witness with their spirits that they were the children of God. . . . My plea was, "that we might be in the favour of God, and not be assured that our sins were forgiven." I granted, "that some very peculiar holy people might be assured of the divine favour; but that it was not the privilege of all the children of God."

This work of prevenient grace was continued, as Rankin joined the society which was formed as a result of the soldiers' witness; and he was further "awakened" by the visit of some

Methodist preachers. Even though he did not "remember that [they made] any particular impression" upon him, he did remember a conversation with a woman who belonged to the society, and who took him to task for not attending his class meeting regularly. This brought him sufficiently close to his spiritual crisis to make him leave home to seek a resolution to his dilemma.

> The short of the matter was this: I had a sincere desire to serve God and to save my soul, as also to be thought a religious young man; but I had not learned to "sell all for the pearl of great price."

The point of surrender was brought nearer when Rankin heard George Whitefield preaching in Edinburgh; and the tension heightened when the time came for the sacrament to be administered. He went to the table, receiving the bread "with a broken, melting, and expectant heart." But when the cup was passed to him, a little of the wine was spilt on the floor, and "that very moment Satan suggested that 'Christ's blood was spilt for me in vain!' . . . Hopes and fears alternately prevailed, and thus I went on for several weeks." Finally, he came to "wrestle with God in an agony of prayer."

> I called out, "Lord, I have wrestled long, and have not yet prevailed: Oh, let me now prevail!" The whole passage of Jacob's wrestling with the Angel came into my mind; and I called out aloud, "I will not let Thee go, unless Thou bless me!" In a moment the cloud burst, and tears of love flowed form my eyes; when these words were applied to my soul, many times over, "And he blessed him there." They came with the Holy Ghost, and with much assurance; and my whole soul was overwhelmed with the presence of God. Every doubt of my acceptance was now gone, and all my fears fled away as the morning shades before the rising sun. I had the most distinct testimony that all my sins were forgiven through the blood of the covenant, and that I was a child of God, and an heir of eternal glory. What I now felt was very different from what I had experienced of the drawings of the love of God for several years past, and when I first partook of the sacrament. I had now no more doubt of my interest in the Lord Jesus Christ than of my own existence.

Rankin's association with Methodism in Scotland continued, and when he was asked by a relative to undertake a business trip to South Carolina, he clearly missed the fellowship which the societies had afforded. On his return, he noted that his soul had suffered "a real declension," and he saw as never before "the whole economy of Methodism in the most favourable light—the class and band meetings, meeting of the society, body-bands, lovefeasts . . . ; the whole was calculated to promote the great end for which they were designed—the glory of God in the salvation of souls."

Rankin's account then describes his quest for Christian perfection, which, as with his spiritual birth, came to a point of spiritual crisis:

> [As] I was one evening meeting my class, and happy in my soul, I was all on a sudden seized with such horror as I had never known from the time I knew the pardoning love of God. As soon as the meeting was finished, I went home, and retired to private prayer; but all was darkness and painful distress. I found no intercourse with heaven, and faith and prayer seemed to have lost their wings. For five days and nights I went through such distress of soul as made sleep, and the desire of food, depart from me. I could attend to nothing but my painful feelings, and mourn and weep.
>
> On the fifth day two friends called to see me, and we joined in prayer, and I found more liberty than I had experienced during the time of this painful distress. As soon as my friends were gone, I fell down on my knees, and continued in prayer till I went to bed. I now found a degree of sweetness, and communion with my Lord once more; and I closed my eyes with the pleasing sensation. I awoke very early next morning, and with a change in my feelings, that I could scarce allow myself time to dress before I fell upon my knees to praise God; and when on my knees, had such a view of the goodness and love of God as almost overcame every power of body and soul.

Soon thereafter, he felt the call to preach, and began to "exhort" at local society meetings. But the call did not come easily. He found that reactions to his preaching were very mixed, and this caused him on a number of occasions "to resolve to preach no more." Yet the spiritual struggle continued, as Rankin sought "the great salvation, deliverance from inbred sin." Finally, in the September of 1761, he records that the Lord gave him such a discovery of His love as he had never known before:

> I was meeting with a few Christian friends, who were all athirst for entire holiness, and after several had prayed, I also called on the name of the "Deliverer that came out of Zion, to turn away ungodliness from Jacob." While these words were pronounced with my heart and lips, "Are we not, O Lord, the purchase of Thy blood? let us then be redeemed from all iniquity," in a moment the power of God so descended upon my soul, that I could pray no more. It was
>
> That speechless awe which dares not move,
> And all the silent heaven of love![70]

Rankin felt that this was indeed the token of Christian perfection, the "second blessing," which brought him the maturity of perfect love and cleansing from inbred sin. But he continued to have doubts about his calling, and it was Wesley who came to his aid by telling him quite bluntly that he would have no peace until he devoted himself full-time to the work of proclaiming the gospel. He accepted this challenge, became an itinerant Methodist preacher, and then knew the full assurance "thát the Lord Jesus has purified my heart by faith in His blood, and that I felt nothing contrary to the pure love of God." He was admitted to a select society, and placed himself at Wesley's disposal.

From 1773–78, Rankin served as Wesley's superintendent in North America,[71] and these years provide us with a convenient introduction to the next phase of Methodist spirituality, which proved to be North American in origin. For some years after his death, Wesley's influence continued to prevail in British Methodism. His joint emphasis on inward witness and the practical outworking of discipleship continued to find expression through the class meeting and other forms of Methodist spiritual practice.[72] But it was not long before the pressures of nineteenth-century English social change, to some extent engendered by Methodist working class leadership, led to polarities and divisions within the movement.[73] As a result, the spirituality of the class meeting in the main body of Wesleyan Methodism became increasingly pietistic to the point of inbred religiosity, while the momentum of social involvement passed to the breakaway groupings. In particular was this true of the Primitive Methodists, whose spirituality owed much to the North American influences we must now examine: the Second Great Awakening, and the interaction between Christian perfection and revivalism which produced the holiness movement.[74]

IV. THE HOLINESS TRADITION

1. The North American Context: Revivalism and Camp Meetings

It is clear from Rankin's account of his North American ministry that the doctrine of Christian perfection was a normative dimension of his preaching. On Sunday, July 4, 1773, for example, he "found freedom and tenderness to apply the word in a particular manner to those who were groaning for pardon of sin and for purity of heart." And on Sunday, June 30th, 1776, while preaching from Revelation 3:8 [I know thy works: behold, I have set before thee an open door . . .], "the very house seemed to shake, and all the people were overcome with the presence of the Lord God of Israel. . . . From the best accounts we could receive afterwards, upwards of fifty were awakened and brought to the knowledge of a pardoning God that day; besides many who were enabled to witness that the blood of Jesus had cleansed them from all sin."

Yet the preaching and practice of the doctrine in North American Methodism seems from an early date to have had a characteristic emphasis on the instantaneous experience of the gift of perfect love rather than on the process which led to it. Ironically, it was on this very point that Wesley had found the doctrine to be most controversial in England. In the late 1750s, there had been a sharp increase in the number of society members who professed to have received the gift, and in the early 1760s, two of Wesley's preachers, Thomas Maxfield and George Bell, had taken a position which was sufficiently extreme to cause a major reaction against the doctrine altogether.

Wesley's response had been cautious. He had continued to

affirm the instantaneous experience of Christian perfection as a gift of grace, but had warned against isolating the experience from its proper grounding in faith and works.[75] And while the conflict had caused him considerable anguish,[76] it had led to serious examination of the doctrine, culminating in the definitive theological treatment of John Fletcher's *Checks to Antinomianism.*[77]

In North America, however, the context of the doctrine was from the beginning the evangelical fervor of revivalism. The Methodist societies were planted in soil already well fertilized by the spirit of the First Great Awakening, in which the preaching of Jonathan Edwards and George Whitefield had focused on the immediacy of decision, and in which the invitation to the sinner was very direct.[78] The evidence of response to this was a divine inruption of grace, changing the will from the waywardness of sin to God-fearing obedience.[79]

Towards the end of the eighteenth century, there were many in the Congregationalist and Presbyterian Churches who were embarrassed to concede that such an intensive and emotional event could have proceeded from their tradition, which was predominantly Calvinist. Methodist evangelism, on the other hand, was quite openly Arminian. "Whosoever will may come," was the cry. Not only did this adapt well to the revivalist approach to evangelistic outreach; it harmonized well with the democratic theory of the new nation, and was admirably suited to the frontier spirit which stressed enterprise and self-sufficiency.[80] Moreover, by the time the Methodist Episcopal Church was established in 1784, North America was on the threshold of the Second Great Awakening.

Signs of this had begun to emerge in the 1790s, emanating initially from Kentucky—indeed, it was often called "The Great Kentucky Revival."[81] As a movement, it was noted most of all for the camp meeting. Not that the idea of bringing people together for an extended weekend of preaching and devotional renewal was new.[82] But to do it with organized accommodations, thereby establishing it as an institutional gathering, was an innovation; and this is what happened when James McGready, a Presbyterian minister, gave advance notice of a sacramental service to be held at Gasper River, Kentucky, in July of 1800. Hundreds came from miles around, and many brought their own tents, since the crowd was far too large for the Gasper River church to accommodate. It was followed by an even larger gathering the following year at Cane Ridge, where again the sacrament of the Lord's Supper was announced as the culminating act of worship.

The atmosphere of the camp meeting was to set the tone for the revivalism of the nineteenth century. It retained the directness of the challenge to the sinner, and the necessity of an inruption of divine grace upon the human will; but the focus was on the experience of this inruption, rather than the change it wrought per se. The new birth was now something to be measured by the intensity and impact of its manifestation in the convert. Leaping, shouting and convulsive jerking were normative, and Methodist leaders, such as Francis Asbury, Peter Cartwright and William McKendree, who endorsed camp meetings to the point where they became identified as a Methodist institution, found themselves on the crest of a wave of emotional expression which was highly evocative of scenes at Wesley's early outdoor preaching, and which sometimes were difficult to control.[83]

The descriptions of conversion experiences are predictably vivid, as in the testimony of a little girl at the Gasper River camp meeting:

> O he is willing, he is willing—he is come, he is come—O what a sweet Christ he is—O, what a precious Christ he is—O, what a fullness I see in him—O, what a beauty I see in him— O, why was it that I never could believe! that I could never come to Christ before, when Christ was so willing to save me?[84]

Or in an eyewitness account of the Cane Ridge meeting:

> I attended with 18 Presbyterian ministers; and Baptist and Methodist preachers, I do not know how many; all being either preaching or exhorting the distressed with more harmony than could be expected. The governor of our State was with us and encouraging the work. The number of people computed from 10, to 21,000 and the communicants 828. The whole people were serious, all the conversation was of a

religious nature, or calling in question the divinity of the work. Great numbers were on the ground from Friday until the Thursday following, night and day without intermission, engaged in some religious act of worship. They are commonly collected in small circles of 10 or 12, close adjoining another circle and all engaged in singing Watt's and Hart's hymns; and then a minister steps upon a stump or log, and begins an exhortation or sermon, when, as many as can hear collect around him. On Sabbath I saw above 100 candles burning at once and I saw 100 persons at once on the ground crying for mercy, of all ages from 8 to 60 years. . . . When a person is struck down he is carried by others out of the congregation, when some minister converses with and prays for him; afterwards a few gather around and sing a hymn suitable to the case. The whole number brought to the ground, under convictions, were about 1,000, not less. The sensible, the weak, etc., learned and unlearned, the rich and poor, are subjects of it.[85]

Given the pedigree of this critical experience of the indwelling Spirit in Methodist spirituality, it was altogether predictable that Methodism should have embraced and been embraced by the revivalism which received this tremendous second wind at the turn of the century. What provided the distinctive catalyst was the energy and the fervor of a new nation, which rendered the spiritual experience at once a cultural as well as a spiritual phenomenon. As with the common people to whom Wesley had taken the gospel in the previous century, hard labor and long hours perforce rendered their communion with God something which had to be apprehensible in the world where they lived and worked.

The significance of a critical experience in response to the divine initiative cannot therefore be underestimated. There was little time on the frontier for niceties of argument, nor yet for subtleties of spiritual nuance. When life was lived in a tension of survival, the alternative was all too often death. The revivalist preachers therefore attacked human sin head-on. Resistance was to be broken if grace was to inrupt. And what began in the intensive experience of the camp meeting was replayed and relived throughout the year in pulpits and churches across the land.

2. The Way of Holiness

Even so, the emphasis on critical decision was not distinctively Methodist. Nor had it been in Wesley's England, for that matter, where Methodism was by no means the only component of evangelical revival. Where Methodist spirituality proved distinctive in North America was in the affirmation of a second blessing, a critical experience in which the believer was brought to a "cleansing from sin," a further inruption of grace, marked by an overwhelming sense of God's love. The Christian pilgrimage would thereafter be sustained by a total subjection of the human will to the divine initiative.

While this was preached during the early years of Methodism in North America, and was a dimension of the Methodist contribution to the Second Great Awakening, it does not seem to have been prominent in Methodist spiritual life until the 1840s.[86] As a doctrine, it had been incorporated into the first Discipline of the new Methodist Episcopal Church at Baltimore in 1784, at the urging of Thomas Coke and Francis Asbury, the joint superintendents, and with the firm support of the traveling preachers. Provision had been made for bands and select societies to foster its expectation and to nurture those who were so blessed. Yet it was traditioned during the first half century of the new Methodist church primarily through its literature.

Of the leadership responsible for this, perhaps the most important was that of Nathan Bangs. In his widely read *Letters to Young Ministers of the Gospel,* for example, published when he was head of the Methodist Book Concern, he recommended the British Wesleyan scholars, Adam Clarke and Richard Watson, both of whom assumed the doctrine of Christian perfection to be normative. Clarke in particular stressed the importance of the instantaneous experience of Christian perfection.[87] The influence of these writings, along with many American editions of relevant works by Wesley and Fletcher, began to gather momentum in the 1830s, and in 1839 Timothy Merritt, who had already published a treatise on the subject, started a monthly periodical entitled the *Guide to Christian Perfection,* which in the next thirty years was to reach a circulation of some forty thousand.

As with all aspects of Methodist spirituality, however, the impetus for what became known as the Holiness Movement came from the experiences of Methodists themselves, and perhaps the most influential of these was Phoebe Palmer, wife of a noted New York physician, Dr. W.C. Palmer. In 1835, she and her sister sponsored a joint prayer meeting for women of the Allen Street and Mulberry Street Methodist Churches in New York City, which was subsequently opened to men in 1839. Its specific purpose was to promote entire sanctification, and Phoebe emerged as a leading exponent and exemplar of this form of spirituality, declaring her own experience of entire sanctification in 1837. She published hundreds of tracts, and a number of books, though the most important was *The Way of Holiness* (1846), in which she expounded the discovery by one of "the children of Zion" of the "shorter way of getting into this way of holiness" without the "waiting and struggling with the powers of darkness."

SECTION VII

"They are not of this world, even as I am not of the world. I pray not that thou shouldest take them out of the world, but that thou shouldest keep them from the evil."—The prayer of Jesus for his Disciples.

"'Tis done! thou dost this moment save,
With full salvation bless;
Redemption through the blood I have,
And spotless love and peace."

Now that she was so powerfully and experimentally assured of the blessedness of this "shorter way," O, with what ardor of soul did she long to say to every redeemed one, "Ye have been fully redeemed; redeemed from all iniquity, that ye should be unto God a peculiar people, zealous of good works!" . . .

Her now newly-inspired spirit could scarcely conceive of a higher ambition, in the present state of existence, than to be endued with the unction of the Holy One, and then permitted, by the power of the Spirit, to say to every lover of Jesus, "This is the will of God, even *your* sanctification." Jesus, *your* Redeemer, *your* Saviour, waits even now to sanctify you wholly: "and I pray God that your *whole spirit,* and *soul,* and *body,* be preserve blameless unto the coming of our Lord Jesus Christ. Faithful is he that calleth you, who also will do it."

It was in that same hallowed hour when she was first, through the blood of the everlasting covenant, permitted to enter within the veil, and *prove* the blessedness of the "way of holiness," that the weighty responsibilities, and also inconceivably-glorious destination of the believer, were unfolded to her spiritual vision, in a manner inexpressibly surpassing her former perceptions. . . .

Have you brought yourself into this state of blessedness? Is it through your own exertions that this light has been kindled in your heart? were the inquiries which were now urged upon her attention. She deeply felt, as her rt espoinded to these interrogatories, that it was *all* the work of the Spirit; and never before did such a piercing sense of her own demerit and helplessness penetrate her mind as at that hour, while her in ost sould replied, 'Tis from the "Father of lights," the "Giver of every good and perfect gift," that I have received this precious *gift.* Yes, it is a *gift* from God, and to his name be all the glory![88]

Not that the holiness movement was confined to Methodism. It emerged in other denominations with different emphases, as, for example, in the person of Charles Grandison Finney, whose methods in the 1820s in the northeastern states pioneered many of the methods of modern revivalism.[89] Finney turned to a theological career in the 1830s, and was particularly influenced by Wesley's *Plain Account of Christian Perfection,* which he read in 1836, the year after his appointment to the faculty of the newly founded Oberlin College. It was perhaps inevitable that his presence should have quickened the pace of spiritual life at the college, and he records in his memoirs how, during a revival season in 1839, a student asked whether entire sanctification was possible in this life. The president, Asa Mahan, in what seems to have been a very moving reply, affirmed that indeed it was possible, and from then on, as Finney records it, the faculty members committed themselves to seeking perfection in their own lives. This spiritual blessing, along with the declared purpose of the college to pursue the reform of human institutions, made Oberlin a powerful and distinctive force within the holiness movement.[90]

Indeed, the impact of the holiness movement on society was perhaps its most significant dimension, as it had been with the Second Great Awakening. An important outcome of Finney's work in the 1820s had been a host of societies and associations for the improvement of social life, and as revised editions of his works appear, restoring the excisions of the late nineteenth century editions, it is becoming clear just how committed he was to the work of anti-slavery and social reform. Take, for example, this extract from his "letters on revivals," first published in *The Oberlin Evangelist* in 1846:

> Now the great business of the church is to reform the world—to put away every kind of sin. The church of Christ was originally organized to be a body of reformers. The very profession of Christianity implies the profession and virtually an oath to do all that can be done for the universal reformation of the world. The Christian church was designed to make aggressive movements in every direction—to lift up her voice and put forth her energies against iniquity in high and low places—to reform individuals, communities, and governments, and never rest until the kingdom and the greatness of the kingdom under the whole heaven shall be given to the people of the saints of the most High God—until every form of iniquity shall be driven from the earth.
>
> Now when we consider the appropriate business of the church—the very end for which she is organized and for which every Christian vows eternal consecration, and then behold her appalling inconsistencies everywhere apparent, I do not wonder that so many persons are led to avow that the nominal church is apostate from God. When we consider the manner in which the movement in behalf of the slave has been treated by ecclesiastical bodies, by missionary associations, by churches and ministers, throughout the land, is it any wonder that the Church is forsaken of the Spirit of God? . . .
>
> It is amazing to see what excuses are made by ministers for remaining silent in respect to almost every branch of reform.[91]

It was no coincidence that, as the country came to face its severest crisis over the issue of slavery, much of the momentum for abolition of that "peculiar institution" came from the explosive chemistry of revivalism and perfectionism grounded in a sure sense of social justice.[92]

3. The Test of Methodist Spirituality

In the decades leading up to the Civil War, the question of slavery proved to be the crisis of discipleship for the Methodist Episcopal Church. Increasingly, the experience of revivalism was stressed rather than its social obligations; and even Phoebe Palmer found herself compromised on the issue of abolitionism.[93] As a result, the decades saw divisions in the Methodist Episcopal Church. In 1843–44, under the leadership of Orange Scott, the Wesleyan Methodist Church was organized in protest against the absence of a stand on slavery. And at the General Conference of 1844, the issue was avoided by the agreement to divide the Methodist Episcopal Church between north and south—a portent of the war to come. The Wesleyan Methodists became increasingly a holiness church after their separation, and it was the emphasis on entire sanctification which led to the formation of the Free Methodist Church in 1857 following the expulsion from the Genesee Conference of a minister who had taken a stand on the doctrine.[94]

Most important of all, however, and generative of a spiritual tradition in its own right, were the divisions which had early taken place to constitute the African Methodist Episcopal Church (1816), and the African Methodist Episcopal Zion Church (1820). As the heritage of black spirituality emerges from the liberation of a distinctive Christian identity in our own day, it points us to the radical worldliness of a discipleship which follows a Christ who is always to be found in the midst of suffering and oppression.[95]

This is not the place to chronicle the further developments of the holiness movement.[96] It gathered fresh momentum during the years following the Civil War, and for a time it was embraced by the main body of Methodism as the cutting edge of its evangelism. The Palmers conducted highly successful tours, and in 1867 there was formed the National Campmeeting Association for the Promotion of Holiness. As a result of American initiative, the teaching and practice of entire sanctification were further developed at the Keswick Conventions in England, which met annually after 1875.[97] And in turn, the Salvation Army, which grew from the work of William Booth in the east end of London, spread to the United States.[98]

But the movement, always rich in its diversity, found its connection with mainline Methodism increasingly tenuous. In spite of much effort on both sides to maintain unity, separatist tendencies developed, and in the closing years of the century the holiness groups were seen as a threat to church order.[99] The tensions became polarized, and a number of new denominations were formed, the most significant of which was the Church of the Nazarene.[100] The fractures to the spiritual tradition of Methodism caused by these divisions remain with us to this day.

With the stimulus of a bicentennial celebration in 1984, the United Methodist Church is re-examining its spiritual heritage with vigor. *The Upper Room,* founded as a spiritual devotional guide in 1935, and now published in sixty-one editions and forty-three languages throughout one hundred and twenty-five countries, has become the parent organization for a wide range of spiritual ministries at the General Board of Discipleship of the United Methodist Church.[101] Methodists are also discovering that the mutual accountability of the early class meeting is rich in spiritual potential, with its emphasis on the realities of Christian discipleship empowered by the means of grace.[102] Yet there remains the need for renewed dialogue between United Methodism and the churches which comprise the Methodist traditions—the Free and Wesleyan Methodists, the Nazarenes, and the black Methodist denominations. In company with a number of Pentecostal denominations, they have common roots in the spirituality of entire sanctification, and the disputes which led to these divisions have proved to be mutually impoverishing. Not least among the casualties has been the spirituality which once impelled to service in the world, but which now renders social involvement all too often an optional corollary of the inward witness.

For in the final analysis, Methodist spirituality is nothing if not a responsiveness to the divine initiative. And on this, Wesley's word remains definitive and timely: as we yearn for the Spirit to move in our lives and across the world, let us wait, "not in careless indifference, or indolent inactivity; but in vigorous, universal obedience, in a zealous keeping of all the commandments, in watchfulness and painfulness, in denying ourselves and taking up our cross daily, as well as in earnest prayer and fasting, and a close attendance on all the ordinances of God."[103]

NOTES

1. For a full treatment of the spirituality of John Wesley, see the volume edited by Frank Whaling in The Classics of Western Spirituality, *John and Charles Wesley: Selected Writings and Hymns* (New York: Paulist Press, 1981).

2. *The Journal of The Rev. John Wesley, A. M.* Standard Edition, 8 vols., ed. Nehemiah Curnock (London: Robert Culley, 1909): 1:83.

3. "A Plain Account of Christian Perfection," in *The Works of John Wesley*, 14 vols. (London: Wesleyan Conference Office, 1872; repr. ed. Grand Rapids, Michigan: Baker House, 1979), 11:366. Cf. Whaling, *Wesleys*, p. 299.

4. Jeremy Taylor, "The Rules and Exercises of Holy Living" [1650]; "The Rules and Exercises of Holy Dying" [1651], in *The Whole Works of the Right Reverend Jeremy Taylor*, ed. Reginald Heber, rev. & corr. Charles Page Eden, 10 vols. (London, 1862), 4:183. See also 4:49ff., 132ff.

5. Wesley, *Works*, 11:366; Whaling, *Wesleys*, p. 299.

6. This was the title of the contemporary translation of the *Imitatio Christi* which Wesley used. See *The Oxford Edition of the Works of John Wesley, Vol. 25: Letters I:1721–1739*, ed. Frank Baker (Oxford: Clarendon Press, 1980), p. 162, n. 7. See ibid. 9ff. for correspondence between Wesley and his mother on the formative influences of his readings at this time.

7. William Law was a Non-Juror, one of those Anglican clergy whose high view of the church prevented them from taking an oath of allegiance to the king. Initially the Non-Jurors consisted of eight bishops and some four hundred priests who refused to swear loyalty to William and Mary after the ejection of James II in 1688 on the grounds that their oath to the old king was still sacrosanct. For a large part of the eighteenth century, they continued to attract others whose high view of the church

engendered similar sympathies—such as William Law, who, having been ordained in 1711 and elected fellow of Emmanuel College, Cambridge, refused to take the oath of allegiance to George I in 1714, and was deprived of his fellowship. As a group, they made a highly significant contribution to Anglican scholarship.

8. William Law, *A Serious Call to a Devout and Holy Life* (London, 1729), p. 27.

9. Ibid., pp. 18–19.

10. See Richard P. Heitzenrater, *The Elusive Mr. Wesley*, 2 vols. (Nashville: Abingdon Press, 1984), 1:50ff., 63ff. Cf. "A Scheme of Self-Examination," in Whaling, *Wesleys*, pp. 85–87.

11. *The Bicentennial Edition of the Works of John Wesley, Vol. 1: Sermons I: 1–33*, ed. Albert C. Outler (Nashville: Abingdon Press, (1984), p. 75, n. 27. See also ibid., pp. 66–96, where Outler provides a definitive overview of Wesley's sources. This brilliant statement has set the agenda for Wesley studies for the next generation. See also Albert C. Outler, *John Wesley*, Library of Protestant Thought (New York: Oxford University Press, 1964), pp. 8ff., 252.

12. This is best stated in what is arguably Wesley's most significant theological essay, *Thoughts Upon God's Sovereignty, Works*, 10:361–63.

13. John D. Walsh, "Origins of the Evangelical Revival," in *Essays in Modern Church History; in Memory of Norman Sykes*, ed. G.V. Bennet and J.D. Walsh (London: Adam & Charles Black, 1966), p. 142. See also John Walsh, "The Cambridge Methodists," in *Christian Spirituality: Essays in Honor of Gordon Rupp*, ed. Peter Brooks (London: SCM Press, 1975), p. 255.

14. Cited in Martin Schmidt, *John Wesley: A Theological Biography*, Vol. 1 (Nashville: Abingdon Press, n.d.), pp. 161ff.

15. *The Oxford Edition of the Works of John Wesley: Vol. 7: A Collection of Hymns for the use of the People called Methodists*, ed. Franz Hildebrandt and Oliver Beckerlegge, asst. James Dale (Oxford: Clarendon Press, 1983), p. 250n.

16. Ibid., pp. 250–52. See also Whaling, *Wesleys*, pp. 192–94.

17. Wesley, *Journal*, 1:475–76.

18. "Methodism and the Catholic Tradition," in *Northern Catholicism: Centenary Studies in the Oxford and Parallel Movements*,

ed. N.P. Williams and Charles Harris (London: SPCK, 1933), p. 526.

19. *The New Covenant, or The Saints Portion. A Treatise unfolding the All-sufficiencie of God, and Mans Uprightnes, and the Covenant of Grace* (London, 1629), 2:155.

20. As Perry Miller has observed, when Puritanism is considered in the broad perspective of human history, it is not a unique phenomenon. It is "one more instance of a recurring spiritual answer to interrogations eternally posed by human existence . . . yet another manifestation of a piety [which I venture to call] Augustinian . . . simply because Augustine is the arch-examplar of a religious frame of mind of which Puritanism is only one instance out of many in fifteen hundred years of religious history." The Puritan frame of mind, suggests Miller, was "a reliance on the moment of aesthetic vision" as opposed to "a dialectical effort to prove the justice of fact" (*The New England Mind: The Seventeenth Century* [Boston: Beacon Press, 1961], pp. 4–5, 18).

21. For a detailed study of these sources in Wesley, see Robert C. Monk, *John Wesley: His Puritan Heritage* (Nashville: Abingdon Press, 1966). See Appendix I, pp. 255ff., for a listing of the authors as they appeared in the first edition of *A Christian Library*.

22. Henry Scougal, *The Life of God in the Soul of Man; or, The Nature and Excellency of the Christian Religion with Nine Other Discourses on Important Subjects* (London, 1726), p. 4. Scougal is represented in *A Christian Library*, as are many of the mystical writers Wesley read at Oxford. The circumspection with which the selections for this major publication were made is an indication of the richness and diversity of Wesley's own spirituality.

23. "An Earnest Appeal to Men of Reason and Religion," in *The Oxford Edition of the Works of John Wesley, Vol. 11: The Appeals to Men of Reason and Religion and Certain Related Open Letters*, ed. Gerald R. Cragg (Oxford: Clarendon Press, 1975), p. 46.

24. Sermon, "The Scripture Way of Salvation," in *John Wesley*, ed. Albert C. Outler, p. 273. Outler notes that if the Wesleyan theology had to be judged by a single essay, this one would do as well as any and better than most (ibid., p. 171). In addition to the volume already published in the Bicentennial Edition (see above, note 11), three further volumes are in preparation by Outler, to provide a definitive edition of all of Wesley's sermons.

25. *Journal*, 2:101.

26. "A Plain Account of Christian Perfection," in Whaling, *Wesleys*, pp. 327–28. Cf. *Works*, 11:394–96.

27. *Works*, 8:359–74.

28. The standard history of the societies is by Josiah Woodward, *An Account of the Rise and Progress of the Religious Societies in the City of London, &c.* (London, 1698). See also David Lowes Watson, *The Early Methodist Class Meeting: Its Origins and Significance* (Nashville: Discipleship Resources, 1985), where the appendices include all of the various *Rules* which helped to form early Methodist polity, beginning with those of Anthony Horneck.

29. In 1699, the *Society for the Promoting of Christian Knowledge* was founded, becoming a resource for the movement with its literature, and in 1701 the *Society for the Propagation of the Gospel in Foreign Parts* became a missionary wing—helping to sponsor the Wesley brothers in Georgia in 1735.

30. The history of the Moravian communities at Herrnhut, and then in North America, is a study in spirituality in its own right. See Gillian Lindt Gollin, *Moravians in Two Worlds,* (New York: Columbia University Press, 1967).

31. Henry Rimius, *A Candid Narrative of the Rise and Progress of the Herrnhuters, commonly called Moravians, or, Unitas Fratrum* (London, 1753), p. 21.

32. Cited in Clifford W. Towlson, *Moravian and Methodist: Relationships and Influences in the Eighteenth Century* (London: The Epworth Press, 1957), p. 185.

33. *Journal*, 1:197–205. See also ibid., pp. 318–19, and "A Short History of the People Called Methodists," in *Works*, 13:305–06. Wesley regarded the Oxford Holy Club as the "first rise" of Methodism.

34. *Journal*, 2:3–63. Wesley's account of this visit remains a major primary source for Moravian history.

35. *Oxford Edition, Letters I,* pp. 592–93.

36. The *Rules for the Band-Societies* are reproduced in full in Outler, *John Wesley*, pp. 180–81. See also Watson, *Class Meeting,* Appendix E.

37. Frank Whaling's identification of five main streams in the Revival is extremely helpful in this regard. See *Wesleys*, pp. 26ff.

38. "A Farther Appeal to Men of Reason and Religion," in *The Oxford Edition, Vol. 11: The Appeals,* p. 306.

39. "A Plain Account of the People called Methodists," in *Works*, 8:249.

40. Martin Schmidt makes an important observation in this regard, which may explain why Wesley increasingly found himself at odds with the Moravians:

> John Wesley for his part . . . left his followers in their original situations [in contrast with] German Pietism, which set out to make the rebirth or new creation of the whole man and humanity visible in an adequate external form and to extend the work of God into the material sphere, the community of Brethren determining the social structure. Wesley gave full right to the order of creation. . . .

John Wesley: A Theological Biography, Vol. 2 Pt. 1 (Nashville: Abingdon Press, 1972), p. 99.

41. *Journal*, 2:528.

42. *Works*, 13:259.

43. "A Plain Account of the People called Methodists," *Works*, 8:253.

44. Ibid., p. 254.

45. Ibid., pp. 254f.

46. Both women and men served as class leaders, except where the class consisted of men only. This was a mark of the role of women in the movement as a whole.

47. The most detailed contemporary account of a class meeting, and of many other early Methodist practices, is in Joseph Nightingale, *A Portraiture of Methodism* . . . (London, 1807), pp. 181ff.

48. *Oxford Edition, Vol. 26: Letters II: 1740–1755*, ed. Frank Baker (Oxford: Clarendon Press, 1982), p. 95.

49. *Journal*, 3:449–50.

50. See Watson, *Class Meeting*, Appendix L.

51. *Journal*, 2:315.

52. Ibid., pp. 329–30.

53. Outler, *John Wesley*, pp. 177ff.; Whaling, *Wesleys*, pp. 108ff.

54. In a striking analogy, Wesley describes in his sermon, "The New Birth," the similarities between a baby in the womb

and a person who has yet to be "born again." See *Works,* 6:69f. This sermon will appear in Volume 2 of the *Bicentennial Edition,* ed. Albert C. Outler, forthcoming from Abingdon Press.

55. "Minutes of The Second Annual Conference, 1745," in Outler, *John Wesley,* pp. 148–53.

56. "A Plain Account of the People called Methodists," *Works,* 8:257–58.

57. See, for example, Wesley, *Journal,* 1:377; 2:121ff. The best source book on the lovefeast remains Frank Baker's monograph, *Methodism and the Love-Feast* (London: Epworth Press, 1957).

58. "A Plain Account," *Works,* 8:260.

59. Ibid.

60. "A Plain Account of Christian Perfection," in Whaling, *Wesleys,* pp. 335–36. See also *Works,* 11:402–03.

61. *The Letters of The Rev. John Wesley, A.M.* Standard Edition, 8 vols., ed. John Telford (London: Epworth Press, 1931), 8:254.

62. "The Large Minutes," in *Works,* 8:322–24.

63. *Oxford Edition, Vol. 7: A Collection of Hymns,* pp. 90–92. Cf. the list of contents, pp. 77f., which differs in some details from the list cited from my personal copy. See also the very good selection of 121 hymns reproduced in Whaling, *Wesleys,* pp. 175–295.

64. *Arminian Magazine. Consisting of Extracts and Original Treatises on Universal Redemption* (London, 1778–97); renamed the *Methodist Magazine,* 1798–1821; further renamed the *Wesleyan Methodist Magazine,* 1822–1913.

65. Thomas Jackson, ed., *Lives of Early Methodist Preachers,* 4th ed., 6 vols. (London: Wesleyan Conference Office, 1871). An expanded edition, edited by John Telford, includes some annotation and additional biographical material, but lacks the fine index of the fourth edition: *Wesley's Veterans: Lives of Early Methodist Preachers told by Themselves,* 7 vols. (London: Robert Culley, vols. 1 & 2, n.d., vols 3–7, 1912–14).

66. This follows the narrative in *Wesley's Veterans,* 3:1–197, passages cited *passim.*

67. "In the ancient Church, every one who was baptized communicated daily. So in the Acts we read, they 'all continued daily in the breaking of bread, and in prayer.'

"But in latter times many have affirmed that the Lord's Supper is not a converting, but a confirming ordinance.

"And among us it has been diligently taught that none but those who are converted, who have received the Holy Ghost, who are believers in the full sense, ought to communicate.

"But experience shows the gross falsehood of that assertion that the Lord's Supper is not a converting ordinance. Ye are the witnesses. For many now present know, the very beginning of your conversion to God (perhaps, in some, the first deep conviction) was wrought at the Lord's Supper. Now, one single instance of this overthrows the whole assertion.

"The falsehood of the other assertion appears both from Scripture precept and example. Our Lord commanded those very men who were then unconverted, who had not received the Holy Ghost, who (in the full sense of the word) were not believers, to do this 'in remembrance of' Him. Here the precept is clear. And to these He delivered the elements with His own hands. Here is example equally indisputable" (*Journal*, 2:360–61).

68. This follows the narrative in *Wesley's Veterans*, 6:113–97, passages cited *passim*.

69. Haime's ministry among the dragoons, and his subsequent itinerancy as one of Wesley's preachers, is related in *Wesley's Veterans*, 1:11–59.

70. See above.

71. Years which, of course, placed him in the turmoil of the Revolutionary War, though on which he declared it was not his intention "to give a detail, or my judgment . . . suffice it to say, that the business belongs to the historian" (*Wesley's Veterans*, 6:175).

72. On this, see Gordon S. Wakefield, *The Spiritual Life in the Methodist Tradition 1791–1945* (London: Epworth Press, 1966), pp. 44ff.

73. On this, see Robert Currie, *Methodism Divided: A Study in the Sociology of Ecumenicalism* (London: Faber and Faber, 1968). The relatedness of Methodist spirituality to these social changes remains an area of dispute in nineteenth century historiography. See the excellent introductory chapter in Robert Moore, *Pitmen, Preachers and Politics: The Effects of Methodism in a Durham Mining Community* (London: Cambridge University Press, 1974), pp. 1–27.

74. Wakefield, *Spiritual Life*, pp. 56ff.

75. See, for example, "Thoughts on Christian Perfection (1760)," in Outler *John Wesley*, pp. 283–98; "Cautions and Directions Given to the Greatest Professors [i.e. of Christian Perfection] in The Methodist Societies" (1762), ibid., pp. 298–305; and, of course, "A Plain Account of Christian Perfection" (1766), in Whaling, *Wesleys* pp. 299–377.

76. See, for example, the letter to his brother Charles in June 1766, cited, with transcriptions from Wesley's shorthand, in Richard P. Heitzenrater, *The Elusive Mr. Wesley*, 2 vols. (Nashville: Abingdon Press, 1984), 1:198–200.

77. A fine example of Fletcher's craftsmanship can be seen in his exposition of whether Christian perfection is gradual or instantaneous. His answer is disarmingly simple: "Both ways are good." See "The Last Check to Antinomianism," in *The Works of the Rev. John Fletcher, Late Vicar of Madeley*, 8 vols. (London: John Mason, 1846), 5:172ff.

78. Jonathan Edwards' account of this phenomenon in *A Faithful Narrative* made an impression on Wesley when he read it in 1739, and he subsequently published edited versions of several of Edwards' works. See Outler, *John Wesley*, pp. 15f and note.

79. See, for example, *The Works of Jonathan Edwards*, General Editor, Perry Miller, *Volume 2: Religious Affections*, ed. John E. Smith (New Haven: Yale University Press, 1959), pp. 205ff.

80. See Bernard A. Weisberger, *They Gathered at the River: The Story of the Great Revivalists and Their Impact upon Religion in America* (Boston: Little, Brown and Company, 1958), pp. 43ff.

81. Theodore L. Agnew, "Methodism on the Frontier," in *The History of American Methodism*, General Editor, Emory Stevens Bucke, 3 vols. (Nashville: Abingdon Press, 1964), 1:506.

82. Ibid., p. 508.

83. Cf. *The Autobiography of Peter Cartwright*, Centennial Edition, intr. Charles A. Wallis (Nashville: Abingdon Press, 1956), pp. 45–46, and John Wesley, *Journal*, 2:187–91, 139–40, and *passim*. See also Sydney G. Dimond, *The Psychology of the Methodist Revival: An Empirical & Descriptive Study* (London: Oxford University Press, 1926).

84. Cited in Bernard A. Weisberger, *They Gathered at the River*, p. 29.

85. Cited in William Warren Sweet, *The Story of Religion in*

America, repr. (Grand Rapids, Michigan: Baker Book House, 1973), pp. 228–29.

86. John Leland Peters, *Christian Perfection and American Methodism* (Nashville: Abingdon Press, 1956), pp. 97ff. This volume is an important contribution to the study of the doctrine per se, quite apart from its helpful focus on the North American context.

87. Nathan Bangs, *Letters to Young Ministers of the Gospel, on the Importance and Method of Study* (New York: N. Bangs and J. Emory, 1826). Most noteworthy in their writings were Clarke's monumental *Commentary on the Bible*, completed in 1826, and Watson's *Theological Institutes*, published in 1829. Both works have gone through a number of American editions.

88. Phoebe Palmer, *The Way of Holiness* (Kansas City, Missouri: Publishing House of the Pentecostal Church of the Nazarene, n.d.), pp. 34–36. A lengthier extract, comprising Sections I & II, can be found in Thomas A. Langford, *Wesleyan Theology: A Sourcebook* (Durham, North Carolina: The Labyrinth Press, 1984), pp. 86–90. This volume is a valuable introduction to the writings of many whose names have appeared thus far in our narrative— Wesley, Fletcher, Clarke, Bangs, Watson, Asbury—as well as contemporary Methodist authors.

89. See his *Lectures on Revivals of Religion,* ed. William G. McLoughlin (Cambridge: Belknap Press of Harvard University Press, 1960).

90. Cited in Timothy L. Smith, *Revivalism and Social Reform* (New York: Harper & Row, 1965), pp. 103ff. Cf. George M. Marsden, *Fundamentalism and American Culture: The Shaping of Twentieth Century Evangelicalism 1870–1925* (New York: Oxford University Press, 1980), pp. 72ff.

91. *Reflections on Revival (1845–46),* comp. Donald Dayton (Minneapolis, Minnesota: Bethany Fellowship, 1979), pp. 113ff. See also Donald W. Dayton, *Discovering an Evangelical Heritage* (New York: Harper & Row, 1976), pp. 15ff.

92. See Smith, *Revivalism,* pp. 148ff., 178ff., 204ff.

93. Ibid., pp. 211ff.

94. See Dayton, *Evangelical Heritage,* pp. 73–84.

95. See the seminal volume by James H. Cone, *The Spirituals and the Blues: An Interpretation* (New York: Seabury Press, 1972).

96. On this, see Marsden, *Fundamentalism,* pp. 72–101. See

also Timothy L. Smith, "The Holiness Crusade," in Bucke, *American Methodism*, 2:608–27, and "A Historical and Contemporary Appraisal of Wesleyan Theology," in *A Contemporary Wesleyan Theology: Biblical, Systematic, and Practical*, gen. ed. Charles W. Carter, 2 vols. (Grand Rapids, Michigan: Francis Asbury Press of Zondervan Publishing House, 1983), 1:88–94.

97. See J.C. Pollock, *The Keswick Story: The Authorized History of the Keswick Convention* (London: Hodder & Stoughton, 1964).

98. Dayton, *Evangelical Heritage*, pp. 116ff.

99. The bishops' address to the General Conference of the Methodist Episcopal Church South in 1894 was heavy with innuendo:

> The privilege of believers to attain unto the state of entire sanctification or perfect love, and to abide therein, is a well-known teaching of Methodism. Witnesses to this experience have never been wanting in our Church, though few in comparison with the whole membership. Among them have been men and women of beautiful consistency and seraphic ardor, jewels of the Church. Let the doctrine still be proclaimed, and the experience still be testified.
>
> But there has sprung up among us a party with holiness as a watchword; they have holiness associations, holiness meetings, holiness preachers, holiness evangelists, and holiness property. Religious experience is represented as if it consists of only two steps, the first step out of condemnation into peace, and the next step into Christian perfection. . . . We do not question the sincerity and zeal of these brethren; we desire the Church to profit by their earnest preaching and godly example; but we deplore their teaching and methods in so far as they claim a monopoly of the experience, practice, and advocacy of holiness, and separate from the body of ministers and disciples.

(Cited in Peters, *Christian Perfection*, pp. 147–48.)

100. Ibid., pp. 148f.

101. These include: the Academy for Spiritual Formation, for the systematic study of spirituality; the Disciplined Order of Christ, a nationwide organization committed to the spiritual disciplines of the faith; and the United Methodist Renewal Services

Fellowship, a network of charismatic groups in the United Methodist Church.

102. See David Lowes Watson, *Accountable Discipleship* (Nashville: Discipleship Resources, 1984).

103. Wesley, "A Plain Account of Christian Perfection," in Whaling, *Wesleys*, pp. 335–36.